Forgiving and Reconciling

BRIDGES TO WHOLENESS AND HOPE

Everett L. Worthington Jr.

InterVarsity Press
Downers Grove, Illinois

InterVarsity Press
P.O. Box 1400, Downers Grove, IL 60515-1426
World Wide Web: www.ivpress.com
E-mail: mail@ivpress.com

InterVarsity Press® is the book-publishing division of InterVarsity Christian Fellowship/USA®, a student movement active on campus at hundreds of universities, colleges and schools of nursing in the United States of America, and a member movement of the International Fellowship of Evangelical Students. For information about local and regional activities, write Public Relations Dept., InterVarsity Christian Fellowship/USA, 6400 Schroeder Rd., P.O. Box 7895, Madison, WI 53707-7895, or visit the IVCF website at <www.ivcf.org>.

Cover design: Cindy Kiple

Cover image: Peter Holt/Illustration Works

ISBN 0-8308-3244-0

Printed in the United States of America ∞

Library of Congress Cataloging-in-Publication Data

Worthington, Everett L., 1946-
   Forgiving and reconciling: bridges to wholeness and hope/Everett
Worthington.
     p. cm.
  Rev. ed. of: Five steps to forgiveness. ©2001.
  Includes bibliographical references.
   ISBN 0-8308-3244-0 (pbk.: alk. paper)
   1. Forgiveness. 2. Reconciliation. I. Worthington, Everett L.,
  1946-
  Five steps to forgiveness. II. Title.
  BF637.F67W67 2001
  158.2—dc21
                                               2003006825

P	20	19	18	17	16	15	14	13	12	11	10	9	8	7	6	5	4	3	2	1
Y	19	18	17	16	15	14	13	12	11	10	09	08	07	06	05	04	03			

In memory of two, now departed,

who directed me toward helping others forgive—

my mother, Frances McNeill Worthington,

and Lewis Smedes

Contents

Preface to the Revised Edition

In September 2000 I finished writing *Five Steps to Forgiveness: The Art and Science of Forgiving* (Crown Publishers). It was published in October 2001. Bad timing for a book on forgiveness—just a month after the horror of September 11, 2001.

September 11 changed things. Many Christians—hearts overflowing with love, compassion, sympathy and empathy—rushed to New York to help. They gave money. They prayed for the victims.

Some Christians were more interested in justice than compassion; they were among the most likely to endorse extreme retribution toward the terrorists. How can Christians be among the most willing both to give and to get even? This speaks to the heart of three important virtues: forgiveness, justice and reconciliation.

Since I wrote *Five Steps to Forgiveness,* we have lived in a world sensitized by awareness of evil. We have seen scandals in the Roman Catholic Church; apologies did not appease, and Cardinal Bernard Law was forced to resign. Republican majority leader Trent Lott made segregationist comments; apologies again failed to satisfy, and he was forced to resign. The submarine captain who surfaced under a boat, killing eight Japanese adults and children, also apologized, but his career was ruined. Public outcry for justice appears ever more certain these days—even when wrongdoers apologize.

In our research at Virginia Commonwealth University (VCU), we have learned a lot in the three years since I wrote *Five Steps to Forgiveness.* We have examined forgiveness and health, justice, apology, restitution, personality and Christian beliefs. We have examined forgiveness in restorative justice, medical and business settings. We have almost completed a six-year study of teaching forgiveness and reconciliation skills to early-married couples, and we have published a study in which we taught forgiveness to longer-married couples. We have studied forgiveness in Christians and people of other faiths. Finally, we have refined the five steps described in *Five Steps to Forgiveness*. Our scientific studies during the last few years have added richness to my understanding of forgiveness. I want to pass along my understanding, but not destroy the easy-to-understand method of forgiving and reconciling that I described in *Five Steps*.

Because the *Five Steps* book was written with a general audience in mind, it did not incorporate explicitly the Christian view on which my approach has, from the beginning, been built. In this new book, *Forgiving and Reconciling*, as I add new research findings on forgiveness, I also place forgiving within a Christian context. My theological understanding has been informed by studying Scripture, reading theologians (e.g., Augsburger, Jones, Volf) and interacting with Christians around the world—in academia, the pulpit, the counseling room and the pews.

I retain the core organization of *Five Steps to Forgiveness*, but I have condensed chapters to make space for new findings and discussions that are specifically Christian. I believe there are four languages that people use to communicate about forgiveness. People on the street speak of human experience. Theologians relate forgiveness to church history, writings of other theologians and Christian leaders, and Scripture. Psychologists speak of scientifically revealed understandings of emotion, behavior, mental activity and motivations. Neuroscientists talk of the ways our bodies (including our brains) and our experiences are connected. I am attempting to craft a language that, in some small way, helps people from these four language groups talk with each other.

I pray that this new version of the book will be true to the heart of the triune God, and that it will thus enrich and edify you. And I pray that your understanding, experience and practice of forgiving and reconciling will be blessed so that you make a positive difference in God's kingdom.

Acknowledgments

I have been studying forgiveness at VCU since about 1984. It is impossible to acknowledge properly all the contributors who have shaped my ideas. If I start naming names, I'll create a list that will last pages, so I hope my friends, collaborators, colleagues, clients, couple-consultants, students and fellow church members will accept my heartfelt thanks and forgive me for not listing everyone by name.

I do want to acknowledge supporters of our research, the John Templeton Foundation (grant #239), the Fetzer Institute (grant #1653.3 to Jack Berry and myself) and VCU's General Clinical Research Center (NIH M01 RR00065). Without such financial assistance, very little of what has been done since 1997 would have been accomplished. Gail Ross and Jenna Land (at the Gail Ross Literary Agency) and Elizabeth Rapoport and Stephanie Higgs (at Crown Publishers) helped me get the original book into good shape. I'm grateful.

I also want to thank Fuller Theological Seminary for inviting me to give the Fuller Integration Lecture series in 2000, arranged by Al Dueck. The Fuller series allowed me to think about the fit between scientific research and Christian theology. These lectures provided a stimulus for preparing talks on the topics, and much of that thinking has been incorporated into this book. Fuller also provided respondents who formally critiqued my lectures—David Augsburger, Randy Sorenson, Sherwood Lingenfelter, Terry Roberts and Kindra Nickerson, who gave challenging and lively critiques that pushed me to clarify much of my own thinking afterward. The intellectually inquiring collection of faculty, students, administrators and attendees also offered their comments and questions. The Fuller Lectures were formative in assisting this integration of the science and theology of forgiving.

My family, friends and Christian family have provided a safe holding place for me to learn about Christianity. My church, Christ Presbyterian Church in Richmond, under the leadership of Pastor Doug McMurry, has been a great support for almost twenty-five years. Doug is a long-term friend and coauthor who has shaped many of my ideas about love and its centrality in all of life.

I have been blessed to travel in countries besides the United States, and this travel has given me a perspective on Christianity that is not locked into our borders. God is working mightily on the African continent. I enjoyed a twenty-three-day trip to South Africa, which was sponsored by the Association of Christian Counselors in South Africa and hosted by Mervin van der Spuy. The government of South Africa also designated me a Visiting Scholar, allowing me to visit eight colleges or universities. In Soweto, where the uprisings began, I met one of the most amazing, unselfish ministers I have ever known, Pastor John Tau. Pastor Tau spent six days each week away from his family. He counseled South Africans, mostly from Soweto, within his two-room house. People stood in line to benefit from Pastor Tau's unselfish love and wisdom. He is an inspiration to me and an exemplar of Christian service.

God is also at work in Asia. I have visited Wesley Methodist Church in Singapore on two occasions, hosted by Danny Ng and Tony Ting. Those conferences and my visits to the National University of Singapore and Nanyang Technological University were wonderful opportunities to interact with Singaporeans in church, profession and university. I was also able to get into Malaysia on those visits. In 2002 I taught a graduate course on forgiveness at Alliance Theological Seminary in the Philippines, where I found the people to be warm and giving. Fred and Heather Gingrich also promoted talks at the University of the Philippines and at Ateneo de Manila, which allowed me interaction with academics, who always have such challenging minds.

God is at work in Latin America. I visited Brazil first on an educational tour funded by VCU through the International Council on Educational Exchange in 1996. The trip introduced me to the country and caused me to fall in love with the Brazilian people. I have been back twice for Christian counseling conferences sponsored by David Kornfield and Robson Gomes.

God is active in Europe. Michael Wang invited me to England to share with Christian counselors there, and Fraser Watts and Nicholas Gibson had me down to Cambridge University to speak to a research group.

Thanks to each of the members of the Network of Christians in Psychology and the Psychology and Christianity Project group at Cambridge.

God is at work in North America as well. Les Greenberg, of York University in Toronto, invited me to Canada for a seminar at their department of psychology, and I am grateful to him for his sponsorship. Tim Clinton and Gary Collins before him have both been wonderful at inviting me to Christian-oriented events throughout the United States. Many, many Christian psychological and counseling conferences, churches and Christian organizations have invited me to speak. Christian counseling programs at Denver Seminary, Liberty University and (soon) Rosemead School of Psychology (Biola University) have allowed me access to their students through graduate courses. Universities, too numerous to name, also have been kind at opening their doors and classrooms for special talks or classroom visits. I am very grateful.

God is alive, well and active all around the planet. And the Lord cares deeply about forgiveness. People throughout the world seem to have a universal concern about whether they have been or can be forgiven by God, whether they can forgive the people who have offended them throughout their lives, and whether they can be forgiven. We live in times of international tensions and wars, national stresses and strains among groups, community violence and turmoil, church factions and splits, and family division and pain. Justice seems to increasingly come up against mercy. Conflict negotiation and communication skills can help ease some of those tensions, but how can the damage be healed?

I believe this very basic truth: *Damage can be repaired in many ways, but complete healing and restoration can come only through forgiveness and reconciliation.* First, we must be forgiven by and reconciled to God. Christians are ambassadors of reconciliation to bring that about (2 Cor 5:17-20). Second, we must live out the gospel. We must seek forgiveness when we wrong others and eagerly rush to grant forgiveness. I believe that reconciliation and forgiveness are not joined at the hip, but God's heart wants to bring them together at every possible opportunity. I am pleased to be able to talk about both within the same book. I acknowledge that apart from God, we—and specifically I—can do nothing. And yet I believe that through Jesus we can do all things. If there are works and words within this book that are lasting, I give the triune God all the glory.

PART 1

Why We FORGIVE

Chances are you have experienced transgressions against you. They have come from well-meaning helpers, parents who are sure they know what's good for you, oblivious friends, stressed-out caretakers, children who disappoint, bosses who have their own agenda, or simply people with a mean streak. Humans get hurt and offended. That is part of being human.

Chances are also high that, with at least one of those transgressions, you still worry it around like a piece of chomped-on skin inside your cheek. Perhaps you sometimes catch the bitterness in your tone of voice. Maybe you have taken petty revenge and hate yourself for it. Perhaps you plot revenge on a larger scale (while, at the same time, you don't like the way your mind is working).

Perhaps the problem occurred in the past. Maybe you are divorced and cannot get beyond the resentment. Maybe your father died without giving you a chance to make things right with him. You want to forgive. You need to forgive.

Perhaps you are in an ongoing relationship that has gone sour—at home, at work or with a romantic partner. You have invested in that relationship and don't want to give it up. You want to reconcile. But how?

This book is for you. My colleagues and I have conducted research for years on how people can forgive and, if they wish, work toward reconciliation. I have distilled our research into a five-step model for how to forgive, which I call the Pyramid Model to REACH Forgiveness. I have also boiled down our thinking about reconciling to a four-step Bridge to Reconciliation. I have been delighted and amazed at how many have learned to apply these models to forgive and reconcile.

Forgiving is never as simple as merely "Apply these 5 steps in 30 minutes and poof—instant forgiveness!" That trivializes a serious and personal experience.

Reconciliation between two parties in conflict is even more complicated. Each person can run aground on the rocks of self-protection and good intentions.

You can employ the five steps you need to forgive and the four steps you need to reconcile. In this book, I suggest concrete ways to apply the steps. I show you how to get back on track after temporary setbacks.

Forgiveness and reconciliation are not simple. They require courage, commitment and conscious effort. But if you are willing, there are great relational treasures to be given—and sometimes even received—when you forgive and try to reconcile. I pray that you will have great success in applying these ideas.

1

Why Forgive?

Like a bee, we distill poison from honey for our self-defense—what happens to the bee if it uses its sting is well known.

DAG HAMMARSKJÖLD

On New Year's Eve in 1995, my mother was murdered in her home by a young burglar. Even today, my pain still occasionally bobs to the emotional surface.

When I received the call from Mike, my brother, on New Year's morning, I was stunned. "Something terrible has happened," he said. "Mama's been murdered. There was blood on the carpet, the walls . . ."

As I got ready to drive from Richmond to Knoxville with my sister, Kathy, and her husband, Damian, I threw clothes in a suitcase, hustling furiously to and fro, numbing my feelings with the narcotic of action. After I packed, I sat at the table. Kirby, my wife, was reading to teenage Becca the children's stories that Grandma used to read her. Preteen Katy Anna walked by, face wet with tears. I reached out to comfort her. Her hugs broke through my defenses, and I wept.

On the drive to Knoxville, Kathy and I recalled many of the good and the bad times with my mother. I remembered doing a radio call-in show with a station in Knoxville only months before. At the end, the interviewer said, "We have time for one more call. I think this is a special one. Go ahead." I then heard the slow, soft, East Tennessee voice of my mother. "Sonny"—she drawled my childhood nickname through four diphthongs—"I've been listening to you. I wanted you to know. You're a good boy, Sonny." I was forty-nine at the time.

Mama was a comfortable grandmother, enfolding our children in her arms, hugging them to her soft and cuddly body. She liked to sing to my kids. She read books, bought them toys that Kirby and I couldn't afford, and had a stash of M&Ms and sweet breakfast cereal that kept our kids on a sugar kick throughout our visits. Ever since my dad had died of cancer five years before, Mama had seemed more vulnerable.

Now she was gone. I wouldn't feel her arms again. I wouldn't hear the music of her East Tennessee mountain drawl. My mind could sort of grasp the loss, but my heart wouldn't accept it.

CONVERSATION IN THE BACK ROOM

After arriving in Knoxville, my brother, my sister and I sat in Mike's back room amid the seventeen loaves of bread, twenty pies and five plates of cold cuts—Southern comfort food that generous neighbors and friends had provided. We talked about the details of the murder that we knew only because Mike had discovered Mama's body. "I called Mama all morning to wish her Happy New Year," said Mike. "When she didn't answer, I got worried. I thought she might have fallen."

Mike had bundled eight-year-old David into the car and chugged over to the house. "I opened the front door. When I stepped into the living room, I couldn't believe the mess. I stumbled with David at my side toward the hall. As I stepped into the hall, I saw the blood-splattered wall. Then her body.

"I slapped my hand over David's eyes and pulled him with me as I walked out to phone the police. The violence in the house, the blood and the position of Mama's body made it clear she was dead—beaten with a crowbar."

THE CROWBAR AND THE BASEBALL BAT

Mike told us the facts the police had shared. Apparently a burglary had gone awry. The police suspected that two youths were involved.

Mama had been smashed three times with a crowbar. Blood was everywhere—on the door, on the walls, soaked through the carpet. The assailant had also violated her with a wine bottle, and then he and his accomplice had completely trashed the house. All mirrors and reflecting surfaces in the house were ruined.

Rage spewed forth. I heard myself say, "I'd like to have him alone in a room with a baseball bat for thirty minutes. I'd beat his brains out."

Kathy said, "I'd take just ten minutes."

Mike added, "I'd take two hours so it would last a long time."

We were furious.

That night, sleep was impossible. I roamed my room. I stormed about, rehearsing scenes of violence and anger, replaying the death scene as I imagined it in the late-show reruns of my mind, seeing the blood in my mind's eye.

I confess that during most of that night, forgiveness never entered my mind. But as I wrestled the covers and paced a path in the carpet, I began to ask myself questions. *Can I ever forgive this? Is it good to forgive? What if the police catch the youths? Will I want them to get the death penalty?* I was eyeball to eyeball with my convictions—carefully thought out in times unclouded by emotion. But the impact of this death and the horror of my images of what my mother must have experienced were an in-your-face confrontation. They rocked my sense of identity. I thought I knew my own character. Yet someone once said, "Character is who we are when no one is looking." Well, who was I in that bedroom when no one was looking?

SELF-SEARCHING

So who was I? I was a Christian. Was it wrong for me to indulge my rage? Was it wrong to want both the law and God to punish that assailant? Christianity is the cross where justice and mercy intersect. At that moment I was happy to seek justice, even the wild vigilante justice of raw revenge. I wanted my hands on that murderer. I did not even want to consider mercy.

I was a counseling psychologist. I had seen people deny experiences, stuffing their worst feelings deep inside. Was it wrong to think of forgiving while I was so angry and sad? I knew that if I sought too quick a resolution to trauma by denying anger, fear and sadness, I could arrest the grieving process. Was it wrong to try to calm myself when feeling intense, legitimate anger that was normal? But I was in a quandary. I didn't want to deny my negative feelings, but I knew that denying my positive side, my morals and my self-control, was just as bad. I dared not *just* rage. Not only psychology, but also Mama, had taught me that. I was a researcher who, ironically, studied forgiveness. I had read philosophical, religious, devotional and literary accounts of forgiveness. I had pored over psychological studies of forgiveness. Yet throughout most of this day I hadn't even thought the word *forgiveness.* Perhaps I heard the whisper of the word at the door of my consciousness, but each time I kicked the door shut.

I had helped numerous couples and individuals to forgive. My colleagues and I had developed an intervention that helped people forgive if they wanted to forgive. To further the irony, only a couple of weeks before the murder, Mike McCullough, Steve Sandage and I had delivered to Inter-Varsity Press the manuscript for *To Forgive Is Human: How to Put Your Past in the Past.*[1] I knew forgiveness might be possible, but did I really want to forgive?

Questions. The poignant question that pierced my heart was this: To whom did my life's work—teaching people to forgive—apply? Was it for other people but not for me? Or did it include me too?

Forgiveness requires both letting go and pulling toward. A forgiver must release the resentment, hatred and bitterness of unforgiveness. A forgiver must release the desire to avoid or to seek revenge against the perpetrator. But the act of forgiving—of reaching out *toward* the perpetrator—is sharper. It pricks the heart. A forgiver replaces unforgiveness with a sense of agape love. A forgiver wishes the perpetrator well. A forgiver could even enter a relationship with the perpetrator if it were safe, prudent and possible to do so. Forgiveness means giving a gift that embodies freedom and love. Should I offer this gift? Should I forgive?

THE GREAT DEBATE

"Don't you dare forgive!" I'd heard many arguments against forgiveness. Jesus said, "If your brother sins, rebuke him, and if he repents, forgive him" (Lk 17:3). The youth who attacked my mother certainly had not repented. So I didn't need to feel bound to forgive, right?

Some argue, "If you forgive, it will reduce your motivation to catch the perpetrator. Forgiveness obstructs justice." Yet I knew that any forgiving I could give would be *my* act, *my* gift. The justice system could consider pardon. God might someday grant divine forgiveness. Those were out of my hands. Whether I forgave or didn't, legal crime, punishment and pardon were not at stake. The murderer should be incarcerated so he would not kill again. To protect others from violence is simply good sense. It did not affect whether I ought to forgive.

I'd heard people argue that unforgiveness is beneficial. "Unforgiveness empowers people to do good," said a bitter man whose child had been murdered. "Because I refuse to forgive, I also help other victims of crime." Righteous anger can motivate acts of charity. Betty Williams, who won the Nobel Peace Prize, was angry about mines planted during warfare that ambushed people long after the war ceased. She organized a campaign to remove those mines. She saved lives, reduced pain. But I can be angry with HIV/AIDS and work to stamp it out without bitterness, resentment and hostility. Righteous anger is not the same as bitter, resentful, hateful, hostile, ruminative unforgiveness.

"If you forgive, it's cowardly," I've heard. Having faced a major hurt and struggled with whether to forgive, I can't buy that. For me, it's harder to forgive than to hate. It's not cowardly to want to give up the hatred that makes a person feel powerful (and makes us wish the perpetrator were weak). It takes courage to grant love that can help *both* people feel stronger and better as people.

Take Chris Carrier, for example, whose story has been told in *Reader's Digest.*[2] I heard him when we appeared on the same day on television's *Leeza.* At ten, Chris was abducted. He was stabbed in the chest and stomach with an ice pick and shot through the temple and eye. Left for dead in a Florida swamp, he awoke later. Chris forgave the man.

Then came the acid test. When Chris was an adult, he heard that the man who had done these things to him was dying. Chris went to the man and comforted him during his final days. Chris's forgiveness was refined into pure love. Was that cowardice? No. It was courage personified.

"It's not my place to forgive," said one man whose child had been kidnapped and murdered. "My child was harmed. She is the only one who could forgive. But she's dead and can't forgive. Murder is unforgivable."

I understood his pain. I wanted to ask him, "If the murder was not also a sin against you, how can you hate? How can you be unforgiving?" It seemed to me that his child's murder had hurt him too. If he could hate, why couldn't he forgive? His forgiveness wouldn't pardon the killer. It wouldn't do away with all of the killer's guilt. But it would introduce an element of good, and perhaps someday even redemption, in a horribly bad situation.

"Forgiveness short-circuits grief," some say. Yet forgiveness does not deny that a true offense or hurt occurred. It doesn't deny the pain and sadness of a true loss. In fact, forgiveness works hand in glove with grieving to help resolve grief faster and more thoroughly.

"Forgiveness is loving toward the wrongdoer but not the victim," some people argue. As Cynthia Ozick has recalled, "The rabbi said, 'Whoever is merciful to the cruel will end by being indifferent to the innocent.' Forgiveness can brutalize. . . . The face of forgiveness is mild but how stony to be slaughtered."[3] Yet once a wrong is done to a victim, does it help the victim if we seek punitive justice? If the wrong involved property, fair restitution is indeed kind. But my mother had been murdered, and no restitution could restore what the locust of death had devoured. Whether I forgave or not would not affect Mama. But I could honor her memory by living out the values of love and mercy she had bequeathed to me.

Don't you dare not forgive! I also knew some of the counterarguments made by apologists for forgiveness. I had heard four arguments that said that we should forgive for our own sake.

First, I knew the Scriptures. Jesus instructed the disciples to pray:

Forgive us our debts
    as we also have forgiven our debtors. (Mt 6:12)

He even made God's forgiveness of us conditional on forgiving others (Mt 6:14-15). Jesus said, "Love your enemies" (Lk 6:27). But I didn't feel like forgiving or loving my enemies. *If I forgive and still feel hatred*, I thought, *won't I still be unforgiving in my heart?* Yes, I knew about the fact-faith-feeling train, but somehow, simply declaring forgiveness in spite of my rage seemed hypocritical. *Doesn't God care about truth?* I wailed internally. *Of course he does,* I answered myself. Jesus said, "I am the way and the truth and the life" (Jn 14:6).

Second, "You can't hurt the perpetrator by being unforgiving, but you can set yourself free by forgiving." I had made that argument myself to psychotherapy clients and friends. It is true to some degree, but I knew from research that it wasn't as simple as it sounds.

Third, "Unforgiveness is a heavy burden to carry." True. Resentment, one of the core elements of unforgiveness, is like carrying around a red-hot rock with the intention of someday throwing it back at the one who hurt you. It tires us and burns us. Who wouldn't want simply to let the rock fall to the ground? Harry Emerson Fosdick said, "Hating people is like burning down your own house to get rid of a rat."

Fourth, "You'll be healthier and happier if you forgive than if you stew in your unforgiveness." I knew the research literature. Maybe I would be healthier. Evidence suggests that hostility causes cardiovascular problems. Chronic stressfulness leads to poor immune system functioning. However, at that time, research on forgiveness was so new that researchers could not make strong statements about its effects. Forgiveness *probably* reduced health risks, I thought. But that wasn't nearly as well supported back in 1996 as it is now.

Maybe I would be happier. "Forgiveness can help reconcile damaged relationships," some argue. Forgiveness can indeed give me more joy with a partner, friend or coworker than staying bitter. Forgiveness is a conduit of love from person to person. Yet again, research on forgiveness in relationships was in its early stages in 1996. I didn't want to claim the matter as fact. Besides, I didn't have a relationship with the youth who killed my mother. So, the jury was still out about my health and happiness if I forgave.

I knew both the do-forgive and don't-forgive arguments. As I paced the bedroom, I didn't know which to listen to.

Why did I try to forgive? Lots of thoughts flashed through my mind that night. I didn't evaluate them like Mr. Spock or Data. I considered point and counterpoint, but my thoughts were jumbled. On the whole, I thought that I *ought* to forgive. Even the mental picture of a blood-soaked carpet could not dislodge that conviction.

Honestly, though, I did not *want* to forgive. Even if I came around to wanting to forgive, I did not know if I *could* forgive.

In the end, however, it was not relentless reasons or even Christian conviction that tipped the scales against ugly unforgiveness. I merely became weary of struggling against hatred. My emotions drove me to try to forgive.

At the emotional crest of that excruciatingly dark night, I wanted relief from my anger. I needed a rock that would steady my reeling views of the world and myself. I wanted to know and do what God wanted me to do. But Scriptures seemed to line up on both sides. My head and heart were spinning. I wanted to forgive if it would help me deal with my pain, anger, hurt and sadness. *If only I could forgive*, I thought, *I could have peace*. I wanted a powerful base that could neutralize the acid of hate and rage that gnawed at me.

Forgiveness: Is It for Giving or for Getting?

Even as I thought of being free of my struggles, I recalled our research programs for helping people forgive. We helped people who wanted to forgive but had tried and failed—often for years. We usually compared two conditions, which we called a self-benefit condition and an empathy-based condition.

Forgiving is for getting. In the self-benefit condition, we asked people to forgive for their own good. We detailed the likely health effects of chronic unforgiveness. We suggested positive health effects of forgiving. We told them, "Forgive. You'll be free. You'll be able to move on with your life." We showed people how to use imagery, let go of anger, release resentment, cut the chains that bound them to the person who had hurt or offended them. We helped people relax. We taught them how to lower the stress of unforgiveness. In short, we appealed to the same motives and emotions that cried within me: *Forgive so you'll feel better*.

I remember a person I'll call Marci.[4] Marci wanted the freedom of forgiveness. She was forty-five years old, but she felt at least sixty. She knew that she should forgive. But knowing and doing are different.

Her difficulties began with a little thing. Her husband's car was rear-ended by a city bus. The car wasn't damaged much, but Bruce, her husband, continued to have pain in his neck. Finally, his physician suggested that surgery might repair the damaged disks between the vertebrae. During the operation, something went terribly wrong, and the surgeon cut the spinal cord. Bruce had not walked for eleven years.

Bruce's injury put an enormous burden on Marci and their two children. Every day Marci cursed the bus driver who hadn't paid attention, the physician who had recommended neck surgery and the surgeon who had botched it.

Now Marci was getting sick. She felt run-down. The demands of caring for Bruce and rearing two adolescents never ended. Her stomach was always upset. Her mother, herself a crotchety sixty-five-year-old, called Marci "old before your time." Marci knew her mother was right. Bitterness was poisoning Marci and had stripped her of happiness. But she didn't seem to be able to do anything about it. She wanted to forgive the targets of her hatred because she wanted to feel better. Forgiveness was the royal road to health, she thought. Our self-benefit intervention would have been tailor-made for Marci if she had only known about it.

Forgiving is for giving. In the empathy-based condition, we asked people to forgive because the perpetrator needs forgiveness. "You are the only one who can give him [or her] what he [or she] needs: forgiveness." We appealed to people's altruistic motives to give a gift of forgiveness because the other person needed it, rather than in order to get relief from unforgiveness.

Frankly, this is a difficult sell. When people are angry, resentful and bitter toward a person, the last thing they want is to do something nice for that person. Yet most people, if they hang with us, change their hearts. They come to see that anger, resentment, hostility, rage and hatred destroy. They know that, while destroying a hated object can feel good for a while, lasting satisfaction comes more often with creating.

Before Kirby and I married, I lived alone in Boston far away from Tennessee where she was in school. I was in love with her and very lonely. I would sit in Storrow Park along the Charles River and watch happy lovers laugh and talk with each other. I wrote poetry. That urge to fill the hole of sorrow was born of a longing to experience something more in my life. I could have raged against fate, circumstances or a hateful God that kept Kirby and me apart. Instead I wrote poetry. I created something that had not existed before—poems that expressed my love and passion. I was proud of my creations. I was pleased to show them to Kirby.

An amazing change took place. I put a piece of myself into creation, yet I was not diminished. In fact, I somehow felt I was more than what I had been. By creating, I used a piece of my heart to bless someone else. Yet my heart grew larger within me. I did not write poetry to grow a larger heart. I wrote to share a piece of my heart and to bless the one I cared about. The surprise was, I grew in the process.

In our empathy-based groups, we appealed to people's altruistic motives. "Empathize with the one who hurt you until you can identify with his or her humanity," we would say. "Then consider whether you have ever hurt people. We are connected to all people. We all do despicable acts at times. So in that way you are similar to the one who hurt you. Now consider whether you would like to do something good for the one who hurt you. There's a wonderful gift that only you can give: forgiveness for that injury to you."

The comparison: for getting or for giving? When we compared people's responses to the self-benefit and empathy-based conditions, we found consistent results. One study involved brief one-hour programs. The other involved eight-hour programs. When we compared one-hour programs, people who forgave in the self-benefit condition achieved more *immediate* forgiveness than did those who forgave in the empathy-based condition. Even when we followed up with people weeks later, we found the self-benefit program had produced twice as much lasting forgiveness as the empathy-based program.

In the eight-hour program, though, things were different. The amount of forgiveness in the eight-hour self-benefit program was the same as in the one-hour program. However, the forgiveness in the eight-hour empathy-based program was three times as large as in the self-benefit program.

Also, weeks later when we retested the people in the eight-hour programs, the people in the empathy-based program were about five times as forgiving as those in the self-benefit program. My conclusions from these two studies are clear. If a person had little time to consider forgiving, the person would probably forgive more easily to benefit his or her own physical, mental and relational health. But if the person was willing to spend more than four hours trying to forgive, then forgiving in order to bless the person who hurt him or her would produce *more* and *longer-lasting* forgiveness than forgiving just for the person's own benefit.

We've all heard "Forgive and forget," but forgiving seems to be for *giving*, not for *getting*. When we forgive, we get a quick jolt of personal peace. If we practice forgiving over a lifetime, chances are we will be healthier in the long run. Our immune systems may function better. We may have less risk of cardiovascular disease. If we forgive, we can also give a gift of peace to the person who hurt us—and we might repair the relationship and therefore have more harmonious social support systems. If we forgive, our entire community might focus less on revenge, avoidance, unforgiveness and past problems and focus more on future possibilities. Away from hurt and toward healing.

Forgiveness does benefit us. But if we forgive mainly to get, we get just a trickle of benefits. If we give a gift of forgiveness to a needy perpetrator, though, we receive freedom, peace, health and relational repair. Forgiveness gushes like water from a fire hose. It washes us clean. It frees us.

In a way, forgiveness is like air. If we close our fist, trying to grasp air, it squirts through our clutching fingers. But if we simply breathe deeply and exhale, then we can get oxygen plus warm those whom our breath passes. In the same way, if we try to clutch the benefits of forgiveness for ourselves by forgiving *because* we want better health, *because* we want more peace, then we seem to contaminate the source of the power of those benefits. We get a discounted version of the benefits. But if we try to bless others by forgiving, then paradoxically we ourselves are flooded with blessing. Forgiving is for giving, not for getting.

HOW MY STORY AND YOURS MIGHT MEET

I already knew many of these things about forgiveness when I found that Mama had been murdered. That event rocked me. I questioned what I knew and what I believed. I wrestled with my emotions. Since the murder, I have changed and grown through my struggles, and I will tell you some of those struggles as we move through this book.

Now, over seven years later, I want to share with you my journeys through personal experience and scientific study—through the heart and science of forgiving. I will show you how to forgive those events and people you might have tried to forgive but could not. You'll learn how to pursue reconciliation if you are in relationships with damaged trust. You'll be able to practice a more forgiving lifestyle. And you'll be able to do all this while acting consistently with Scripture.

If I am successful with this book, you may understand and experience forgiveness and reconciliation differently than ever before. I hope to gently challenge the story of self-focus that, in our culture, we seem to have adopted to explain the miracle of forgiveness. I hope to reconcile the tension between biblical commands to forgive and encouragement to forgive from the heart, so that there is not as much distance between the head and the heart when it comes to handling transgressions. I hope to arm you with new ways to handle transgressions. I hope to help you never look at or practice forgiveness the same way again.

ROAD RAGE AND A LITTLE GIRL

I experienced such a change in perception one day. It was a July summer day in Richmond, Virginia, and the temperature was about 104 degrees Fahrenheit. A brief thundershower had just ended, and the steam was rising from the pavement in waves that distorted vision. Traffic had become snarled in one lane, perhaps because of a fender-bender down the street somewhere, and the second lane was barely moving.

As I walked down the street, a drama unfolded before my eyes. I saw a man in the lane that was barely moving almost literally go crazy. He pounded on his horn furiously, slamming his hand onto the steering wheel again and again. The car in front of him had stopped, and the driver had left the car in the middle of the lane of traffic, noxiously belching exhaust fumes, and was hustling toward one of the university psychology buildings. The steam coming from the pavement was nothing compared to the steam that seemed to be shooting from the ears of the irate driver behind the stopped car. He jerked open his door, fought his way out of his vehicle, kicked the door shut, and stalked toward the car in front of him. I thought I was going to see road rage. "Driver throws automobile two city blocks," the news anchor would say. "Details at eleven."

Just as the irate driver reached the abandoned car, the door to the psychology building opened and the driver of the abandoned car struggled out, holding a child in his arms. The child's legs were withered. She had braces on both feet. The man lurched toward the car as fast as he could, carrying his crippled burden.

When the irate driver heard the steps approaching from behind, he whirled with a scowl and almost took a step toward the driver who was carrying the child. Suddenly, the irate driver realized what was happening. His eyes widened. The squint softened. The jaw muscles slackened. He stepped back and, like a doorman at the Ritz Carlton, opened the car door with a flourish for the man to place the child inside the vehicle. I could almost hear his heels click.

This irate driver experienced a change in his view of the situation, making all of his old ideas irrelevant and setting him on a path of compassion because of his empathy for the man carrying the child.

If you follow my reasoning in this book, you may see forgiveness differently from before. I hope that you'll think of forgiveness as a way to give to others something they need. You may not believe it could happen, but I hope that by the end of this book you might even wish well to those who have offended and hurt you.

LONG-TERM REWARDS OF DEVELOPING A FORGIVING CHARACTER

I was alarmed at the hatred, anger and bitterness that had suddenly revealed themselves in my own life. The violence of the attack against my mother had stripped away some of the tenaciously held self-delusion that kept me believing that I am habitually kind, loving and forgiving. Confronting my own unforgiveness was a powerful shock.

As a Christian, I long to live a virtuous life that honors Jesus, my Savior.

Yet I know enough of my dark side to know that my motivations are always tainted. Looking back, I now see how—even as I was consumed by unforgiveness, fantasies of revenge, resentments at life and society, and the beginnings of bitterness—a small voice whispered for me to at least *consider* forgiving the murderer. We often underestimate our basic desire, born of the Holy Spirit, to have a virtuous character. Yet the small voice pulls us along if we but listen.

Pursuing forgiveness—not just as an act, not just as a response to a particular troublesome person, but as a character trait—is a goal for many people. Christians, out of gratitude for all God has done to bless us, want to honor God by reflecting his character. We are like mirrors that catch the rays of the sun and reflect them into dark places. We follow this path toward virtue. We find ruts, side trails that lead us into the bushes, landmarks that allow us to evaluate our progress, obstructions that block our way, widened parts of the trail that speed our progress in relationships, and even bridges that must be crossed.

The way of forgiveness is hard. Forgiveness isn't for wimps. In many ways, the destructive path of unforgiveness is much easier than the tough, steely pull of forgiveness. Still, if we follow forgiveness, we will become more loving.

YOU CAN FORGIVE

In this book I tell my story, bit by bit in each chapter, as a way to help you forgive those with whom you are having difficulty. In part one, I consider why we forgive, including practical and theological reasons. In part two, I describe how we forgive—whether we are in a continuing relationship with another or whether the person is estranged, has moved away or is dead. Then in part three, I describe how to reconcile with a person with whom you want to or must continue to interact.

Both Christianity and modern culture have much to say about forgiving. I have learned from both. In this book, I concentrate on the aspects of how to forgive that are informed both by Christianity and by science, by the humanities and by our personal experiences. I believe that those voices blend in intricate harmony. So I try to combine the voices into the song I sing to you about how we can more deeply forgive.

Each step in the Pyramid Model to REACH Forgiveness is easy to understand. Each practical exercise is easy to do. Thousands of people have tried them. If you put these ideas into practice, you can forgive events that have troubled you for years. Yet do not be deceived. Forgiveness is as mysterious as love. I have forgiven some horrendous offenses in hours and nursed petty grudges for years.

I invite you to come with me as I describe my experiences—personally, as a counselor and as a researcher. If you have been devastated by a gaping emotional wound or if you have a nagging personal abrasion, let's walk this path together.

DISCUSSION QUESTIONS

1. In the author's studies to help people who want to be successful at forgiving, he and his colleagues use two conditions (as well as a control group). Describe the self-benefit condition. Describe the empathy-based groups.

2. Do you believe that forgiveness is always, in all cases, required?

3. Do you believe that the bigger the traumatic event, the more difficult it is to forgive? Can you give examples of times when it was hard to forgive—either in your life or in the lives of people you know?

4. The author is a scientist and a Christian, and he believes that there are valuable truths to be learned both from Scripture and from science. Do you agree or disagree? What do you think the roles of each should be? Does Scripture teach us everything we need to know to live out our lives in a godly way?

5. Have you ever had one of those man-seeing-the-crippled girl moments, when things looked suddenly and drastically different? If so, can you share it with the group?

6. Is forgiveness something that Christians can do particularly well because they are followers of Jesus? Can people who are not Christians truly forgive?

2

Unforgiveness, Justice and Forgiveness

We talk a good forgiving line as long as somebody else needs to do it,
but few of us have the heart for it while we are dangling from one end of a bond
broken by somebody else's cruelty.

LEWIS B. SMEDES

Unforgiveness is a jumble of emotions. Resentment, hostility, hatred, bitterness, simmering anger and low-level fear interlace in the tapestry of unforgiveness.

Unforgiveness is not a "hot" (i.e., immediate) reaction to a transgression. It is ignited by the spark of perceived hurt or offense, fanned by the hot emotions of anger and fear, damped to a slow burn by time, and scuffed into a stack of dangerous coals by rumination. Unforgiveness is emotion served "cold" (i.e., delayed). But like dry ice, so cold it can burn the fingers, unforgiveness can still scorch the gut. Unforgiveness motivates people to get rid of those unpleasant emotions.

Maybe the best way to understand unforgiveness is to look at a flow chart that illustrates the process of moving from an initial transgression to full-blown unforgiveness (see figure 2.1).[1] A *transgression* is perceived as a *hurt* or an *offense*. A hurt stimulates fear (of being hurt again) and anger (like when I painfully bump my head and slam the offending door in rage). An offense makes us angry. Important: *Fear and anger, immediate responses, are not unforgiveness.* Unforgiveness must ripen through rumination. Only after mentally replaying the transgression, the motives of the transgressor and the consequences of the transgression do we become unforgiving. It takes time and reflection to develop unforgiveness.

Rob was unforgiving. When I met him, he was wearing a shirt picturing a flaming city against a black background. The caption read "Rage Against the Machine," the name of a rock band known for its angry protests against social injustices. Rob had recently been released from his drug rehabilitation program. Living on the street in the Northeast, he had paid for his drug habit by borrowing until his friends ran out, begging until his patience ran out and bartering until the stolen goods ran out. With the approach of winter, he scraped up enough money for a bus ticket and headed south. Picked up for vagrancy and drug intoxication in Florida, he served his time and headed for a reha-

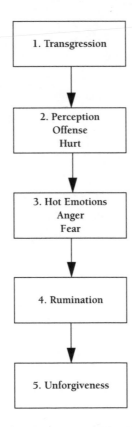

Figure 2.1. Understanding forgiveness. Reprinted from Everett Worthington, "Is There a Place for Forgiveness in the Justice System?" *Fordham Urban Law Journal* 27 (2000).

bilitation center. Rob was twenty years old.

Rob blamed a lot of people for his troubles. He
had kicked him out after Rob struck his mother d
broke out when Rob came home high on drugs.
school love, who introduced him to the party scene
philosophy professor, who preached hedonism. N
"friends," who took him in after his father rejected him, bled him of everything he owned, then turned him out on the street.

Rob could quickly name the transgressions against him. He recalled each as a personal offense by "the bastards." His dominant emotion was anger, with a sub-theme of hurt and fear etching a whine into his complaints. Rob ruminated continually about his situation. He complained. He ranted. He mumbled about "the bastards" to himself and to anyone who would listen (and some who would not listen). Rob was a poster boy for unforgiveness.

Unforgiveness can be defined as *delayed negative emotions, involving resentment, bitterness, hostility, hatred, residual anger and residual fear, which motivate people to reduce the negative emotions.* There are two important parts to this definition. Unforgiveness is an emotion. Unforgiveness motivates people to get rid of or avoid negative emotion. Let's consider each part.

UNFORGIVENESS IS AN EMOTION

Rumination—repeatedly reflecting on what has hurt us—changes fear and anger into the delayed emotion of unforgiveness. The key to this model, and to my description of how you might forgive, is my understanding of *emotion* (see figure 2.2).

Emotions are not feelings. Feelings are the ways we label emotions in a part of the brain where the working memory exists. We say, "I feel angry," or "I feel loving." That feeling is our conscious mind's way of using a word to describe what is going on all over our body and is being communicated to the brain.

Emotions are *embodied* experiences. Antonio Damasio, perhaps the leading expert on emotion in the world, has studied them for years.[2] Damasio points out that when we experience an emotion, each part of our body tells the brain precisely what emotion we are experiencing by sending either chemical messengers through the blood or chemical and electrical messengers through the nervous system. These messengers activate the memories of past emotions in the part of our brain called the association

, located in our prefrontal lobe. The pathways from these associa-
...s project into the working memory.

As the messengers travel through our nervous system, electric currents

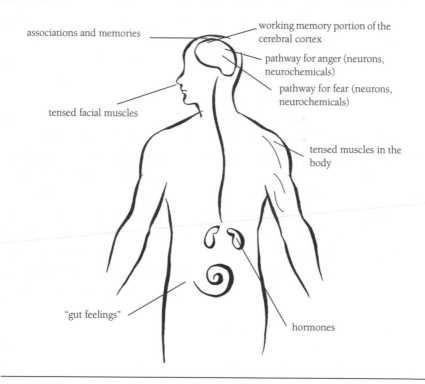

Figure 2.2. Understanding emotion

rush along neurons through brain structures such as the amygdala and
hippocampus, saying, "This path means, 'I'm afraid,'" or "This path means,
'I am happy.'" Neurochemicals squirt into parts of the brain when we're
sad and other parts when we're angry, afraid or happy. Patterns of neurochemical release identify our emotions—without our being consciously
aware of it—to our working memory.

As chemicals travel through the bloodstream, they trigger the release of
hormones. One mix tells the working memory we're angry. Another says
we're afraid. The patterns of hormones are sensed, and our working memory receives that information.

Our muscles get into the act. When we're angry, we clench our fists,
hunch our shoulders and grind our teeth. When we're afraid, we widen

our eyes, draw backward and inhale. When we're calm our face relaxes or we smile. Facial muscles send strong unconscious messages to the working memory.

Even our gut sends unconscious messages to the working memory. Damasio has found that a person's gut shouts *alarm!* over a risky decision long before the brain can figure out the message consciously.[3]

Our working memory is a supercomputer that decodes the body's unconscious chemical and electrical messages, coming up with a conscious *feeling*. "I feel angry," we might say to ourselves.

Because emotions are whole-body experiences, they often blend if they are relatively similar. For instance, anger, fear and sadness are all perceived negatively, especially if they are experienced intensely. Joy, happiness and satisfaction are also relatively similar and are perceived positively. Similar emotions can blend with each other to form a secondary, more complex emotion. For instance, the negative emotions of resentment, bitterness, hatred, hostility, anger and fear blend into the feeling that our working memory labels "unforgiveness." This blending makes it very difficult for scientists to disentangle discrete emotions, but our brain seems able to make those distinctions.

However, when emotional states are very different, they don't blend together. Rather, they compete with each other. For instance, when we grimace in anger, that grimace edges out a soft smile of happiness. The patterns of hormones in the blood or neurochemicals in the brain also compete. Different emotions light up different pathways and structures in the brain.

For instance, try this experiment. Look in the mirror and make a face that might show you are angry. Then look afraid. Now look angry and afraid at the same time. With effort you can make the two negative emotions blend on your face.

Now do this. Look angry. Then look happy. Try to put them together. Your face simply won't cooperate. The brain will get only one signal at a time. Maybe you could confuse your brain by switching rapidly between anger and happiness, but with naturally occurring emotions, fooling the brain wouldn't be easy. Thought processes can change quickly, but hormones dumped into the blood or neurochemicals squirted into the brain respond more slowly. That is why we can be in a sad mood and laugh at a joke but return immediately to feeling sad.

UNFORGIVENESS MOTIVATES US TO GET RID OF
OR AVOID THE NEGATIVE

Unforgiveness is a hot potato—people try to unload it as soon as they can. All negative emotions are unpleasant when they are intense. We usually like to get rid of those feelings quickly. Sometimes our goal is simply to get rid of the unpleasant feelings. Other times it's to radically change from negative to positive feelings.

Perhaps one of the strongest examples can be seen in the case of parents needing to forgive their children. Njeri was an educator who often spoke publicly on parenting. She was also the single-parent mother of Rashid. Rashid obviously had a mind of his own. He was flunking sixth grade and was often in trouble with his teachers. One night, a month earlier, he had been caught breaking windows at the school. Njeri knew that her reputation as an educator and trainer of parents was damaged by Rashid's willfulness.

She felt like a failure at parenting. She had tried the hard line. She had taken away Rashid's privileges, restricted television and monitored his friends. Still he acted out. She knew he now would have to face the juvenile authorities, and it wasn't just he who was on trial. Her parenting was going to be judged along with her son.

Over the month, Njeri's resentment had grown. She sometimes thought, *I hate that boy.* She knew that her negativity was pushing him farther into deviance. If things were going to turn around, she would have to do something drastic.

Njeri instinctively knew that she needed new emotions. She didn't want merely to reduce her anger toward Rashid. She wanted to feel more compassion and love for him, not just less rage. She needed to forgive him, so they could start afresh and rebuild their mutual love. Eventually she was able to forgive Rashid and develop a more positive attitude. Rashid didn't respond immediately, but he finally changed his group of friends and moved away from the troubled path he had been following.

Forbearance. Most people think of forgiveness as "the way you reduce unforgiveness." But there are many ways people reduce unforgiveness besides forgiving.[4] Some people head off unforgiveness even before it develops. They forbear a transgression. Forbearance is the suppression of negative emotion through invoking the will or using psychological denial or distraction. Some simply practice forbearance; they seem to almost effortlessly suppress negative emotion. Others exert a lot of effort and willpower to forbear.

When forbearing is the result of effortful self-control, it behaves like a moral muscle.[5] Practicing forbearance can make the moral muscle stronger. Transgressions that could not be forborne a year ago seem almost weightless after a year of practice. So forbearance can come to seem effortless. However, trying to forbear many transgressions at the same time can exhaust us. With overuse, the moral muscle of forbearance is weakened. As a personality trait, forbearance is high in some people and low in others.

Successful revenge. There are many other ways to lower or avoid unforgiveness. To take a trivial example, I could reduce my unforgiveness through successful revenge. Suppose I am walking out of my office holding my ever-present cup of coffee in my forever-coffee-cup-molded right hand. A mysterious stranger bumps into me, spilling coffee on my favorite seventies pink-with-polka-dots power tie. (I love that tie.) After an initial burst of anger, I seethe with the lust for revenge. Donning my genuine Arnold Schwarzenegger *Terminator* trench coat, complete with an arsenal of weaponry that would make any National Rifle Association member envious, I track down the mysterious stranger and blow him away. I have reduced, perhaps eliminated, my unforgiveness by successful revenge.

Effective? Yes. Appropriate? No. It's like overeating. It might feel good while you're doing it, but it will give you a sour stomach in the morning and health problems if it becomes habitual. And is blowing somebody away really a fitting response to a coffee stain?

Seeing justice done. Another method to reduce unforgiveness involves experiencing justice. Justice often seems to run head-on into forgiveness.[6] Remember the argument I considered in the first chapter that forgiving means letting someone off the hook. We often think that when we forgive, we cannot hold a person accountable for his or her acts. We don't want to forgive; we want justice.

Justice is fairness. It balances both sides. The icon of justice is blindfolded and holds scales in her hands, symbolizing that she seeks to bring about a balance of fairness without regard to individual personalities. When a transgression occurs, things are put out of balance. I like to say that a transgression creates an *injustice gap*—the difference between the way I want events to settle out ideally and the way I perceive them to be at present. A large injustice gap is usually associated with more unforgiveness than is a small injustice gap. Thus, a larger injustice gap usually means a transgression will be harder to forgive.

Seeing justice done can reduce unforgiveness. It moves the way I perceive things to be closer to the way I want them to be. In the movie made from Sister Helen Prejean's book *Dead Man Walking*, the murderer was about to be put to death by lethal injection. He faced the parents of the two youths he killed. To one father he said, "I hope that seeing my death will give you peace." He instinctively knew that seeing justice done would reduce unforgiveness but not necessarily lead to forgiveness.

Justice can also be personal rather than civil or criminal. Personal justice balances the personal books. For instance, my daughter Katy Anna had a falling out when her friend failed to carry out a task that they had planned for a year. I asked Katy Anna how their relationship was. "I could easily forgive her," said Katy Anna, "if she would just apologize. She doesn't even have to mean it." Katy Anna meant that she could forgive if her friend narrowed the injustice gap by lowering herself through apologizing—even if the lowering was very slight. When a person transgresses against us, the person effectively says, "I am better than you because I can inflict this transgression on you." If the friend apologizes or makes restitution, then the friend puts the relationship back into balance by lowering himself or herself—thereby reducing or eliminating the injustice gap.

Sometimes a justice of natural consequences can reduce or eliminate unforgiveness. For example, I used to ride my bicycle to work. On Skipwith Road, a narrow two-lane road with a 40 miles-per-hour speed limit, I stayed well to the right. The traffic whizzing in both directions kept me alert. To complicate things, there was a several-inch dropoff instead of a wide shoulder.

One morning, rush traffic was moving steadily and briskly in both directions. I was as far to the right as I could get, but a truck behind me was extra-wide. It was a huge monster, periodically roaring in frustration. Because the road was narrow and the truck was wide, the driver was reluctant to try to pass me. I could tell he was getting more frustrated. Finally, oncoming traffic thinned just a bit, and he roared up beside me and loudly blared his horn.

I promptly ran off of the road into the ditch. The roughness rattled my teeth. I gamely fought the bike back onto the road. The truck zoomed ahead. In exasperation, I spread both hands wide in a questioning motion—kind of a "why me?" gesture. Suddenly I saw the truck's brake lights flare. His speed slowed dramatically until I rode my bike alongside. He matched my speed. Then he leaned across the cab and extended his right hand. His middle finger—how can I say it delicately?—seemed to be pointing the way to heaven. (He was probably witnessing to me.) Discretion, as they say, is the better part of valor. I was way too discreet to look at him. With oncoming traffic making its appearance again, he blasted away, very fast, spinning gravel.

About three minutes later, nearly a mile up the road, I saw blue flashing lights. When I rode past, a police officer was writing a ticket for the driver of the monster truck. I guess I have a bit of a mean streak, but I couldn't help waving to the truck driver. And smiling. Friendly—that's me. (Yes, I repented later.) The justice imposed by natural consequences reduced my injustice gap for having been run into a ditch.

Restorative justice seeks to find ways criminals can be returned to society. On March 14, 2002, I was speaking at an American Association of Christian Counselors conference in Los Angeles. As I changed clothes between sessions, I turned on the television. The *Montel Williams* show was on. The show's guests had each recently met with the murderer of their child. Excerpts of the meetings were shown.

The first woman's daughter, at the time of her murder, had a young child, age five, and was pregnant with a second child. The victim's mother and another daughter met with the accomplice of the killer. He had served fifteen years. The accomplice's story was gut-wrenching. The two men abducted the young woman. They planned to rape her and then shoot her in the leg to allow their escape. But after the rape, in a lonely field, they realized she had seen them and was a threat to their safety. So they talked in front of her about killing her. She asked, "Why?" She promised not to tell anyone. She told them about her five-year-old and about the baby growing in her womb. She begged them not to kill her. "Take the car. Take everything I have," she said. "I won't tell."

When they walked behind her and put the gun to her head, she said, "I forgive you, and I know God will forgive you too." She bowed her head, and the man shot her.

The accomplice was contrite. He wept as he told the story of the murder. He was clearly sorry. He wasn't just going through the motions of telling a story. The memory itself was painful to him. He seemed consumed by guilt.

At the end of his story, the mother and her daughter responded. The women forgave him. They hugged.

This contrasted with the second woman's experience. She also met with the accomplice of the killer of her daughter. He had been sentenced to seven years, served two and was paroled. The woman's attitude before the meeting was hard. She said that she wanted only to tell him how much he had hurt her.

The accomplice described the scene of the murder. The boyfriend of the victim was in money trouble over dealing drugs. So the supplier of drugs put out a contract on the boyfriend. When the contract killers found the boyfriend, he was with his girlfriend, who knew nothing of the drug dealing. The killers shot the boyfriend and, because the girl was a witness, shot her as well.

As the accomplice told the story, he was nonexpressive. He said he was sorry. He mouthed the right words, but he showed nothing in his face. He experienced guilt, it seemed, but he could not show regret.

With both the victim's mother and the accomplice being "hard" and reluctant to express softer emotions, they didn't reconcile. As the mother talked with Montel, she said she could never forgive the accomplice. At the end of the interview, Montel asked if the meeting had helped. She said it did simply because she had a chance to tell the accomplice how much she had been hurt.

The contrast was dramatic. When sincere apology was offered, its costliness brought some justice back into the first mother's life. That narrowed the injustice gap and promoted forgiveness. But when the second mother attempted only to inflict guilt on the accomplice, only a small narrowing of the injustice gap occurred. No forgiveness seemed to occur, even though the mother felt a little better.

Giving up the right to judge. People can reduce unforgiveness by giving up the right to judge. In 1996 I visited South Africa and met some survivors of the Cape Town St. James Church massacre. Pan African Conference terrorists tossed explosives into a worship service, and people were maimed and killed. The survivors I talked to all said the same thing. "I don't hold it against the terrorists. I have given judgment over to God." Some people seemed to give up judgment to God because they didn't think it was their place to judge (Mt 7:1). Others seemed to be hoping that God would enact divine justice on the terrorists (Rom 12:19).

Telling a different story. People can also reduce unforgiveness by telling a different story about the transgression or transgressor. "He was just under stress" might excuse the transgression. "I was rude to her, so I deserved what she said" might justify it. Excusing or justifying a transgression will reduce the storyteller's unforgiveness.

Accepting the transgression. Or people can reduce unforgiveness by simply accepting a transgression. "What's done is done," a person might say. "I'm just going to accept it and move on with my life."

Sometimes our best course of reducing unforgiveness is seeking justice. At other times, we tell a different story or simply accept the transgression and move on with life. Sometimes, though, we want to do more than reduce the negative feelings. That is where forgiveness enters the picture. Forgiveness is not merely reducing unforgiveness. It is something far more.

TWO TYPES OF FORGIVENESS

Forgiveness as a decision. Sometimes we make a decision that we will forgive. A friend might say, "I forgot your birthday. Can you forgive me?"

Without hesitation we might say, "Of course." We might be hurt and disappointed, but we are quick to assure the friend that we have canceled the debt and do not intend to hold the mistake against the friend. I call this type of forgiveness "decisional forgiveness."[7] When we grant decisional forgiveness, we agree to control our negative behavior (avoidance or revenge) toward the other person and restore our relationship to where it was before the transgression occurred. We hope later to reduce or eliminate our negative emotions and motivations—that is, our *desires* to act—if possible. However, we usually realize that it will take a lot longer to change emotions and motivations than to say we intend to control our behavior. There is a great distance between head and heart.

Forgiveness as emotional replacement. We may grant decisional forgiveness, hoping that it will change our behavior. But the type of forgiveness that changes the heart is "emotional forgiveness." I will call emotional forgiveness simply *forgiveness* to differentiate it from decisional forgiveness. Forgiveness is defined as *the emotional juxtaposition of positive emotions (such as empathy, sympathy, compassion, agape love or even romantic love) against (1) the hot emotions of anger or fear that follow a perceived hurt or offense or (2) the unforgiveness that follows ruminating about the transgression, which also changes our motives from negative to neutral or even positive.* Positive emotions are juxtaposed against—or experienced at the same time as—the negative emotions. At first, the positive emotions reduce the intensity of the negative emotions. If the emotional juxtaposition is strong enough and lasts long enough, the unforgiveness is changed so that it can never be experienced in the same way again. Emotional "replacement" has occurred. In the most complete forgiveness, the positive emotions of empathy, sympathy, compassion, agape love or romantic love remain without any negative feelings. Instead of wishing to avoid or seek revenge against the transgressor, the forgiver is left with feelings of good will toward the person who hurt him or her. Complete (emotional) forgiveness is experienced.

It is important to understand what I mean by emotional replacement. Our hurtful memories are not really wiped out. We almost never really forget serious hurts or offenses. We remember them differently after we forgive. Hate, bitterness and resentment are replaced with positive thoughts and feelings. The memory of the hurt remains, but it is associated with different emotions. When we completely forgive, amity is substituted for enmity.

There are two ways to eliminate unforgiveness. First, you can chip away at it by replacing a little unforgiveness with a little forgiveness in hundreds of experiences. Second, you can whack unforgiveness with a giant dose of empathy, sympathy, compassion or love, and simply overwhelm it. (One woman I know responds to perceived slights by sending the transgressor a "love bomb," which blows her bad feelings to bits—a vivid way to describe how positive emotion can disarm hurt feelings.)

Forgiving emotions motivate attempted conciliation or reconciliation if—and sometimes it is a big *if*—it is safe, prudent and possible to reconcile. Reconciliation is defined *as reestablishing trust in a relationship after trust has been violated.*

Note that forgiveness does not erase a transgression. It does not change the nature of the transgression to somehow turn a wrong into a right. When we forgive, we change the emotional attachments to the transgression. That reduces negative emotions and increases positive emotions. And we reduce our negative motivations and in the best case replace them by positive motivations (that is, acting to benefit the transgressor).

How emotional replacement works. Emotional replacement is possible because emotions are "embodied experiences" involving those gut feelings, rushes of hormones, muscle contractions, facial expressions, brain pathways, neurochemical patterns, memories and associations that I described earlier. Our working memory sorts out the messages from our body. Basically, we are simpleminded. When we think about a transgression, our body sends messages to the working memory. Our brain detects our hormones. Are our hormones those associated with resentment, bitterness, hostility and hatred? Or are our hormones compatible with empathy, sympathy, compassion and love? Are our muscle contractions, facial expressions and all the other indications more like unforgiveness or forgiveness? The working memory struggles for and arrives at a label for our feelings. If all the signs translate into negative emotions, we think, *Ah, I must be unforgiving,* even if we don't consciously use that term.

Here's how replacement occurs. If we can think of or picture the transgression again, but this time while experiencing strong forgiving emotions, the positive overpowers the negative. The forgiving emotions attach to the memory. We conclude, *Ah, I'll forgive the one who hurt me.* The attached forgiveness won't let you experience unforgiveness in the same way again—unless you have another negative experience or allow yourself to ruminate about the old transgression.

"Here's looking at you, kid." A good example comes from the classic movie *Casablanca.* Rick (Humphrey Bogart) and Ilsa (Ingrid Bergman) are lovers. Then Ilsa finds out that her husband, Victor Laszlo, whom she thought was dead, is still alive. Ilsa loves Rick, not Victor, but she feels duty-bound to return to Victor. So she leaves Rick at the train station. Jilted. Rejected.

Rick nurses his grudge. Later Ilsa and Victor walk into Rick's club in Casablanca hoping to escape the Nazis. Rick holds the only two letters of transit out of Casablanca. His unforgiveness is fierce. He lusts for revenge.

However, his romantic love for Ilsa is rekindled. It eventually subdues his unforgiveness, and in the end he lets Ilsa and Victor escape into the fog with the two letters while he stays in Casablanca to fight the Nazis. We see step by step how Rick's emotional replacement evolves. And it's the stuff of great cinema.

Forgiveness occurs by emotional replacement of unforgiveness emotions—either by chipping away at them or by replacing them all at once in a corrective emotional experience. That is the foundation on which a structure of how to forgive will be erected.

You've got male (and female). Because the idea of emotional replacement is so important, let me give you another brief example of how forgiveness replaces unforgiveness. I will use romantic love as the positive emotion because in real-life romantic relationships and marriages, re-experiencing romantic love is often the key to defeating unforgiveness.

You've Got Mail is forgiveness in an electronic key. Tom Hanks portrays Joe Fox, owner of a chain of giant bookstores. Meg Ryan owns a family-run bookstore. Hanks drives Ryan out of business. "It's nothing personal," he says. But to Ryan it is nothing but personal. She feels offended, wronged and hurt. She becomes unforgiving.

Meanwhile Ryan and Hanks develop a relationship via e-mail—corresponding with each other using pseudonyms. Neither knows the name behind the pseudonym. Then Hanks discovers Ryan's identity but continues to hide his own. Their love grows as they get to know each other through e-mail (still using pseudonyms) and through personal interaction (in which Hanks tries to win over an unsuspecting Ryan). But Ryan's unforgiveness is still stronger than her love. In the climactic scene, she discovers that Hanks is the same person she has come to know and love through e-mail. That extra amount of affection melts her heart and closes her injustice gap until love enables her to leap over it. "I wanted it to be you," she says.

It took a long time but, when the feelings of love overpowered the feelings of unforgiveness, Meg Ryan forgave. And things changed dramatically. Forgiveness was like flipping a light switch from off to on. Her heart lit up.

Forgiveness is kicking down the Berlin Wall, chipping at it hammer-blow by hammer-blow or blowing it suddenly apart. When the Wall is breached, people can run through the holes into freedom.

FORGIVENESS IS NOT JUST . . .

I have made the case that there are two types of forgiveness. Decisional forgiveness can occur at any time. It might occur soon after a transgression, but it might not. Decisional forgiveness changes our behavior but is not the forgiveness that heals our hearts. Mostly, in this book, I will focus on emotional forgiveness. Properly understood, emotions are far more than merely feelings. Emotions include thoughts, memories, associations, hormones, neurochemicals and feedback from our muscles. Forgiveness is

emotional replacement of unforgiveness wit[...]
changed emotions are connected with change[...]
vations can lead to decisional forgiveness. Or[...]
change the motivations. There is no prescribed[...]

There are many other ways people understan[...]
ple think of forgiveness as merely an *act of the w[...]
that forgiveness must be a *mental activity.* They th[...]
view of the situation, thinking differently about the[...] [...]ning to
understand the meaning of the situation differently [...] result in different
emotions and different behaviors. True, forgiveness often is instigated
when we break out of the ruts gouged by old thoughts. However, sometimes forgiveness occurs and only later does a new understanding occur.
Other people believe that forgiveness is an *action.* They believe that if we
act forgiving toward a person, our changed behavior will result in changed
thoughts and emotions. Sometimes changing my behavior can result in my
experiencing forgiveness.

I argue—I hope convincingly—that it does not matter how forgiveness
begins. It can begin with changed decisions, thoughts or actions. It can begin by the sovereign touch of God the Father, the firm confrontation of
Jesus or the gentle wooing of the Holy Spirit. But regardless of how forgiveness is begun, healing forgiveness will not occur until people's emotions change. Decisional forgiveness—releasing people from the debt
incurred by a transgression—is important, and it can occur at any point in
forgiving. But it does not in itself mean that we have forgiven from the
heart.

How does this view of forgiveness fit with Scripture? Let's look next at
the scriptural foundation of this view. That foundation, we will find, is
consistent with what has been discovered through our scientific studies on
forgiving, which is not too surprising if you know that I started out to investigate scientifically what I thought Christianity taught. I've been surprised with new insights, but I have not found Scripture to be wrong.

DISCUSSION QUESTIONS

1. Define unforgiveness. The author treats it as an emotion that motivates revenge and
   avoidance. Do you agree?

2. What is forbearance? Is forbearance scriptural? Can you find verses in Scripture
   that support your position?

difference between emotions and feelings?

author argues that people reduce unforgiveness (and close the injustice gap) in many ways that are consistent with Scripture. What do you think? Should forgiveness be the sole response of the Christian? Does the scriptural teaching that Christians must forgive prevent Christians from forbearing, accepting and seeking new understanding of a transgressor's motives, or pursuing justice?

5. Define decisional forgiveness and tell how you think it differs from emotional forgiveness. If a person grants decisional forgiveness but still feels negative toward the person who transgressed against him or her, has the person really forgiven? Would decisional forgiveness satisfy Matthew 6:12, 14-15?

6. Define reconciliation. According to Scripture, must Christians always reconcile with people with whom they have had conflicts, whom they have hurt or by whom they have been hurt?

3

The Christian Foundation
of Forgiving

He has shown you, O man, what is good.
*   And what does the LORD require of you?*
To act justly and to love mercy,
*   and to walk humbly with your God.*

MICAH 6:8

Divine and interpersonal forgiveness are cut from the same cloth but are shaped into different garments. In this chapter, I outline a theology of both divine and interpersonal forgiveness. Our goal is to treat the transgressions of others and our own transgressions in ways that gladden God's heart. To reach that goal, we must search the Scriptures.

DIVINE FORGIVENESS AND THE HEART OF GOD

God's heart of love revealed from the origin of humanity. Throughout history, people have been wronged and have wronged others. When Adam and Eve sinned (Gen 3:6), they hurt God. God responded in love and mercy. He sacrificed an animal to clothe their nakedness (Gen 3:21). But God also was just (Gen 3:14-19). He pronounced the fulfillment of his law: that Adam and Eve would be separated from the intimate fellowship of the Garden (Gen 3:23) and would die (Gen 2:17; 3:22). From the beginning, justice and mercy flowed from the Lord.

People soon began to transgress against each other. Cain killed Abel (Gen 4:8) and was banished. However, God showed his merciful heart by forbidding people from exacting retributive violence on Cain (Gen 4:11-16).

God's heart of love revealed in the Hebrew Scriptures. Judaism developed over the centuries. Within the Hebrew Scriptures, there were notable examples of interpersonal forgiveness. For instance, Joseph forgave his brothers (Gen 50:20). David forgave Saul many times, and he also forgave Nabal when Abigail asked him to. Hosea was a paragon of forgiveness for Gomer.

But the most attention was given to God's forgiveness of the people of Israel. Early in Israel's history, perhaps the most important passage concerning forgiveness in the Hebrew Scriptures was attributed by Moses to the Lord, "And he [the Lord] passed in front of Moses, proclaiming, 'The LORD, the LORD, the compassionate and gracious God, slow to anger, abounding in love and faithfulness, maintaining love to thousands, and forgiving wickedness, rebellion and sin. Yet he does not leave the guilty unpunished; he punishes the children and their children for the sin of the fathers to the third and fourth generation'" (Ex 34:6-7). This passage—or portions of it—was quoted throughout the Hebrew Scriptures (Ex 20:5-6; Num 14:17-18; Deut 24:16; Neh 9:17; Ps 86:5, 15; 103:8-10; 130:3-4; 145:8-9; Jer 31:34; Dan 9:9; Joel 2:13; Jon 4:2; Mic 7:18-19). The passage emphasizes God's love and mercy—more so as time passed—but it clearly does not give up the notion of justice. Justice and forgiveness are the twin edges of the sword of love.

The Hebrew Scriptures often showed God to be merciful *and* to remain true to the principle of justice. For example, when Abraham appealed to God over God's intended destruction of Sodom (Gen 18:22-33), their conversation showed how justice and forgiveness work together. God stated that he intended to destroy the wicked city of Sodom for the sake of the righteous. Abraham appealed on the basis of mercy (vv. 23-24), "Will you sweep away the righteous with the wicked? What if there are fifty righteous people in the city? Will you really sweep it away and not spare the place for the sake of the fifty righteous people in it?" God relented (v. 26), "If I find fifty righteous people in the city of Sodom, I will spare the whole place for their sake." Then, in turn, Abraham inquired about forty-five righteous people, then forty, thirty, twenty and even ten. God always agreed to exercise mercy. Abraham was basically inquiring about the relationship between justice and forgiveness—how much injustice God would forgive. Abraham was asking about the relationship between the Lord's "injustice gap" and his willingness to forgive. The Lord showed that his mercy was big enough to overcome a huge injustice gap.

God's heart of love revealed through Jesus. Systems of morals, ethics, philosophy and relationship were also developing throughout the non-Jewish world. Many world systems focused on justice and fairness. Others emphasized beneficence and love. However, most love-based systems were fundamentally reciprocal. People behaved kindly toward each other because they expected kindness in return.

When Jesus set aside his divinity (Phil 2:5-7) and later gave up his life (Phil 2:8), he illustrated nonreciprocal love at the heart of Christianity. He showed that God initiates salvation for humans out of love. Based on this divine initiation of love, Jesus advocated a radical personal and communal moral system, which transformed social relations—at least as Christianity understood them.

God the Father's role in divine forgiveness. God is the source of forgiveness. Let's think about the role of forgiveness within the Godhead. We know that the fundamental character of God the Father includes justice as well as mercy. We see this in Romans 11:22, which says, "Consider therefore the kindness and sternness of God: sternness to those who fell, but kindness to you, provided that you continue in his kindness. Otherwise, you also will be cut off."

Transgressions violate trust and cause pain and anger. Over the course of all human history, God the Father has been hurt, offended, betrayed and disappointed by humans countless times. God's injustice gap—the gap between reconciliation and all the pain inflicted by all of humanity—is huge. God's character, which demands perfection and justice, rightly condemns every person to an eternity of lack of fellowship with the Godhead (Rom 3:23). We simply don't measure up.

When Jesus died for humans, he was the complete propitiation for our sins. He paid the debt, satisfied the demands of the law and took our sins on himself so we could be healed. This death could satisfy God's justice because (a) Jesus was perfect and did not deserve death himself, and (b) Jesus was not only human but simultaneously divine. Theologians (including writers of Scripture) have used these forensic metaphors for centuries. Yet by themselves they are inadequate to explain all that the death of Jesus accomplished. By analogy, if someone stole $100 from me and then someone paid off the whole debt, I would still have emotional turmoil. A murderer who dies through capital punishment fulfills the demands of the law but still leaves victims in pain. Justice can move people toward complete elimination of the injustice gap, but it can rarely close the gap. Forgiveness can heal the pain within the injustice gap that justice did not eliminate.

The same might be true of God the Father when dealing with the accumulated transgressions of humanity. God through mercy had forborne previous sins (Rom 3:25). When Jesus willingly agreed to be crucified for the sins of many (Rom 3:24-25; Eph 5:2; Heb 7:26-27; 10:12; 1 Jn 2:2), he fully satisfied God's sense of justice. I hypothesize that such justice reduced God the Father's anger and hurt. People were justified (Rom 5:9). God the Father thus forgave humans (juxtaposing divine love over the pain), using Jesus' finished work (Ps 103:3; Col 2:13; 1 Jn 1:9; 2:12) to meet the demands of justice. God the Father's anger and hurt were appeased through his love for people, which replaced the negative emotions of hurt and anger with positive other-oriented emotions.

Jesus' role in divine forgiveness. Jesus is a part of the Godhead. He is the Son of God, and his heart is joined to God the Father. In his loving, self-sacrificial act of offering himself for sinful people (Phil 2:6-9), he willingly presented himself to be the object of God's justice. He thus personified love. But he also was the demonstration of the empathy, compassion and love of God the Father. He acted in accord with God the Father's loving heart.

The Holy Spirit's role in divine forgiveness. Four functions of the Holy Spirit are especially relevant for forgiveness—regeneration, sanctification, empowering for ministry and promotion of fellowship. The Holy Spirit is active in drawing the believer toward forgiveness by justifying him or her and giving new life. Forgiveness is worked into the Christian believer through the Holy Spirit by Jesus' substitutionary and sacrificial death. So the Holy Spirit actively promotes people's receipt of forgiveness—calling them when they are lost, wooing them, and bringing them to a profession of faith—to bring forth regeneration. Without the Holy Spirit there can be no regeneration. The Holy Spirit sanctifies; he calls the believer to holiness. Receiving divine forgiveness sets people apart as holy, and the Holy Spirit pulls people toward that holiness. The Holy Spirit empowers for mission and service. Thus the Holy Spirit prepares people to serve others through implanting altruistic love in their hearts—the love that flows from the Godhead. He gives gifts to those who become Christians (Rom 12:6; 1 Cor 12:4; 14:1; Eph 4:7; 1 Pet 4:10). The Holy Spirit promotes fellowship. He calls people into an adopted family and unites them into one body (1 Cor 12:27; Eph 4:4-6, 16; Col 1:18; 2:19). Forgiveness is essential to repairing disunity and thus creating a unified body of Christ.

IS ALL FORGIVENESS THE SAME?

Divine and interpersonal forgiveness are similar but different. A frequent debate sheds light on the similarities and differences. Is repentance needed before forgiveness is granted? On one side, people argue, "The perpetrator must repent before I forgive. I want to be like God. God requires repentance before forgiving. Therefore, I should too." The opposition counters, "The perpetrator should not have to repent before forgiveness is granted. I want to be like God, and Jesus is God. Jesus did not require repentance before forgiving. He prayed from the cross, 'Father, forgive them, for they know not what they are doing' (Lk 23:34). He forgave the paralytic (Mt 9:2; Mk 2:5; Lk 5:20) without being asked. So, if I am to be like Jesus, then I should offer forgiveness freely."

I believe that both sides are reasoning incorrectly. People are not God. God can know people's motives; humans can't. So God can look into our hearts and require repentance. I cannot look into another person's heart and know his or her true motives. (I can't even know my own true motives.) So interpersonal forgiveness, throughout Scripture, does not require repentance of the offender.

David Stoop (2001) suggests another argument against repentance being required prior to our forgiving.[1] People are required to forgive, and we're held accountable if we don't (Mt 6:12, 14-15; Lk 6:37-38). If repentance of the offender were required before we could forgive, then *we* would be damned if a perpetrator refused to repent. Yet surely God would not hold us accountable for something not under our control.

In Scripture we see a division between divine and interpersonal forgiveness. Fred DiBlasio, a professor of social work at the University of Maryland, Baltimore County, tallied Scriptures concerning forgiveness by God and by people.[2] Most that deal with divine forgiveness make forgiving by God conditional on repentance. Jews—who base their theology on the Hebrew Scriptures and on interpretations of those Scriptures by teachers and scholars—usually conclude that interpersonal forgiveness is embedded within offender repentance (teshuva).[3] Literally, the word teshuva means return to the path of God. Thus, when an offender sins, the offender must return. Jewish rabbi Maimonides (A.D. 1140-1204) taught that if the offender repents and asks for forgiveness, then the victim must forgive. If the victim refuses to forgive three times, then the victim has strayed from the path of God and needs to repent of that sin.

The New Testament is full of references to interpersonal forgiveness. Such forgiveness, according to the verses listed by DiBlasio,[4] is based on humility. Humans cannot know the motives of the transgressor's heart. So the victim should be merciful and humble, willing to grant forgiveness without requiring repentance.

Some might point to Luke 17:3-4. Jesus said, "So watch yourselves. If your brother sins, rebuke him, and if he repents, forgive him. If he sins against you seven times in a day, and seven times comes back to you and says, 'I repent,' forgive him." Does this verse argue for required repentance? No. It doesn't say what to do if the offender doesn't repent. Based on the weight of New Testament Scriptures and the witness of Jesus' life, I suggest that we must forgive anyway. Jesus did not mention an offender's repenting when he told Peter to forgive seventy times seven times (Mt 18:22).

Divine forgiveness differs from interpersonal forgiveness, but there are still lessons to learn about interpersonal forgiveness from studying divine forgiveness. For example, some people argue that forgiving could lead to condoning an offense. However, God forgives sin without condoning it. No one is let off the hook for immoral behavior because God forgives (Rom 6:1-2).

Some people draw on 1 John 1:9, "If we confess our sins, he is faithful and just and will forgive our sins and purify us from all unrighteousness." Based on that verse, some people say that God instantly forgives when we confess; thus, forgiveness is always decisional, never emotional. I don't believe that reasoning is correct. God's time is certainly different from human time. We observe that God will "purify us from all unrighteousness" when we forgive, but does the purification from all unrighteousness occur instantly? Or does it occur over time? Will it take place only in heaven? My analysis prompts me to conclude that in interpersonal forgiveness, decisional forgiveness might be granted instantly, but (like purifying) emotional forgiveness usually takes longer.

INTERPERSONAL FORGIVENESS: THE HUMAN SIDE

Let's formulate a brief theology of forbearance, decisional forgiveness and emotional forgiveness.

I described my understanding of unforgiveness, justice, forbearance and forgiveness in chapter two. *Forbearance* is the inhibition of initial revenge and avoidance acts and motivations. Unforgiveness—negative emotions of resentment, bitterness, hostility, hatred, anger and fear—might still creep in if a person ruminates about an injustice. The person, in spite of his or her feelings, might grant decisional forgiveness. This will eliminate the debt that was owed and satisfy the demands of justice. Decisional forgiveness promises not to act in revenge or avoidance, but it doesn't necessarily make a person feel less unforgiving. Emotional forgiveness is the emotional juxtaposition of positive other-oriented emotions against the negative unforgiveness. Those positive emotions first neutralize unforgiveness and eventually, if things work well, replace unforgiveness with a sincere agape love.

Scripture supports this understanding. Forbearance is not the same as forgiveness (Ps 4:4; Eph 4:26). Paul even contrasts forgiving and forbearing within the same passage (Eph 4:1-3; Col 3:12).

We see decisional forgiveness in the parable of the unforgiving servant (Mt 18:23-35). The servant received forgiveness based on mercy from the king. Yet the servant was unwilling to grant decisional forgiveness to his debtor. The king responded to the servant's lack of mercy and agape love by reversing his decision and holding the servant accountable for his debt. Justice was returned with justice.

Jesus speaks of decisional forgiveness in the disciples' prayer (Mt 6:12, 14-15). He says, "Forgive us our debts, as we also have forgiven our debtors." And later, "For if you forgive men when they sin against you, your heavenly Father will also forgive you. But if you do not forgive men their sins, your Father will not forgive your sins." Decisional forgiveness is changing our intentions to act. Instead of wanting harsh justice-at-any-price retribution, we give mercy to one who has transgressed against us.

Contrast that release-of-debt forgiveness with the father's forgiveness in the parable of the prodigal son. We see the heart of the father in action (Lk 15:11-32). The father was wounded deeply by the first son, who demanded his share of the father's estate. The son was unwilling to wait for the father to die. What an insult! Then the prodigal squandered his inheritance on sinful living. He returned to the father hoping to work for him. Instead, the father granted instant decisional forgiveness—canceling the debt derived from the son's insult. (The father didn't want work from his son; he wanted a father-son love.) But the father also experienced emotional forgiveness. He had no resentment, bitterness, hostility, hatred, anger or fear—no unforgiveness. He replaced those emotions with agape love for his son, based on empathy, sympathy and compassion.

The second son then expressed his resentment of the father. He accused the father of favoritism. Again, what an insult! Yet the father did not put the son in his place, lecture him or justify himself to his son. Rather, from his heart, the father forgave the second son.

This is a superb portrait of a heart overflowing with love and forgiveness. Our heavenly Father wants us to have this same forgiving heart. He wants us to forbear hurts, grant decisional forgiveness quickly, and replace negative emotions with positive emotions of love, empathy, sympathy and compassion for the person who harmed us. Both decisional forgiveness and emotional forgiveness are seen in Scripture, but people usually prefer one definition over the other. They emphasize the duty of decisional forgiveness or the experiential freedom of emotional forgiveness. Why?

Personal values in forgiveness. Virtues are personal qualities that people think of as desirable. Many virtues exist.[5] For example, self-control, truthfulness, responsibility, accountability, honesty, conscientiousness, attention to detail, obedience, faithfulness, righteousness, honoring justice and doing one's duty are each considered virtuous. We could find scriptural references that support each of those as a Christian virtue. In our research, we call them "conscientiousness-based virtues." Other virtues might include love, compassion, sympathy, mercy, gratitude, forgiveness, kindness, tenderheartedness and humility. We call those "warmth-based virtues." Conscientiousness-based virtues seem to be related to each other, and warmth-based virtues seem to be related to each other. In general, some people will simply be more virtue-minded than others. But most people value one set of virtues more than they value the other.

Knowing which virtues we value the most seems to be one key to understanding many of our choices in life. Christian denominations usually preach both the conscientiousness-based and warmth-based virtues. But you can probably think of denominations that emphasize self-control, responsibility, obedience and accountability, and others that emphasize love, compassion, empathy and sympathy. The same is true of congregations within each denomination and people within each congregation; some value one set of virtues more, and some value the other set more.

People who value conscientiousness-based virtues more tend to zero in on decisional forgiveness. They usually describe forgiveness as making a decision that cancels a debt. They stress not succumbing to unforgiving behavior. They say, "Forgive. Don't worry about what you feel. If you grant forgiveness, the feelings will follow." They often advocate that holding a transgressor accountable is good for the transgressor.

People who value warmth-based virtues tend to emphasize emotional forgiveness. They are drawn by compassion toward the people who need forgiveness. They talk about and act on agape love because they feel tender feelings or because they are convinced that gratitude springs from having been forgiven by God. Gratitude, empathy, sympathy and compassion make up the bricks of forgiveness, and agape love provides the mortar. If they don't feel forgiving, they are troubled. They might pray that the Lord will help them *feel* forgiving, and if someone suggests that they "grant forgiveness, the feelings will follow," they might think that this is hypocrisy.

In fact, though, as in most of Scripture, we are called to walk on a knife edge between conscientiousness-based and warmth-based virtues. Romans 11:22 says, "Behold the kindness and severity of God." God himself is both a conscientiousness- and warmth-based God. He endorses in Scripture both kinds of virtues. We should not denigrate either. We should esteem both.

By extension, decisional and emotional forgiveness are two sides of forgiveness, both of which need to be experienced. God does not want us grudgingly to forgive a debt. God wants us to grant decisional forgiveness eagerly (Mt 6:12) and also to forgive from the heart (Mt 18:35). That is, we are to forgive the debt, but also to experience a heart change in which the bitterness, resentment, hostility, hatred, anger and fear of unforgiveness are replaced with the sympathy, empathy, compassion and love of emotional forgiveness.

Other Christian-consistent ways of dealing with unforgiveness. All Christians are admonished to grant decisional forgiveness, but what if they cannot experience emotional forgiveness? Are people who are unable or unwilling to emotionally forgive doomed to misery? No. As I said in the previous chapter, people cope with the stress of negative emotions by using many strategies. Many of those strategies are consistent with Scripture. Only a few—like revenge (Lev 19:18; Deut 32:35; Rom 12:19; Heb 10:30)—are explicitly forbidden.

For instance, we might simply accept the event and move on with our lives. Or we might turn judgment over to God and disavow our right to judge (Gen 18:25; Mt 7:1). Or we might convince ourselves that the transgression wasn't as harmful as we had thought. For example, instead of holding a grudge against his brothers, Joseph said, "You intended to harm me, but God intended it for good to accomplish what is now being done, the saving of many lives" (Gen 50:20). Understanding why a person's actions, which we had assumed were wrong, were in fact just and fair can also reduce unforgiveness, just as understanding mitigating circumstances behind a wrongdoer's actions can help us forgive. Or we might just forget with the passage of time.

We might also seek justice to reduce the injustice gap. Forgiveness and justice can sometimes seem to clash,[6] but they also can work together. Justice is certainly consistent with Scripture.

> It is unthinkable that God would do wrong,
>   that the Almighty would pervert justice. (Job 34:12)

Further, Scripture says:

> This is what the LORD says:
>   "Maintain justice
>   and do what is right,
>   for my salvation is close at hand
>   and my righteousness will soon be revealed. (Is 56:1)

The prophet Amos says:

> But let justice roll on like a river,
>   righteousness like a never-failing stream! (Amos 5:24)

So, we might reduce our feelings of unforgiveness by seeing justice enacted (Deut 16:20; Mt 7:1-5) by the courts. For example, if someone notes that a court has convicted and punished a criminal offender or decided fairly in a civil dispute, then justice reduces the injustice gap. If a person observes ironic natural consequences or perceives God to have punished an offender (Acts 5:1-11), then that natural or divine justice also reduces the injustice gap. In each case, unforgiveness is reduced even though emotional forgiveness does not occur.

Personal justice can also reduce unforgiveness. When a person transgresses against a victim, the transgressor essentially sets himself or herself superior to the victim. A transgressor *ipso facto* says, "I can wound you and get away with it." But if a transgressor tries to balance the emotional books through confessing, repenting, expressing regret, apologizing sincerely, offering restitution and punitive damages (Lk 17:3-4), and making amends (Eccles 10:4), then personal justice is perceived. Unforgiveness is reduced, and forgiveness might be stimulated.

Emotional forgiveness is difficult. How easy it is to forgive depends on the size of the injustice gap. If we can narrow the injustice gap, we can lessen negative unforgiving emotions. As negative emotions subside, they are more easily neutralized by positive other-oriented emotions. Forgiveness from the heart is more likely.

INTERPERSONAL FORGIVENESS: THE DIVINE SIDE

There are various roles within the Godhead in stimulating interpersonal forgiveness.

God the Father. God the Father is sovereign. He is the one who shapes our character and acts to stimulate justice, mercy and love in us. The works of God the Father appeal to both: those who naturally gravitate toward warmth-based and toward conscientiousness-based virtues. God's justice, while essential to forgiveness, is mixed with God the Father's love, mercy, grace, compassion, caring and empathy for the human condition to bring about full forgiveness. God's love is at the root of forgiveness.

Jesus. Jesus, through his sacrificial death, became our example of how to lay aside our rights when we have been offended. Jesus did no wrong, but he laid aside his rights to retaliation or to justice (Mt 26:42; Lk 22:42). On the cross, he forgave (Lk 23:34) from his heart. If we take Jesus as our example, we will work for justice, as Jesus did during his lifetime. However, when we are wounded, we too must lay aside our right for justice and, instead, forgive as Jesus did. Jesus was a model to both: those who favor warmth-based and conscientiousness-based virtues.

The Holy Spirit. Forgiveness plays an essential part in each of the four doctrines of the Holy Spirit.

The Holy Spirit works *regeneration*. The Holy Spirit works to regenerate relationships in the same way that he helps regenerate the spirit of a believer. He calls people toward reconciliation (Eph 2:14-16). He woos people to forgive and mend their bonds. He brings them to a decision to forgive and, if conditions are right, to pursue reconciliation.

The Holy Spirit *sanctifies*. Sanctification is the growth of the character of God within us. God's character includes a heart of love, justice and forgiveness. Those are the essential components of the nature of God. As I have argued, part of the way that we see love is in the balance of forgiveness and justice. That is, the Holy Spirit is active in helping us reduce unforgiveness through the pursuit of justice, the furthering of social justice, forbearance and all the other biblically consistent ways of reducing unforgiveness. But the Holy Spirit is also active in sanctifying us by building empathy, sympathy, compassion and agape love into our character—in short, the Holy Spirit directs us beyond ourselves to other-oriented emotions showing mercy and grace. Without the Holy Spirit there can be no sanctification.

The Holy Spirit *empowers* for mission and service. The Holy Spirit empowers Christian believers to carry out the Great Commission of going into the whole world and baptizing and making disciples (Mt 28:19-20). This requires forgiveness because people throughout the world are not reconciled with each other. Conflicts and tension are endemic to human life. Without the Holy Spirit there can be no empowerment for mission.

In addition, the Holy Spirit empowers Christians for service. Power is the fundamental motivation of the fallen person. Service kneels to help while power stands to rule. People are inherently hurtful and manipulative. Offenses and hurts will inevitably be inflicted upon each Christian throughout his or her life. Offenses make us want to stand and fight. We can resist the devil without fighting (Jas 4:7; 1 Pet 5:9). Those who serve God through the Holy Spirit must build a forgiving character that can resist the cry for the reassertion of power stimulated by the inevitable hurts and offenses that we receive. This, of course, is intertwined with the sanctifying work of the Holy Spirit. If humility, gratitude, compassion and love are not built into a person's character, there is little will to listen to the Holy Spirit's whispers that coax costly service. Without the Holy Spirit there can be no empowerment to service.

The Holy Spirit promotes *fellowship* (see Acts 2). Forgiveness is essential to any bond of unity. People *will* violate trust and *will* betray us. Without the Holy Spirit's work in promoting forgiveness, there can be no fellowship of Christians or even a fellowship of trusting life together between Christians and non-Christians. Without the Holy Spirit there can be no sustained fellowship.

I believe that God, in each part of the Trinity, works to promote forgiveness in the world as one essential part of carrying out his relationship of love with a fickle humankind. Through the work of God the Father, Jesus the Son and the Holy Spirit, we humans are called to promote forgiveness and reconciliation. We learn how to forgive through Scripture, through human examples or models, through the Lord's dealing with us in our sins and failures, and by experiencing gratitude for the forgiveness we have received.

HOW CAN GOD FORGIVE? DOES GOD EXPERIENCE UNFORGIVENESS? CAN PEOPLE FORGIVE GOD?

Because I have taken a position that forgiveness is of two types, decisional and emotional, another question arises. How can God forgive? Of course, we know that God is a forgiving God (Ex 34:6-7), but how can this forgiveness come about?

Someone might say, by claiming that God is forgiving, does that mean God had to experience unforgiveness? Not at all. Unforgiveness is a sin (Mt 6:14-15), and God cannot sin.

Let's consider decisional forgiveness. God could be motivated to vengeance (Deut 32:35; Ps 94:1; Jer 50:15; Rom 12:19; Heb 10:30) and avoidance (Is 14:22). God can, by granting forgiveness, thus give up those motivations (Ex 32:14; 1 Sam 15:11; Jer 18:8; 26:13, 19; Jon 3:9; see also Num 23:19).

What about emotional forgiveness? God can feel anger (Ex 4:14; Num 11:1; 12:9; 22:22; Ezra 5:12; Ps 103:8; Nahum 1:3). God can thus forgive by replacing the righteous anger (Ps 60:1; Hos 11:9) with positive emotions and conciliatory motivations *before* unforgiveness develops. Therefore, using my definitions, we can see how God can forgive both decisionally and emotionally.

At times people become angry, disappointed or even unforgiving toward God.[7] A tragedy occurs. A woman wonders, *Why?* She ruminates until she is bitter and resentful that God would allow or, worse, cause such a tragedy. Can she forgive God? If so, what does it mean to forgive God?

Many people have trouble with the concept of forgiving God because God cannot do wrong. They are treating forgiveness as being appropriate only for an objective wrong. I do not believe this is the best understanding of forgiveness. Many times people become unforgiving when a misunderstanding occurs or when a decision goes against their wishes. They might become unforgiving if a natural disaster injures them. Unforgiveness is prompted by hurts as well as by wrongs.

As I've argued, I believe that unforgiveness is an emotion that motivates revenge or avoidance (or both). The fact that unforgiveness is not justified—against a friend or against God—does not invalidate the emotion and does not reduce the motivations to avoid or seek revenge.

To take the position that forgiveness can occur only when an objective wrong occurs, one must then say either that such unforgiving feelings are invalid or that somehow the feelings are not *really* unforgiveness. I think neither of those options is acceptable.

Rather, people can forgive God by decisional forgiveness. They declare their intention not to avoid God or not to reject him. They declare conciliatory motivations toward God, which prepares their way to move back toward God. If emotional unforgiveness has developed, people can change their negative emotions toward God. When they emotionally forgive God, they replace unforgiveness with love. After people deal with the emotions and motivations, they can confront their accusations against God.

Should people feel guilty about blaming God? I believe that after we have dealt with any anger or disappointment at God, then we will come to repent of our accusations. We will recognize our disappointment for what it was—our damaged pride and our lack of trust. If we are particularly graced, we might even recognize and repent before we deal fully with our anger and disappointment with God.

When we are in the midst of emotional upheaval, though, that is not usually the time when we focus on guilt. We cannot destroy unforgiveness by overwhelming it with guilt. We simply cover up the emotions. Instead, we must overcome the negativity of anger or disappointment with God by re-experiencing events that demonstrate God's trustworthiness and love.

Questions may arise about this theology of interpersonal forgiveness. Let's look at some of them.

Do Christians Forgive More and Better Than Other People?

What research tells us. Forgiveness is often associated with Christianity. But Christianity does not own forgiveness. To be human is to have experienced hurt, offense, betrayal and rejection. Forgiving is one way that all creatures can deal with those events that wound the soul. Forgiveness—like love, honesty, justness, truth, responsibility, accountability, altruism, gratitude, compassion, mercy, grace, rationality and creativity—resides in the common grace given by God to all people. To forgive is human.

Yet it seems clear that to the extent that Christians practice Christian virtue—which is characterized by love and gratitude, yielding to God, and agape love that does not ignore justice—they ought to be expected to emotionally forgive more often than people who do not embrace such beliefs and values. Furthermore, to the extent that Christians practice Christian virtue, characterized by responsibility, self-control, justice and accountability, they ought to be expected to grant decisional forgiveness more often than people who don't embrace such beliefs. So can we expect Christians to be more adept at forgiving on the whole than are non-Christians?

From Scripture, we would expect Christians to be forgiving. But just because Christians *should* forgive doesn't mean that Christians always *do* forgive. Neal Krause and Berit Ingersoll-Dayton, of the University of Michigan, interviewed elderly Christians about their experiences with forgiveness.[8] Not everyone experienced forgiveness similarly. Some usually forgave instantly. Others were reluctant forgivers or intentionally held grudges. Still others believed that transgressors had to earn forgiveness through apologizing, groveling, suffering or making restitution. In addition, Christians are not the only people who are grateful, loving, empathic, sympathetic, humble and unselfishly loving. If we are honest, we must admit that we know many people who are high-minded but do not name Jesus as Lord.

Nevertheless, our research[9] and other research by Joann Tsang and her colleagues[10] show that Christians *as a whole* tend to be more forgiving than are people of other religions, who are in turn more forgiving than are people who don't profess a religious orientation. These differences are not as much as Christians might hope, given the centrality of forgiveness in Christianity. Yet the differences are consistent. Why? There are many possible reasons.

Christians accept the importance of forgiveness and practice it. Forgiveness is at the center of Christianity. God, out of mercy and lovingkindness, forgives through Jesus' death on the cross. People become Christians when they accept God's forgiveness, though their acceptance does not cause God to forgive. Rather, God is the agent who brings forgiveness about. When people respond in gratitude to having been forgiven, part of their response is to forgive those who harm them—and to respond in forgiveness afterward. Gratitude, in effect, creates a path where God's life-giving water of forgiveness can flow through Christians to others. We forgive our family members, others in the church, our neighbors and our coworkers. Almost all people can forgive others—especially when it is in their own best interests to do so. But, following Jesus' instruction, example and commands—out of gratitude for what God has done for us—Christians are to forgive even our enemies. That is the radical teaching and example of Jesus Christ.

Mike McCullough and I reviewed the early research on religion and forgiveness in an article we published in 1999.[11] We found that when Christians were asked, "Are you a forgiving person?" they consistently said they were. Yet when the research examined their emotional responses long after transgressions, they were found to be little or no different than nonbelievers in their forgiveness. At that time, we interpreted this paradox as possibly due to the social pressure on Christians to say they are forgiving but not really to feel forgiving. Following the reasoning I have outlined in this book, though, we might suspect that this reflects a difference in decisional and emotional forgiveness. Christians might be more forgiving in the sense of granting decisional forgiveness and making an intention statement not to retaliate or avoid the person. However, their emotions might remain stirred up. Emotional forgiveness might take just as long in Christians as in others.

Another possibility exists. Maybe the 1999 finding was due to not being able to measure forgiveness accurately. Our later research[12] and the research of others[13] have cast doubt on the original finding. Since some of the methodological problems with the early research were corrected, psychologists have found that Christians actually are quicker to forgive than most non-Christians—though there clearly are many exceptions.

Christians respond out of a changed spirit, thus experience changed emotions and motivations. The major emotions and motivations of Christianity, arguably, are gratitude, love, humility, justice and forgiveness. Because God acted first in love, mercy and justice, the Christian response to God's initiation was gratitude. In Christianity, God is always the initiator. Some people have argued that gratitude is *the* basic Christian emotion (Ps 50:14, 23; 1 Thess 5:18).

Agape love is the Christian's response to God's love and is the act we are inspired to do for others. Jesus boiled down the essence of the law into two summary commandments: "Love the Lord your God with all your heart and with all your soul and with all your mind. This is the first and greatest commandment. And the second is like it: 'Love your neighbor as yourself.' All the Law and the Prophets hang on these two commandments" (Mt 22:37-40; Mk 12:28-34). Others took up that refrain (Rom 13:9; Gal 5:14; Jas 2:8). When Jesus identified love as the embodiment of the Law and the Prophets, he named it as a central Christian emotion.

Christianity also emphasizes humility (Phil 2:1-11). Paul urged people to have the same self-sacrificial mind as did Jesus: to lay down one's life on behalf of others and to count others better than oneself (Phil 2:3). Peter counted humility as a cardinal virtue (1 Pet 3:8-9), saying, "Finally, all of you, live in harmony with one another; be sympathetic, love as brothers, be compassionate and humble. Do not repay evil with evil or insult with insult, but with blessing, because to this you were called so that you may inherit a blessing." Also, he admonished the believers to clothe themselves with humility because

"God opposes the proud,
 but gives grace to the humble." (1 Pet 5:5)

God also is a just God (Ex 34:7). He is by nature the essence of justice, and he demands that Christians be fair and just as well. In Scripture, Micah captures these godly human emotions and motivations.

He has shown you, O man, what is good.
 And what does the LORD require of you?
To act justly and to love mercy,
 and to walk humbly with your God. (Mic 6:8)

God is forgiving (Ex 34:6). He is merciful. In response, we are also to be forgiving.

If we practice Christian emotions and motivations over a long time, we may develop more virtuous character dispositions.[14] In an initial study of virtues, we have found that Christians seem to rank warmth-based virtues such as forgiveness, humility, gratitude and love higher than do non-Christians.[15]

The Christian community stimulates forgiveness. Research done by Robert Wuthnow on small groups suggests that people in small groups help each other forgive.[16] To some degree, several things might be happening. Perhaps group members encourage and support each other, empowering warmth-based virtues. Perhaps they hold each other accountable to practice Christian ideals, activating conscientiousness-based virtues. Perhaps they simply exert social pressure to conform to a Christian ethic. Besides these, perhaps there is something mystical about the body of Christ, and the Lord acting in the unseen world empowers the church to be his body.

Why Doesn't Our Experience Match Our Theology of Triumphant Forgiveness?

Christians have experienced God's mercy and grace—God gave Jesus freely to die for us (Rom 5:1; Col 2:13-14). Having received such gifts from God, Christians should be ever-merciful and quick to forgive. We *should*. Christians are a people of the Book, so we are commanded to forgive and commended to mercy. We know that we can do all things through Christ who strengthens us. We should succeed.

But we often fail. Our experience is more in line with Peter. He plaintively whined to Jesus, "Lord, how many times shall I forgive my brother when he sins against me?" (Mt 18:21; Lk 17:3-5). How many, indeed, Lord? Almost daily, we catch ourselves judging others for not forgiving—often for not forgiving *us*. In our moments of honesty, we feel the deserved shame of knowing how short we fall of forgiving anyone seventy times seven times (Mt 18:22). I know in my heart some of the resentments I harbor. I know that my heart is deceitful and that I am not even aware of much of my own sin (Jer 17:9-10). Sometimes my intentions are good. I want to forgive, yet I often fail.

Our inability to live up to our high calling to be forgiving people can motivate us to react in several ways.

• We can fool ourselves into believing forgiveness isn't important. Yet, in our hearts, we know that it is central to the heart of God in a fallen world.

- We can acknowledge forgiveness's importance but pay little attention to it. Yet, we don't want to render mere lip service to forgiveness simply because it is hard to do.

- We can quickly say that we forgive but never really release grudges. When we do this, we eventually confront our own heart. Who are we fooling? Certainly not God, who knows us intimately.

- We can work to forgive but do so in the flesh (as an idol to our own good character). Yet the works of the flesh are dead works, and none of us want to launch off doing dead works apart from God.

- We can work sincerely and diligently to forgive because we want to be transformed by the renewal of our minds (Rom 12:2). We want to put aside impure motives, bring our sinfulness to Jesus—not to be condemned but to be transformed—receive his work within us, and practice forgiving (and thus loving) with all of our heart, soul, mind, and strength. We want to forgive and love our family, friends, coworkers, acquaintances and even enemies, because in doing so we show that God's love is at work within us and we are practicing the love of God.

Clearly, this fifth response is the one we *should* cultivate. Yet how do we do this? I can forgive only by the grace and mercy of God. I cannot forgive in my own strength. But on the other hand, knowing that my own strength is not sufficient for me to truly forgive does not relieve me from the responsibility of trying to forgive. I know that I am accountable for whether I forgive, and I must work at forgiving.

WHY DO WE EXPERIENCE SUCH PARADOXICAL DILEMMAS?

Paradoxes are not easy to understand. Larry Christensen, one of the greatest teachers about Christian families in the 1970s, once described God's truth as like a hula-hoop.[17] Truth is unified and whole. A mind is like a matchbox. Getting the whole truth into our mind is impossible. It is too big, too complex. So it is as if God splits the hula-hoop. One end is inserted in the left side of our head. The other end is inserted in the right. We must whip our attention back and forth from truth to truth to try to make sense of the paradoxes. If we had God's perspective, we could see the unified truth. From the limited human perspective, we see two contrasting sides.

Christensen suggests that God might have done this intentionally. Because our minds cannot contain all of the truth, we must depend on the leading and guiding of the Holy Spirit to discern which side of the paradox to apply in a particular situation. Were this not the case, we would have flawless decision rules and would be tempted to use rules instead of relying on God.

HOW DO WE RELY TOTALLY ON JESUS AND YET WORK CONSCIENTIOUSLY TO FORGIVE?

Our effort and striving alone are not sufficient. The movie *The Mission* captured the essence of forgiveness well. Rodrigo Mendoza (Robert de Niro's character) was a slave trader in South America. He captured Indians to sell as slaves. He got in a fight and killed his brother with a knife. He was imprisoned, and Father Gabriel, head of the mission above the falls, visited Rodrigo in prison. Rodrigo was remorseful for his many sins, but he was in complete despair over his sinful state.

"Nothing can be done to redeem me," he said to Father Gabriel.

"There is a way," said Father Gabriel, "if you are willing to risk it."

"I'll try if you are willing to risk failing," said Rodrigo.

After that, a new scene opened. Father Gabriel, Father John and others were trudging toward the mountaintop Indian village. Rodrigo trailed behind, dragging a bag of heavy Spanish armor. The scene took about ten minutes. Rodrigo dragged the armor over rough ground, boulders and streams. He tugged it up waterfalls. He exerted to the limit of his ability.

Father John, moved by compassion for Rodrigo, begged Father Gabriel to cut Rodrigo free from his burden.

"He doesn't think it's enough," said Father Gabriel. Rodrigo continued to drag his burden behind in true remorse and penance.

At last they reached the Indian village at the top of the falls. The children recognized Rodrigo's coming and ran to tell the elders of the tribe. They gathered to watch Rodrigo drag his heavy burden the final distance. Completed, Rodrigo collapsed to his knees in the depressive knowledge that all his suffering was not enough to cover his guilt. Head back, he awaited his deserved death at the hands of the Indians. The chief motioned. A warrior grabbed a knife and rushed toward Rodrigo. Holding the knife to Rodrigo's jugular, the warrior looked to the chief for instructions to exact justice. The chief nodded. With a powerful stroke, the warrior sliced the rope and kicked Rodrigo's burden over the cliff, where it was covered in clear, fresh water.

Rodrigo collapsed in the joy of freedom. He could not earn forgiveness through his own efforts. Someone else had to grant forgiveness. It was a gift of mercy and grace.

Rodrigo was like the Pharisee in Jesus' parable of the Pharisee and the tax collector (Lk 18:10-14). He prayed. He offered sacrifices. He worked to deserve forgiveness. But forgiveness could not be grasped by hands clenched in effort, only through an on-your-knees open-handed attitude of receiving love, mercy and grace. Forgiveness burst upon Rodrigo by surprise. Father Gabriel was surprised at the love of God. The Indian chief was surprised at his own joy that came in granting forgiveness and freeing his tribe from hatred. Father John, who had wanted to cut the burden away earlier, realized that he would have deprived Rodrigo of the knowledge that he could not earn forgiveness through his own effort. He would have prevented Rodrigo from experiencing true Christianity—that, in the end, forgiveness is a gift of mercy, grace and love. There is a place for human effort, but striving can take us only so far. Justice can take us only so far.

We cooperate with the Lord. We have a part and so does God. We realize that our part is to try to understand forgiveness, discern when we need to practice forgiveness, and admit the limitations of our own self-effort. Basically, we are incapable of truly forgiving in a spiritually meaningful way under our own power. Through Jesus' work applied to us, though, God can do remarkable things. He can work forgiveness through us. Two verses capture this dilemma. "I [Jesus] am the vine; you are the branches. If a man remains in me and I in him, he will bear much fruit; apart from me you can do nothing" (Jn 15:5). Yet, "I can do everything through him who gives me strength" (Phil 4:13).

We are like irrigation structures. As Christians, our motive is to spread the living water of God widely and deeply to the field of living plants (people) that God has placed us near. It is as if we erect a system of movable canals and irrigation pipe for doing that. That system is our abilities, talents and skills. The system can look beautiful to observers.

But if we try to irrigate fields on our own, apart from God, we can only use spit and urine to provide water and nourishment for the plants. Both have good chemicals mixed with small amounts of liquid, but both also have chemicals that can damage plants. On our own we are an elaborate irrigation system in acres and acres of a dying field.

When we draw close to the source of living water and connect with it, life-giving water can gush *through* our structures and spray over a giant field. We can scatter God's love abroad.

We do not draw near to the source of living water merely to have our own pipes filled with water. True, irrigation cannot happen *unless* we are filled. Yet the filling of our pipes—our personal nourishment—is not the object of drawing close to God. It is a by-product. We are structures who are created not to look pretty or to receive the nourishment in our own power for our own benefit, but to be conduits of love to others. If we act properly, as conduits of love, then (paradoxically) we are winsome, are filled and are powerful ministers of love.

Putting off unforgiveness and putting on forgiveness. This does not mean that forgiveness is easy for Christians. We do not forgive because it is easy, but because it is right and is a response to God's love and forgiveness of us. Christians believe that, with the fall of humanity, things became abnormal. Since then, humans cannot "go with the flow" and let nature take its course. Instead we must battle the principle of sin. When we are transgressed against, we must therefore fight unforgiveness instead of giving in to our natural inclination toward emotions of resentment, bitterness and hatred and our motivations of avoidance and revenge. By doing so, we put off the old nature (Rom 6:1-4, 12-14; Gal 5:19-21; Col 3:5-11). We must likewise forbear, forgive and seek justice. By doing so, we put on the new (redeemed) nature (Rom 6:5-11, 17-19; Gal 5:22-26; Col 3:12-17). This battle is not winnable by independent human striving (Rom 7:14-24). We can win only by cooperating with God (Rom 7:24—8:11; Eph 2:8-10; Phil 2:12).

WHAT IS THE ROLE OF THE COMMUNITY IN FORGIVENESS?

In his 1995 book *Embodying Forgiveness*, Greg Jones, theologian and dean of the Divinity School at Duke University, argues against what he calls therapeutic forgiveness.[18] Therapeutic forgiveness is forgiveness for the sake of one's own therapy. Jones suggests that forgiveness is meant to be experienced within the body of Christ—the church. Attempts to make it a type of secular or even Christian psychotherapy are wrong.

Theologian David Augsburger has argued for years that forgiveness is intended to include reconciliation.[19] He suggests that in biblical times the Hebrews did not parse forgiveness into mere emotional forgiveness.

Rather, biblical forgiveness was meant to include both the intrapersonal and interpersonal. He treats forgiveness as an inclusive term that I would say involves both forgiveness and reconciliation. What I call emotional forgiveness he calls agape love; what I call reconciliation, he calls forgiveness.

People often discuss transgressions. Such talk affects whether one forgives. That does not mean, though, that forgiveness includes talking about transgressions. If that were true, people could not forgive an absent or dead person. In part three of this book I will describe how to talk productively about transgressions. For now, let me acknowledge that discussing transgressions can involve requests for explanations, accounts of one's acts, seeking forgiveness, receiving forgiveness and accepting having been forgiven.

Social psychologist Roy Baumeister and his colleagues have described two cases when communication of forgiveness does not match a person's internal experience of forgiving.[20] In "hollow forgiveness" a person says he or she forgives but secretly harbors a grudge. The victim remains upset but may or may not act on the grudge. The transgressor may feel truly forgiven or may sense the victim's hesitancy. Baumeister, Exline and Stillwell also identify "silent forgiveness." The victim internally forgives but does not admit the forgiveness to the transgressor. Rather, the victim uses the trans-

Table 3.1. Seven Characteristics of Biblical Forgiveness

As Christians, when we forgive, we
- **forbear**, limiting our initial reaction through a developed forgiving personality, practice forgiving, suppression of negative motives
- **freely grant decisional forgiveness** as soon as we can, implying our intention not to seek revenge or avoid, but to seek conciliation to the extent possible and to desire good for the person who harmed us
- **find other biblical ways to avoid or reduce unforgiveness** such as seeking justice, accepting the wrong and moving on, turning judgment over to God, telling a different story about the event (see Gen 50:20)
- **focus on the good of the other person** more than we focus on ourselves and the damage we have felt
- **feel agape love, empathy, sympathy, compassion** for the person who harmed us
- **forgive because we have been forgiven** rather than because we receive a blessing when we forgive
- **follow through** on our changed emotions and motivations to not act negatively toward the person but to bless the person

gression to make the transgressor suffer guilt or offer restitution.

Forgiveness does not have to occur within a formal religious setting, but it seems that forgiveness is tied to people's spiritual existence. Friends can help each other forgive. Robert Wuthnow, from Princeton University, has found that people receiving support from friends in church groups report being able to forgive more than church people who do not participate in groups.[21]

In these first three chapters, I have described models of unforgiveness, justice, forbearance, and both decisional and emotional forgiveness. There are seven parts to a biblically based model of forgiving, which I have summarized in table 3.1. We now are ready to move on to learn how we can forgive more easily and quickly.

DISCUSSION QUESTIONS

1. Did God change his character between the time of the Hebrew Scriptures and the time of the New Testament? If not, reconcile the two treatments of forgiveness. Is there a conflict?

2. The author identified Exodus 34:6-7 as the key passage on forgiveness and justice in the Hebrew Scriptures because it was quoted or paraphrased numerous times throughout that portion of the Bible. Look up the verses that quote or paraphrase that passage. Arrange them in roughly chronological order. See whether you see any change in how the divinely inspired authors of Scripture treated that passage as time went on.

3. The author argues that divine forgiveness differs from interpersonal forgiveness. Do you agree or not? Give your reasons.

4. Is forbearance the same as forgiveness? If you forbear a hurt, it is scriptural, but should you be satisfied that you are acting consistently with Scripture if you still hold unforgiveness in your heart?

5. If you decide to forgive and grant forgiveness but still hold hate in your heart, what do you think your responsibility is—if any?

6. The author identified two types of preferences for virtues—conscientiousness-based virtues and warmth-based virtues. Do you favor one cluster more than the other? Do you agree that if you favor conscientiousness-based virtues, you have been drawn to looking at forgiveness more in terms of decisional forgiveness? Do you agree that if you favor warmth-based virtues, you have been drawn to looking at forgiveness more in terms of emotional forgiveness?

7. The author said that forgiveness and justice can sometimes seem to clash. Do you

agree? Can you give an example of such a clash? Can you find any examples in your own life in which you saw justice done and that made you more willing to forgive?

8. Do you agree that the larger the injustice gap, the more the unforgiveness and the harder a transgression is to forgive? Can you give an example from your own life?

9. Have you ever blamed God for a hardship or injustice you experienced? How did you deal with your blame? Do you still harbor disappointment with God?

10. What is the role of other Christians and of family in helping each other forgive? For you, what do you think the line between helpfulness and intrusiveness is? Do you have a responsibility to help a friend or family member who is bitter consider forgiveness? If you were bitter, what would you think if someone pointed that out to you? What kind of relationship would be necessary for such confrontation? How would a person confront you sensitively yet honestly?

How to REACH Forgiveness

The Pyramid Model to REACH Forgiveness is rooted in replacing negative emotions associated with anger, fear and unforgiveness with positive emotions associated with empathy (and perhaps sympathy, love, compassion, even romantic love). It helps people REACH forgiveness through using five steps. First, to get a bird's-eye view, walk with me up the Pyramid. The steps spell out the acrostic REACH. I have pictured it in figure A.

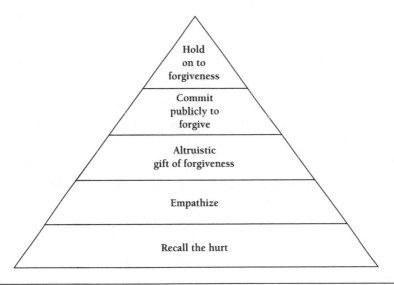

Figure A. The pyramid model to REACH forgiveness

Recall the hurt (R). When we are hurt, we often try to protect ourselves by denying our hurt. To heal, we must recall the hurt as objectively as we can. Don't rail against the person who hurt you, expend fruitless effort in finger wagging, waste time wishing for an apology that will never be offered, or dwell on your victimization. Instead, admit that a wrong was done to you.

Empathize (E). Empathy is seeing things from another person's point of view. To forgive, try to feel the transgressor's feelings. Even though it is difficult, try to identify with the pressures that made the person hurt you. Empathy puts a human face on suffering. How would he or she explain the harmful acts? Empathy is only one of the emotions you can use to replace negative emotions. You also can sympathize with, feel compassion for, experience agape love toward, or kindle romantic love for the transgressor. Each of those can help you replace the unforgiveness.

Offer the altruistic gift of forgiveness (A). Have you ever harmed or offended a friend, parent or partner who later forgave you? Think about your own guilt. Then consider how you felt when you were forgiven. When you remember how you felt, you might be willing to give a selfless gift of forgiveness to those who have hurt you.

Commit publicly to forgive (C). If you make your forgiveness public, you are less likely to doubt it later. Tell a friend, partner or counselor that you have forgiven the person who hurt you.

Hold on to forgiveness (H). When you doubt whether you have forgiven, there are many ways to stop forgiveness from slipping.

PUTTING THE PYRAMID MODEL INTO PRACTICE

Knowing that you must take five giant steps to forgive is not the same as knowing how to take those steps. Sometimes we feel like Lilliputians trying to match Gulliver's giant strides. Forgiving seems impossible. However, in our research over the years, my colleagues and I have been able to help people take those giant steps by having them approach forgiveness in a measured, gradual way.

You will forgive best if you identify specific people whom you wish to forgive. Then practice trying to forgive each one. Apply the five steps to one person at a time. Think through your life and identify some people you want to forgive.

Who might need your forgiveness? Transgressions can occur in almost any setting, but some settings seem to invite transgressions. See whether you can find people you need to forgive.

Romantic relationships put egos on the line. We leave ourselves open to betrayal when we invest our love in another fallible human. Failed dating relationships, terminated cohabitation and divorces provide much fuel for the fires of unforgiveness. Is there a romantic partner you want to forgive?

Note some specific transgressions.

Families of origin influence us. Disappointments, hurts, misunderstandings and just plain cruelty may show up in both parents and children. Siblings often compete and quarrel. Families divide over contested wills. The family is a crucible for pounding out differences, and as such, it is a natural laboratory in which both forgiveness and reconciliation can be practiced. Are there incidents from your family history that still rankle? Write notes.

In the *church*, much of the emotional life of the Christian is lived out. I have seen people who never returned to a church because the pastor wasn't friendly enough or didn't remember their names on the second visit. I have seen churches split with hurt feelings lasting for decades. I have seen disagreements between pastors and board members, or pastors and parishioners. We have all seen the devastation that can arise from clergy sexual misconduct in the crisis in the Roman Catholic Church during 2002. Sexual misconduct in Protestant congregations is also frequent, and parishioners can be wounded for life because a pastor has an affair. Of course, petty power struggles can arise in any group whose members spend time together, and the church is no exception. The church is a garden that should produce fruit, and yet the weeds of unforgiveness often choke off the fruit trees at the root. Do you have any relationships with church members, past or present, that need your prayerful attention?

In the *workplace*, time is spent in ego-involving tasks. Wages and salaries are interpreted as opportunities for valuing and devaluing. Interactions with bosses or subordinates can value or devalue. Scarce resources and power differentials set the stage for hurt feelings.[1] Have you been transgressed against in the workplace?

Healthcare settings provide opportunities to forgive.[2] The Institute of Medicine estimates that between 44,000 and 98,000 medical errors are made each year that lead to death of a patient. Have you or has a loved one been a victim of a medical error? Has an arrogant physician, nurse or health administrator demeaned you? Have you been ignored when you were in pain? Has an insurance company treated you unfairly? Also, when medical problems arise in our own and our loved ones' lives, we often cannot understand why God allows those to happen. Do you hold any unforgiveness of God?

Perhaps you have run up against the *justice system*.[3] Criminals inflict injustice by the nature of their crimes, and many people have been the victim of at least one crime in recent years. Hard feelings can remain against the criminal. Crimes against property and people—even when the criminal is apprehended—are usually met by drawn-out litigation. They usually end in plea bargains or settlements. Hard feelings by wronged parties often persist for years. Wrongdoers feel unfairly judged. Litigants do not believe they received a fair deal in property disputes. Arguments can be heated and hurtful. Have you experienced shortcomings of the justice system?

At the *end of life*, people try to make sense of their lives. They hate to leave the world with grudges. Forgiveness is a way to bring peace to their spirit. Reconciliation can bring peace to their relationships. Are you nearing the end of life? Whom do you want to forgive?

As the world becomes globally connected, we recognize how much our own contexts affect our understanding of others. In high school, the jocks don't hang out with the grunge crowd or the preps. Heavy metal clashes with hip-hop. The roots of *ethnic and class conflict* are often sewn in the wardrobes of in-groups and out-groups. Adult political groups play for higher stakes, such as taxes, political influence, even ethnic cleansing. Unforgiveness can run wild in ethnic conflict. Failed forgiveness can flow like blood. Have you been hurt, offended or discriminated against for your ethnicity, religion, age or gender? Who did it?

THREE QUESTIONS

You have considered several areas in which you might harbor unforgiveness. Perhaps you have recalled several specific incidents that you want to try to forgive. For each incident, ask yourself these questions. *How serious is the transgression?* Small transgressions annoy us. Large ones can turn our world upside down. Put off trying to forgive those that upset the world until you have gained confidence with smaller hurts. *How raw is the wound?* Don't choose wounds while the blood is still wet. *Is the person you want to forgive absent from or present in your life?* In an ongoing relationship, the offending person will react to what you do. He or she can deliberately or accidentally hurt you again, which can compound unforgiveness. In part two of this book, you'll practice the REACH method to speed your forgiveness. Choose absent people for part two of the book. In part three we will consider how to talk about transgressions and perhaps reconcile.

Think of at least four people whom you might practice forgiving as you read the remainder of this book. For example, choose an absent person who inflicted only a few small hurts and whom you have already mostly forgiven. That might be a schoolteacher who shamed you. Perhaps you resented the embarrassment for a while but have since forgiven most of the hurt. Only a thimbleful of unforgiveness remains. Choose a second absent person who inflicted more severe wounds. Perhaps you have not yet forgiven that person.

At the other end of the spectrum, choose two people who are still present in your life—one who did few harms, one who did more. Maybe your best friend made a careless remark that left you a bit miffed. Maybe a parent was abusive as you grew up, and he or she lives across town and expects you to visit often.

You will have the most success if you think of a specific incident in each case. In a notebook that you can use through the rest of the book, write a summary of each event now.

Remember, you can't forgive in the abstract. Forgiveness occurs when you work through *specific events with specific people*. Reading a book about forgiveness will help you forgive a little, but not nearly as much as if you practice on the stories of hurt, betrayal and anger you tell yourself. You must apply what you are reading.

We now have a bird's-eye view of the five steps to climb the Pyramid Model to REACH Forgiveness. In the chapters in part two, let's swoop in on an up-close and personal look at each step.

4

R: Recall the Hurt

We eye the evil face to face and we call it what it is.
Only realists can be forgivers.

LEWIS B. SMEDES

Transgressions wound us. There are many varieties of wounds, from the five-cent variety to the five-hundred-dollar kind.

NICKEL WOUNDS

A nickel wound was inflicted on me as a struggling graduate student at the University of Missouri, Columbia. Kirby and I moved into our first house, a two-bedroom crackerbox that had *just* enough room in the master bedroom for a bed and a chest of drawers. If we got out of bed at the same time, we would bump into each other.

The summer that we bought the house, I planted a garden. I spaded 2500 square feet of hard ground by hand. Rototillers, I thought, were for the weak. The fact that the outdoor work kept me from studying was irrelevant.

When the spading was complete, I planted peas, perfect for an early spring harvest. Soon the tender young shoots shot six inches out of the ground. I admired the six fifty-foot rows of young pea plants. I was the Jolly Green Giant planting in magic soil. Ho, ho, ho. Little did I know.

The next morning I strolled down to the "lower forty." One and one-half rows were leveled. It could only have been a savage attack by a vicious animal. *A rabbit*, I thought grimly. Rage bubbled up inside of me. I concocted a plan.

Before dawn the next morning, I armed myself with the only weapon I owned, a hammer. In my lawn chair, I assumed sentry duty. I sat in Mr. McGregor's garden in ambush for Peter Rabbit.

As dawn neared, motion caught my eye. A rabbit hopped purposefully past the house, underneath the apple tree, and across the ditch between house and garden.

As the rabbit approached, I flung the hammer at it. I missed, of course. (I'm sorry if I have disillusioned you. I was avenging those helpless slaughtered peas.) The rabbit seemed unalarmed. It languidly took four hops back toward the house. I retrieved my hammer and flung it again. Not even close. This time the rabbit hopped, perhaps, eight hops away. It turned to squint at me with what seemed like a Clint Eastwood glare in its eyes. I could practically hear the theme song from *The Good, the Bad, and the Ugly*. I flung the hammer a third time. The rabbit scurried away. I followed it along the path it had come on, across the road, through four other gardens, four blocks away. There I lost the trail. That rabbit had hopped through a half-mile of other gardens to eat my peas. *My* peas! I hated that rabbit. Unforgiveness rose in my heart.

The next morning, wiser, I awaited the rabbit at the edge of the garden. This time, instead of being armed with a one-shot hammer, I carried a bag of rocks. (This is how the arms race in the Cold War got started.) Dawn. As the rabbit approached, we faced off like gunslingers in our own bad Western. This time I had an AK-47 instead of a Smith & Wesson. I peppered the rabbit with the stones that I carried in my arms. After fifty tosses, I hit the rabbit in the side and stunned it.

I closed in on the rabbit with raised stone. I saw its nose twitching and its limpid eyes staring, unblinking. Revenge screamed, "Finish it!"

Empathy whispered, "It's only doing what rabbits do. It's just a little bunny rabbit." How important were those peas anyway? I dropped the rock and walked away. A nickel's worth of unforgiveness was not that hard to deal with. (Three days later, the peas were history.)

FIVE-DOLLAR WOUNDS

Five-dollar wounds are more severe. I had one of those in graduate school too. (Are we picking up a pattern here?) The professor of my behavioral psychology class seemed to be prejudiced against the counseling psychology students. He seemed to prefer the clinical psychology students. This being behavioral psychology, I immediately instituted systematic observation of the professor's behavior. I counted the number of times that he engaged in looking and speaking behavior with counseling as opposed to clinical psychology students. (That's the way behaviorists talk.)

As I suspected, he favored clinical psychology students. Or, as I thought of it, he emitted reinforcement behavior on a different schedule for counseling and clinical students. I even did a statistical test ($p<.05$). (Uh, did I also mention that I was a wee bit compulsive? One of my favorite books of the Bible is Numbers.) Being a counseling psychology student, of course, I was not happy about the professor's prejudice.

At the end of the course, he gave me a B. I was aghast. How could he possibly do this to *me*? So I got even. For probably five years afterward, I nursed a five-dollar grudge against him for his unfair treatment. That showed him.

Another five-dollar hurt arose when my wife and I were attempting to become pregnant with our fourth child. The first three children came almost exactly two years apart. I got overconfident about the pregnancy business. When it was time to attempt to conceive a fourth time, I was confident that it would happen quickly.

Month after month passed. No pregnancy. We tried all of the home remedies. We tried elevating the hips after making love—her hips, not mine—because gravity is our friend. We tried precise timing. Kirby took her temperature regularly so we could make love at the precise time of ovulation. Yes, this led to some interesting phone calls at work. The phone rings. I listen, then say, "Excuse me, but I need to take a brief recess from this meeting. I'll be back in about an hour."

Nothing worked. We began to be concerned. Perhaps (gulp) I needed to have the potency of my semen tested.

I arrived for my appointment at the medical school clinic. In the center of the room sat a woman whom I affectionately think of, even today, as the Dragon Woman. She was armed with a clipboard, and her face was set into a perma-frown. Around the edge of the room, forty men sat on the edges of their chairs. They weren't anxious. Just incredibly alert. I said quietly to the Dragon Woman, "I'm here to have my semen tested."

"What?" she yelled. I looked quickly around the room.

"I'm here to have my semen tested," I said, a little louder.

"I can't hear you!" She shouted like the drill sergeant in a *Gomer Pyle* rerun.

"I'm here to have my semen tested!" I called out. Forty pairs of eyes fixed on me. I felt like crawling under the desk. That took the mystery out of my visit.

"Why didn't you say so?" she said. She reached under her desk. After fumbling around for a moment, she held up (for every eye to see) a flask. It was a *large* flask. A *very* large flask. "Fill 'er up," she said.

I swallowed heavily.

"Just kidding," she said. I took the flask, still looking at it apprehensively. I searched for privacy. I saw nothing available, so I looked inquiringly at her. "The bathroom is right behind you," she said helpfully (and by the way, loudly enough for every ear to hear). Sure enough, the bathroom was right behind me. The public bathroom. And everyone in the room knew why I sauntered, oh so casually, to the bathroom.

So I entered the very public bathroom. Being a keen observer, as psychologists often are, I immediately noticed that there were no doors on the stalls. Swell. Alone in the public bathroom, I went into one of those stalls. I wasn't alone long. Patrons of the bathroom walked in and out. They mumbled about what was going on in this public bathroom. The one with no doors on the stalls.

Finally a miracle occurred. I then pushed the flask underneath my coat and reported to the Dragon Woman. I sidled up to the table. I opened my coat so that she could see the flask, like someone selling "Rolex" watches for $25. I spoke out of the corner of my mouth. "Here's the semen sample."

She took the flask from me and held it up high (for everyone to see). She said, seemingly at the top of her lungs, "That's not very much."

Now, that probably classifies as at least a five-dollar wound, but at that instant I was thinking mega-bucks. She diffused the situation quickly by saying, "Naw, I'm only joking." (At least twenty men in the room let out audible sighs.) Even though I was embarrassed by her jokes, I quickly put the incident behind me. It was painful, but only at a five-dollar level.

Fifty- and Five-Hundred-Dollar Wounds

In contrast to the nickel and five-dollar variety wounds, a fifty-dollar wound leaves a lasting impression on people's lives. Remember the classic movie *Casablanca?* Rick was left standing in the rain at the train station. Rain splattered like tears on his "Dear John" letter. That was a fifty-dollar wound. It changed Rick (and Ilsa) forever.

Five-hundred-dollar wounds irrevocably change people's lives. My mother's murder was an irreversible loss. The death of a loved one cannot be undone. The pain of the grief will remain, regardless of what is done. One can always choose whether to compound the pain of the grief with a search for revenge, but the loss is permanent.

COUNTERFEIT-MONEY WOUNDS

I've heard people say that forgiveness is the way that we deal with "true offenses." With this reasoning, if my father beat me, that would be a true offense—one I might someday forgive. If I thought I overheard my father criticizing me, but he really wasn't, then he didn't truly offend. Forgiveness would not be appropriate. One of the frequent complaints counselors hear is "I cannot forgive God." According to the "true offense" way of thinking, it would be inappropriate to be unforgiving toward God.

I believe, however, that how we *perceive* an event determines whether we feel unforgiveness. Imagine a teacher lecturing a class. Two women students are talking. The teacher believes that she cannot make her point because of the women's conversation, so she says, "You two, please stop talking."

One woman might think, *Who does she think she is? She can't talk to me that way. I have a right to say what I want. I paid my money, and I can talk if I wish.*

The other student might think, *I must be a terrible person for interrupting the class, taking everyone's time and drawing attention away from the lesson. I am not worthy of the air that it takes to keep me alive. She has deeply wounded me by pointing this out to everyone.*

The teacher in this case was not offending either woman in an absolute sense. The teacher was within her rights to ask for silence. Yet one of the women perceived the teacher's fair and controlled reprimand as an offense to which she responded with anger, and the other perceived the teacher's reprimand as an injury to which she responded with pain and hurt. Both women might go home, ponder that event, ruminate about it until it generates a sense of unforgiveness.

Can they never forgive this teacher, because this teacher truly did nothing wrong? Or do the anger and fear, ripening into vengeful rumination, produce perceived transgressions that need forgiveness?

Whether one needs to forgive is not determined by objective circumstances. Who is to decide whether a "true" offense or hurt has occurred? If you experience unforgiving emotions, then you might need to forgive emotionally, even if you do not need to grant forgiveness verbally. Counterfeit-money hurts still wound us.

RESPONDING TO THE HURT

When we are hurt or offended, we may respond emotionally in any of several ways.

Fear. When we are hurt, our body and brain seek to avoid similar hurts. Emotions of fear are alarm bells that surround the memory. If similar threatening events, memories or even thoughts of threat trip the alarm, then fear and anxiety quicken the breath, trigger adrenaline and make us want to head for the hills to avoid hurt again.

Anger. When we are offended, we get angry. Injustices are barriers to happiness. Anger makes us want to kick down the barriers.

Fear and anger are usually mixed, but one is stronger. An event that hurts one person might anger another. It's our perception of an event and its meaning to us, not the event itself, that stokes our emotional fires. Our perception of most events is not pure. I might perceive more hurt than offense, or vice versa, depending on my temperament and past experiences. I usually react with one emotion more than with the other. Some people are easily hurt. They are walking wounded: thin-skinned, tenderhearted and fearful. They expect hurt and rejection. Others are volcanoes of offense and anger looking for a vent.

Avoidance. Perceptions of hurt or offense and the accompanying emotions motivate us to avoid the transgressor. We might be hurt again. We might explode angrily. It's better to avoid the person, we conclude.

Retaliation or revenge. Retaliation is striking back with little forethought. Retaliation is a "hot" response. "Revenge is a dish best served cold," goes the saying. Revenge is plotted, planned and executed in cold blood more than hot blood. Revenge is freeze-dried retaliation; just add heat.

Attack. Some hurts or offenses trigger more than mere retaliation or revenge. We might not be satisfied with a trickle of blood. We want to go for the jugular. We might attack because of hatred—or to defend ourselves from someone we consider to be a serious threat to our physical or psychological existence. Recall the Mel Gibson movie *Ransom.* When Gibson's son is kidnapped and the kidnappers demand two million in ransom, Gibson doesn't knuckle under. He refuses to pay. He even goes on television and offers a reward for the kidnapper—two million dollars. Gibson responds to an offense with an attack. The kidnapper threatens. Gibson responds by increasing the bounty to four million dollars. Attacks—when we are comfortably watching a good guy face down a bad guy—are empowering. But in real life, the stakes usually increase with each attack until one person is completely defeated.

Withdrawal and submitting. Sometimes we are so intimidated by a transgressor that we dare not fight back—can't seek revenge and can't avoid the threat. For survival, we knuckle under.

Self-protection. Sometimes we try to step around the pain through mental processes.

Denial. Mentally, we may respond to transgressions by girding up our loins and protecting ourselves by saying, *It never happened.* Our mind denies hurts or refuses to focus on painful memories.

Justifying the self (by selective perception). The mind also can make us believe we are right, virtuous and pure as the driven snow. We pay attention to and remember what is consistent with our story.

Rumination. Both denial and self-justification are self-protective. In spite of our self-protective efforts, our wounds stir us up. We may ruminate about hurts and offenses. Rumination is what cows do: regurgitating food from one of their stomachs and masticating it ("chewing their cud"). In our case it is spitting up a partially digested memory and chewing it around until it ripens into unforgiveness.

THE BODY TALKS BACK

Some people have their feelers up to detect hurts. They may have reactive nervous systems. Little things grate. Noises startle. Slights wound. Insults cause massive reactions. Because small hurts cause big reactions, such people are often filled with fears.

Other people have personal radar detectors for being offended. They seem hard-wired for anger. Slights are seen as insults. Insults are seen as egregious wrongs. They are anger waiting for a place to happen.

Unforgiveness, though, is neither hurt, nor fear, nor the mixture of the two. Unforgiveness is slow-cooked through vengeful rumination into resentment, hatred, hostility, anger, fear, stress and bitterness. It is cacophony.

These jumbled emotions are likely to have health consequences. This is especially probable if a person practices unforgiveness over a long time. The wages of chronic unforgiveness are eventual illness—physical, moral, relational and spiritual.

In writing about women's health, psychotherapists Deborah Cox, Sally Stabb and Karin Bruchner[1] describe the case of Mary, a seventy-four-year-old great-grandmother. Mary's life was focused on her ill health. That was not surprising given her thirteen surgeries. Mary's past involved severe abuse and punishment by her parents for expressing anger. She had once been imprisoned in a garage for a whole day because she made a face when told to give her favorite toy to a neighbor. Mary's husband was frequently unfaithful.

Mary kept gritting her teeth. She also got sicker and sicker. She had colitis, gall bladder problems, heart problems, upper respiratory troubles, migraine headaches and hernias. Mary's daughters, Janine and Sarah, both in family therapy, recalled that if they expressed their anger, Mary punished them. Unforgiveness sent a cascade rippling through Mary's body and her family, trickling pain down through the generations.

Unforgiveness builds a bone-scattered putrid lair, in which a giant dragon of self-absorption sits on its tin ruminations, thinking them to be solid gold. The dragon protects its hoard from invading counter-impulses of forgiveness and forbearance. Only love, empathy, compassion and humility are strong enough and brave enough to enter the lair, slay the dragon and thus alchemically transform the tin treasure into gold.

How Not to Recall the Hurt

For some of us, whose unforgiving emotions lurk beneath a barely civil surface, allowing ourselves to recall our hurts and offenses can plunge us straight into rumination and thus bitter unforgiveness. To forgive, we must recall the hurt or offense differently from the way we usually do.

Perhaps we usually try to suppress feelings of unforgiveness. We deny that we feel hate. We think, *That hurt didn't matter.* Instead of suppressing our feelings, we must come to grips with them. Instead of turning from the pain and anger, we must face them.

Yet here's the catch. We must not glory in finger-pointing blame. We must not wallow in gut-wrenching self-pity. Remember Rick from *Casablanca*? Eventually he forgave Ilsa, but he made it difficult for himself by recalling Ilsa's rejection while he was drinking and feeling sorry for himself. Rick ordered Sam, the piano player, to play "As Time Goes By"—Rick and Ilsa's song. "If she can stand it, so can I," Rick said without unclenching his jaw. Classic Bogart.

We must try not to think of the other person as a devil or as the personification of ill will toward us. When we have been hurt, it is easy to imagine that the person who hurt us did so because he or she despised us and organized his or her entire existence around ruining us. In the light of the midday sun, such a belief might seem like a paranoid delusion. When we are in the darkness of an angry and unforgiving mind, it seems that the person has dedicated his or her life to destroying us.

As we think logically about our own lives, we know that we ourselves typically do not focus our lives around plotting someone's disaster, even if we hate the person. If we are honest with ourselves, we admit that we usually do not think much about our enemies. Any anger and malice toward them is only periodic. So it's important to give other people the benefit of the doubt. Assume that your offender's motives are not totally negative and directed toward destroying you.

We also need to heed the lesson of social psychology. When people are tempted to harm another, it is easier if they depersonalize the other. They call the person a monster, an animal or a devil. That seems to allow people to inflict harm and feel justified in doing so. Yet as Christians, we know that all people are created in the image of God, and all are redeemable. Jesus died for all people. They are not monsters or devils. So do not recall the hurt by depersonalizing the person who hurt you.

When people recall hurts, they usually express emotion. That's okay. When we have been hurt, we are angry, and expressing anger or sadness is not, in itself, bad. But neither is it good to express emotion without control.

Freud espoused catharsis theory, which advocated letting out the anger or sadness as if it was a release of pressure. Freud thought such expression would reduce pent-up emotions. Freud was wrong. If anything, ranting or sobbing builds up more steam. But psychologist James Pennebaker found that writing about emotionally painful and angering events helped people be physically healthier. Expressive writing helped only if people went beyond mere expression of negative emotion to gain more understanding and make a healthier response to the event.[2]

So, at first, when we write about or talk about the transgression we are trying to forgive, we can feel free to express all the emotions we feel. But we do not want to stop there. When we get down to working on forgiving, we should try to recall the hurt as objectively as we can. We should try to remember accurately what the person did and what our responses were. Sometimes it helps to visualize what happened.

It is normal to remember the events that support our view of any situation. If I am unforgiving toward Mack, I will tend to remember the things that Mack did to hurt me. His insults are at the edge of my consciousness. I'll forget what I did to provoke Mack. I'll remember my pain and unjust suffering. I'll forget my gossip about Mack and how it hurt his reputation. I'll remember his anger. I'll forget his contrition.

Sometimes when we remember a painful event, we can easily think of ourselves as innocent victims who were cruelly abused. While sometimes that is accurate, most of the time events that lead to unforgiveness have more than one side to them. (Of course, I usually look only at my side.)

ONE HELPFUL WAY TO RECALL THE HURT

Begin with prayer. Sometimes recalling a hurt or offense, especially if it is a traumatic memory, can throw us into a tailspin. Gird up your loins with prayer at the outset. Pray for the presence of the Lord as your protector. Invoke the Holy Spirit as your comforter. Then, as you begin to recall the hurt, be sensitive to the leading of the Holy Spirit. Just because we pray for the Lord's protection does not mean we can forge ahead without listening for his guidance.

As you begin to recall the hurt and the details surrounding it, monitor yourself to make sure that you are not slipping into rage, fear or depression. Try to spiritually discern whether you are experiencing any checks from the Holy Spirit. If not, then do a quick recall trying to get full emotional expression. After your first expressive run-through, try a rerun. This second recall is likely to be the helpful one. Remember, you are going to try to replace the negative emotions with more positive emotions, and if you crank up your negative emotions to a fevered pitch, that will make it more difficult to replace them. So on the second run-through, don't dwell on the negative. Try to be objective. Don't be afraid to express some negative emotion, but try to stay under control. Try to remember not only what happened but also what you felt about what was happening.

Create a picture in your mind's eye. Identify your emotions with accurate labels. Don't just think *I was upset*. That might be true, but it's too general. Instead, use precise feeling-words, like, *I was baffled at first, but I got angrier as the misunderstanding continued until I was furious*. Or, *I was puzzled at what she meant at first, but then the implications sank in, and I was deeply hurt*. Struggle to get the precise words to best describe your feelings. Although this might seem like it will make you more aroused, you'll probably find that thinking of precise words to label your emotions will take some of the hurtful or angering edge off the memory.

As you recall the hurt, take deep, slow breaths to keep yourself calm. Be sure to exhale fully. (If you empty your lungs, inhaling will take care of itself.) By exhaling deeply, you activate the parts of your autonomic nervous system that calms you. Calming breaths help you remember objectively.

Even if you breathe deeply, it might be difficult to recall the hurt if the trauma was great. We do not like to re-experience negative feelings. Our mind protects us by shutting out negative memories. You can choose whether to recall painful events. The recall of trauma brings up strong feelings. If those feelings become unmanageable, stop thinking upsetting thoughts. Do something active. If you can't stop unwanted thoughts, seek the help of a psychologist, psychiatrist, counselor or pastor.

However, just because it is painful to recall a trauma does not mean you should stuff the memory. If you consider the pain caused by unforgiveness, you might still want to face the pain of recall. Recalling the hurt or offense is the first step to healing.

Most hurts (painful as they are) are not traumas. In the introduction to part two, when you selected events in your past on which to practice forgiving, I hope you didn't choose the whoppers. To learn to use the Pyramid Model to REACH Forgiveness, choose the nickel or five-dollar wounds. When you have successfully forgiven them, then you're ready for the big money.

HOW I RECALLED MY MOTHER'S MURDER

I was still boiling mad as I paced the floor that first night in Knoxville, but I was convinced that I needed to at least try to forgive my mother's murderer. So I employed the Pyramid Model to REACH Forgiveness. It was, after all, research-tested. Despite its helping hundreds of people forgive, I wasn't sure it would work for such a big wound. But it beat walking the floor.

At the heart of the method was recalling the offense and my hurt, and then overlaying that anger and pain with empathy, sympathy, compassion, or agape love for the youth who killed my mother. Empathy is an understanding, undergirded by emotion, of the perpetrator and the perpetrator's motives for doing the act of transgression—but you'll hear much more of that in chapter five. The same for sympathy, compassion and agape love.

I needed to think through the murder of my mother, as painful as that might be, in as much detail as I could. I knew I had to get inside the heads of those who committed that murder. I didn't *want* to do that. I *needed* to do it.

I imagined how two youths might have felt as they prepared to rob a darkened house. Perhaps they had been caught at robbery previously. This time, though, they knew they wouldn't get caught. Standing in a dark street, they were keyed up.

"This is the one," one might have said. "Ain't nobody home. It's pitch black."

"No car in the driveway," said the other.

"They're probably at a New Year's Eve party." They couldn't know that Mama didn't drive and therefore did not own a car.

"We gotta be careful," one might have said. "I'll knock." So the one with the crowbar walked to the front door, gave a sharp knock to the door— five or six sharp raps. He probably leaped from the porch and slipped around the side of the house, just in case someone was home.

The noise was loud enough that the next door neighbors heard something. "We heard a noise," they later told the police, "but it wasn't repeated."

Mama didn't answer. She was already asleep. She also had a slight hearing problem. The two youths must have believed the coast to be clear.

The one with the crowbar walked to the back door. His breathing must have come in quick gasps. A quick tap on the glass and he snaked his hand through the broken pane. He turned the latch.

He probably stood just inside the door for a minute, straining his ears, listening. He heard the hum of the refrigerator, the tock of the old clock.

He stepped further in, feeling his way in an unfamiliar kitchen. *Bam.* He stumbled in the dark against the refrigerator, leaving a smudged handprint. He made his way to the front door. He clicked the latch, letting his buddy inside.

Feeling more confident together, they began to ransack the living room and hallway, pulling drawers out and dumping their contents on the floor. Maybe one swore as he scattered drawers full of precious memories but worth few dollars.

From behind the one in the hall, a voice must have jabbed his adrenal gland. "What are you doing in here?" said my mother from the door of her bedroom.

He whirled around. *Oh no*, he must have thought. *I've been seen. This wasn't supposed to happen. This was supposed to be a perfect robbery. Where did this old woman come from? Our careful plans are spoiled. This is terrible. Worse, she can even recognize me. I'm going to go to jail. This old woman is ruining my life.*

He probably glanced down at the crowbar in his hand. Savagely he lashed out with the crowbar, slamming my mother across the cheek. She fell backwards. He struck again, landing a blow across her shoulders. She tumbled against the wall and fell, landing on her back. He stepped forward and crashed the crowbar into her skull. She lay unconscious, dying on the floor.

He must have sworn and experienced extreme anger, guilt and fear all mixed together. "What have you done?" his partner might have yelled. Perhaps the partner ran out the back door. The young killer began to smash objects with the crowbar. He ran to the kitchen and threw objects. "That old woman shouldn't have been here!" he might have yelled. The guilt must have been overwhelming. He couldn't look himself in the face at what he had done. He began to smash every object with a reflecting surface.

She caused me to do this. In rage he ran back to my mother's body holding a wine bottle from the kitchen. He viciously assaulted her body, thrusting it under her nightgown. She didn't stir. Her breathing was weak. Then grabbing a change container, he turned and caught his reflection in the hall mirror. He snatched the crowbar and smashed it. He fled the scene, plans ruined, overcome with the shame of murder.

The house would have been silent except for my mother's weak irregular breathing. No one could hear her blood draining into the carpet beneath her head and pelvis.

ANALYZING MY RECALL

As I traced the likely events of that night in my mind, I felt that I understood better what had happened. The youth who had murdered my mom had done a terrible thing—nothing will ever change that. It was an evil act.

But by recalling the events (as they had been "seen" in my imagination all day), I short-circuited revenge motivations born of rumination and replaced them by empathic recall. It was not an empathy that white-washed the facts. It was empathy that tried to understand. Through empathizing with what might have been going on in the youth's mind, I understood that he had lashed out in fear, surprise, guilt and anger. I guessed that he had responded to his own guilt and shame with the destructive anger that he unleashed on the house and my mother's body. I was making up a plausible story.

I could even feel sorry for the youth. He had, through his impulsiveness, poor decisions and uncontrollable rage, ruined his life. I felt sorry that he would have to go through the remainder of his life seeing replays of what he had done to an old woman. It was sad.

Through empathizing and sympathizing with the youth, I stopped indulging the desire to kill or hurt him in return, as I had been doing all day. I felt sorry for what he must have experienced and must be experiencing. *He must be alone*, I thought, *worried about what he has done, sickened by the news report that Mama died.* I knew that the guilt and shame he had shown at the scene of violence must be a powerful force in his life wherever he was at that moment. I could imagine him wrestling with his guilt alone that night, just as I wrestled with my grief. I felt a sense of compassionate understanding for this youth, while still seeing the utter ugliness of what he had done.

As I look back on the experience now and analyze it, I can see that I was experiencing new emotions. Instead of the rage and fear that I experienced before empathizing, I felt compassion. My body was being reprogrammed. The scene, vivid in my mind, was being paired with different events occurring in my body. Different neurochemicals were flooding my brain. Different gut feelings were being experienced. My face softened, my jaw no longer clenched in anger and hatred. Different associations were being made. Instead of associating the event with a fantasy of revenge, I was associating the event with sadness and compassion for a needy person—a person who needed serious help and who needed to be prevented from hurting others.

At no time in my empathic fantasy did I ever construe his act as being justified. At no time did I ever think that he should be pardoned for his crime if he were to be apprehended. His act of murder was not justifiable. It was not excusable. The murder was wrong and evil. After my empathic fantasy, it was more understandable. I thought about what might have been the murderer's experience. I did not judge him from outside.

It was hard to force myself to imagine such a traumatic scene. In fact, my mind rebelled against it. I wanted to flee from the thoughts. Yet I knew that I needed to try to understand an act of a desperate human. So I persevered with my imagined scene based on information from police reports. (If I had thought I was going to be unable to handle this, I would have wanted to dwell on it only with a pastor or counselor available.)

By forcing myself to imagine this scene and arrive at a compassionate stance, even though the memory was traumatic, the process probably helped speed up my forgiveness. Researchers tell us that when people are experiencing a trauma, memory occurs differently than in nontraumatic conditions. Trauma seems to cause the emotional centers of the brain to become extremely active and charge emotional experience strongly. By immediately imagining a traumatic scene and pairing it with the emotion of compassion, I probably reprogrammed my emotions of rage and fear more quickly and more powerfully than if I had tried to imagine the same scene a week or a month later.

Even though the imagination was difficult, in the long run it was good for me. Empathic recall is hard. It is emotional. Yet empathy, sympathy, compassion and love help promote healing.

WHAT YOU SEE IS WHAT YOU GET

You may want to try using this process on an area of deep hurt. First imagine, then forgive.

Imagine vividly. Empathy is the key step in forgiving. To develop deep empathy, imagine the incident vividly from the point of view of the perpetrator—as I did with my mother's murder. Picture the scene as clearly as you can. Run a movie through your head. Instead of seeing the movie from your own point of view, picture it as if you were the person who hurt or offended you. Imagine what you saw (as transgressor). Imagine what you heard, what you smelled, tasted. Make the picture as real as you can. Imagine your thoughts and feelings. What were your motives? Most people do not act from evil motives—although it sometimes seems like that from our point of view. Most people are trying to do what they think is best to meet a perceived need. Later, they might look back and see that their decisions were mistaken or self-motivated.

Forgive a difficult person by focusing on symbolic events. When we become unforgiving toward a person, usually it is because we have generalized our opinion from many accumulated hurts. In a good relationship, we are not usually bothered by small or infrequent hurts. But if the number or size of the hurts becomes large enough, we usually make a mental shift. We move from seeing the relationship as good, the person as trustworthy, and the emotional tone as positive to seeing the relationship as troubled, the person as untrustworthy, and the emotional tone as negative. We whip off the rose-colored glasses and slam the dark glasses in place.

If your relationship with any transgressor has deteriorated to the level of hating the person, you will probably never forgive unless you recall specific events that were hurtful. Recall each event and work through it before going on to the next. Forgiving a *person* often requires accumulating forgiveness from several symbolic events.

It turns out that vividly recalling the hurt is vital to forgiving. Nathaniel Wade and I examined forgiveness interventions from five different laboratories.[3] All recommended spending time on recalling the hurt. Even more important, though, the amount of forgiveness was strongly related to how long people spent recalling the hurt—not ruminating on it incessantly, but recalling it with sympathetic emotions and under control. That opened the doorway for the positive other-oriented emotions of empathy, sympathy, compassion and even love to walk through.

DISCUSSION QUESTIONS

1. The author identifies "counterfeit-money hurts" as hurts that we feel when no objective wrong was done to us. He says that those may still need emotional forgiveness because they create opportunities for unforgiveness. Do you agree, or do you think that a real, objective wrong is necessary before forgiveness is called for? Have you ever been deeply hurt and then found out later that you had misunderstood a person's actions? How did you handle the misunderstanding between the time when you experienced the hurt and when you found out it was a misunderstanding?

2. What are the two ways that the author cautions us to avoid recalling the hurt?

3. Deep breathing helps us relax. Physically, how does it help us relax? Do you think that deep breathing exercises are "New Age" or simply using the body mechanisms God gave us?

4. How does the author recommend forgiving a difficult *person* (in contrast to forgiving one specific transgression) who might have hurt or offended you many times?

5. Do you seem to interpret transgressions more as hurts or offenses? Or are they about fifty-fifty in your life? If you think of them mostly as hurts, can you also see the offense and injustice? If you think of them mostly as offenses, can you also sense that you were hurt?

6. Some people prefer simply to sweep past transgressions under the carpet. That is, they think that recalling such transgressions just stirs up old hurt and anger. Freud argued that such past emotional wounding *will* come out, perhaps in unconscious ways. Some psychologists argue that past wounds can truly be isolated and not cause us any problems. Still others argue that old wounds only resurface if new situations—like being hurt in the same way again, being under lots of stress or seeing the offender again—bring them to awareness. Where do you stand on this?

5

E: Empathize

We must develop and maintain the capacity to forgive. He who is devoid of the power to forgive is devoid of the power to love. There is some good in the worst of us and some evil in the best of us. When we discover this, we are less prone to hate our enemies.

MARTIN LUTHER KING JR.

In Charles Dickens's much-assigned but little-read novel *Great Expectations* lived a character called Miss Havisham. She spent her life in a darkened room, half dressed in her wedding clothes from years before. Her fiancé had sent her a note, breaking the engagement as she was preparing to go to the church for their wedding. Time froze for Miss Havisham. From that day forth, she lived in her room with the hands of the clock stopped at precisely the time she had received the message. Miss Havisham is a clear picture of unforgiveness. Her growth was stunted by poison from a harm she could not forgive.

Miss Havisham adopted a beautiful young girl named Estelle. Estelle was Miss Havisham's revenge on men. Estelle would make men pay. She had been trained to lead men into loving her deeply. At the peak of their love, she struck, rejecting them. She was a beautiful black widow spider.

Pip, the protagonist of *Great Expectations*, visited Miss Havisham. Miss Havisham began to enjoy Pip's company and like him very much. Pip fell in love with Estelle, who led Pip on. In front of Miss Havisham, Estelle broke Pip's heart. As Miss Havisham saw his pain, she was moved with empathy. She fell to her knees and asked Pip if he could forgive her causing him pain. Miss Havisham's empathy was the goad that prodded her to request forgiveness. Her empathy for Pip then helped her to forgive the man who, years before, had rejected her.

LEVELS OF EMPATHY

Empathy can be experienced at three levels.[1] At the shallowest level of empathy, you understand the point of view of the other person. At a middle level of empathy, you identify emotionally with the other person. You feel *with* and think *with* the other person. At the deepest level of empathy, you feel compassion *for* the other person as well as emotional identification. This is called compassionate empathy. Each level adds depth to the previous level. If you want to forgive, you can do so if you achieve this compassionate empathy.

Level 1: Understanding

Level 2: Emotional Identification

Level 3: Compassionate Empathy

Figure 5.1. Three levels of empathy

Recently I was giving a talk at York University in Toronto. Les Greenberg, a noted researcher of psychotherapy, showed me his lab while I was there. He is interested in *how* people forgive others who have deeply wounded them. In consulting on the supervision of one case, I saw the videotape of a counseling session with a man who held a deep grudge against both his mother and father. At age ten, the man had returned from school to find that his mother had killed herself. The boy didn't know how to cope all alone. In his ten-year-old mind, his mother had abandoned him. His father, himself overcome with grief, was depressed, incapacitated, unable to help. The boy asked his father, "Don't you love me?" The father's response: "Of course I love you, but you can never love a child like you love a wife."

During the counseling session, I saw the man—now in his thirties—sit with his arms wrapped closely around him, "I feel out of touch with the whole human race," he said. "My mother bailed out. My father was never there for me." Within the first fifteen minutes, the man said he was *adrift, abandoned* and *alone*. His most vivid memory was being left "alone in a dark room."

In previous sessions, he had told his counselor how he thought his mother abandoned him through her suicide. Near the end of the videotaped session I observed, he began to talk about his father. His anger toward his father seemed to surprise him. The therapist asked him to pretend to talk to his father. "Imagine your father seated in this empty chair." The therapist pulled a chair directly in front of the man. "What would you like to say to him? Tell him how he abandoned you."

"You were never there for me," he began. "I don't even know if I could talk to you." He looked stonily at the empty chair.

After a silence, the therapist urged, "Give it a try."

"It's not that you weren't there. You weren't there *for me*. You came home at night, but you were always thinking of work. Your body was there, but your mind was not. That's the way you always were. Cold. Detached. I was a nuisance to you. An obligation. I felt like you resented me."

The client poured out his unforgiveness. He was angry, bitter and full of hate. Then he was fearful of his father's rejection. He whined. Sadness replaced the fear. It finally gave way to a cynical rejection of his father.

One transgression is hard to forgive. How could this man forgive a person who had transgressed many times? How could he forgive a lifetime of being left to drift alone, out of touch but not out of sight of the person who should have been giving love and comfort?

"Can you think of one time that stands out?" asked the therapist.

"Playing in the band was my salvation," he said after a moment's thought. "I threw myself into music. I can't understand how you never could come to our concerts. Even when I played the solo at the spring concert in my junior year, you didn't come. You said you had a date. You said, 'You understand, don't you?' I said, 'Sure,' but I didn't really. I know it sounds like nothing now, but it was important to me then. It sums up our so-called relationship. You were always somewhere else. I had no mother, and you could never be my father. You were just a biological sperm donor. I could never tell you that. I could never get close enough to tell you."

Anger and hurt competed in the client's face. Hurt seemed to be winning as he gazed in silence at the empty chair.

"What do you think your father's reaction would be?" asked the therapist after the client poured out the litany of his complaints and feelings of abandonment. "Sit in his chair and talk about how he might feel."

The man moved to the father's chair and began to talk for his imagined father. He said, "I'm so sorry, so sorry. I had no idea you were so hurt. So alone. I was so hurt by your mother's death and struggled to cope. I simply had nothing left to give to you. I wanted to be a real father to you. I didn't want to add more hurts to you. I knew you were suffering. I just didn't have what it took to give you what you needed. I knew that concert was important to you. There was no excuse for not going. I'm sorry, so sorry."

"What do you want to say to your father now?" asked the therapist.

The client changed chairs. He said, "I'm sorry too. I see now that you did all you could—all you were capable of. I was only ten when Mom died. I didn't understand. You were wrapped up in your own hurt. I condemned you for that. When I was ten, that made sense. Now I'm an adult and I still have not been able to get past my own hurt. I see now that if we are ever going to be back in touch, I need to reach out to you and not wait for you to reach out for me. I'm not ten anymore."

Watching this videotaped session, I was impressed at how much this counseling resembled the Pyramid Model to REACH Forgiveness. The client recalled (R) a specific hurt. He literally sat in his father's chair and acted out an empathic (E) response. He had to "be" his father. When he was saying, "I'm sorry, so sorry," he felt sorry. Those feelings were like shovels that turned over the soil, covering parts of his own experience. Through empathy he saw his own shortcomings. He came to experience an altruistic (A) forgiveness. He saw how he and his father were alike. That helped him commit (C) to forgive, which I hoped would help him hold on (H) to the forgiveness.

For years, using the empty-chair technique, Les Greenberg has been investigating how people resolve unfinished business.[2] The empty-chair technique is a concrete example of empathy in action. When a person sits in the perpetrator's chair, talks like the perpetrator and explains things from the perpetrator's point of view, then the person must identify with the perpetrator.

To achieve the first level of empathy, the person tries to accurately portray the thoughts and emotions of the perpetrator. To reach the second level, the person literally feels with or thinks with the perpetrator. Whether forgiveness occurs, though, seems to depend quite a lot on whether the person can move to the third level of empathy. Can he or she develop compassion for the one who did the wounding? Can the person care for the wounder, realizing at the gut level that he or she and the transgressor are the same under the skin? If the person cannot feel such compassion, he or she experiences no emotional change and remains glued to unforgiveness. Only after achieving compassion can complete forgiveness take place.

Greenberg, and now Wanda Malcolm, one of Greenberg's former students, have found that when the person portrays the perpetrator gently and with compassion, the person might soon forgive. But when the person remains hard toward the perpetrator, he or she probably will not forgive—at least not until feelings change. Accusing the perpetrator helps resolve anger by leading to an affirmation of the self and one's rights. But it does not lead to forgiving. Therefore, in psychotherapy, empathy has been shown to be a key component in whether people can forgive.

PAY ATTENTION TO OTHER PEOPLE'S EMPATHY

Empathy can be contagious. Seeing another's empathy can heal hurts. Richard and Joan married in their forties, both for the first time. Six months later they were in counseling, talking of divorce. Richard was into computer programming. He was logical, hard-wired to argue. Joan was into art. She was passionate, feeling slights as though they were deep wounds.

Before one session, Joan was told by her boss that she needed to finish some sketches before leaving work. She phoned me and told me to start the session with Richard. She would join us late.

Richard began to complain to me that Joan couldn't understand him. "No matter how I try to tell her about my needs, she won't listen," he said.

"So you don't feel like she understands you."

"She doesn't. She is always working her agenda."

"That feels devaluing—like she couldn't care less about you."

"Right. I get angry. We end up yelling."

"So when you don't feel that she is really hearing you, you feel she doesn't care. That makes you angry, and you express the anger."

"Both of us do. It's not just me. We yell at each other."

"So something makes her angry?"

"Well, I had been thinking more about me, but now that you mention it . . . yeah, I guess she probably doesn't feel like I understand her either."

"Do you?"

"Yes. At least I think so. Maybe I don't. I don't know. She would probably say I don't understand her."

"Do you think I understand how you feel?"

"Yes," he said.

"Why do you think I understand?"

"Because you listen. You sort of repeat back what I tell you and then expand it."

"So when I repeat back what you tell me, it doesn't leave you puzzled about whether I heard you. I tell you what I heard. Then you feel understood."

"Right."

"If I didn't tell you that I understood by summarizing what you say, would you know that I understand?"

"Maybe. I might be able to read it in your face. I guess it would be harder. I might misread you."

"So let's get back to you and Joan. She doesn't seem to understand you, and you think she might not feel understood. If she felt understood by you, what effect do you think that would have?"

"We probably wouldn't get angry as often. She might even be more willing to listen to me. Maybe."

"So if you want her to listen better to you, what can you do?"

"Maybe it would help to assure her that I understand what she is saying. It might not help at all, but, hey, that would be no different from now."

Later that hour, Joan arrived. She was frustrated that her boss had kept her late. She began blowing off steam. "I didn't need this hassle today," she said. She turned to Richard, "I wanted to talk about whose parents we visit over the holidays. I know we'll argue about it. I hate to start out already mad."

I could almost see Richard thinking about our earlier conversation. He had an I-*want*-to-be-empathic look, but he didn't seem to know exactly what to say.

"I know you are frustrated," he said. "I don't want to jump in with my two cents on the holidays. I really want to hear what your feelings are."

Joan's mouth literally fell open. Richard's openness was so different from his usual logical argumentative style that she could hardly take it in. She looked to me. "What did you feed this guy before I got here?"

Richard and Joan said the following talk was the best conversation they had had since they were married. Both felt understood.

Richard saw my empathy for him, and he felt more empathy for Joan. Joan saw Richard's empathy for her, and she returned empathy.

TALK BACK TO YOUR DOUBTS

I have moved fast in this section. Let me summarize. Forgiving depends on feeling differently about a person who hurts or offends you. If you can light that spark of positive feeling—empathy, compassion or love—it can blaze into forgiveness. Sometimes, as the positive feelings build, the negative voices whisper again in our ears. If we are to forgive, we need to talk back to those doubts.

I'm the victim here; he (or she) should be empathizing with me. It is hard to get into the mind of one who hurt you. That is especially true if the hurt left lasting damage that you face every day. A man looks in the mirror and sees a body damaged in an accident with a drunk driver. He thinks, *I'm the victim. Why should I try to understand that idiot woman who maimed me?* Daily his unforgiveness allows her to reinjure him. She keeps torturing him with his own hatred. The hatred makes him bitter. Some day it could cause a heart attack. Yes, he is the victim, but by holding on to hatred he allows himself to remain a victim.

I don't want to empathize with him. As flickers of empathy for my mother's killer sparked in my mind, objections tried to pour cold water on them. *If I understand the killer,* I thought, *will I be betraying my mother?* I had to ask myself, *What did Mom teach me? Did she teach me to hate?* If I bent under the weight of pressure to hate, *that* would betray my mother. By doing the hard thing—looking the killer in the face and trying to understand—I was honoring my mother.

If I empathize, that is the first step down the path to forgetting, and I don't want to forget what they did! My wounded heart wants to remember. The truth is that if I succeed at empathizing, I might forgive. Instead of ruminating, I might feel closure. I will not *forget;* I will *remember differently*. Because I forgive, I want to combat murder and crime more, not less. When I felt unforgiveness toward the killer, I wanted to bash him. I wanted to add to society's violence. After I forgave, I wanted to stop senseless murders.

By empathizing with the killer, we forget the victims. The idea that we forget the victims if we empathize with the killer is not true. I empathized with my mother while also understanding her killer. Those were not polar opposites. Empathizing with one person does not mean we cannot empathize with two, or three, or one hundred. In fact, I want to understand and feel compassion for all people.

I can't empathize with that! When we are horrified with an act, our entire being rebels against understanding it. How can I empathize with a man who sexually molests his child? How can I understand a serial killer? How can I feel what a torturer feels? Sometimes my mind will not let me think about such evil crimes. In those times, I try to sympathize. I think, *How horrible it must be to have a conscience so seared by hatred that he could molest his child. How terrible to feel compelled to kill person after person until forcibly stopped. How tragic to torture another person.* The fact is, no one can empathize with every horrid human act. When my empathy fails, I fall back on sympathy.

But empathy is hard. Too often I give up too easily on doing what is hard. I often don't want to try to empathize. I say "I can't" when I mean "It would make me strain." I say "I can't" when I mean "I don't see how I can." Yet there are some things I can do that will help me empathize.

UNDERSTANDING PEOPLE—THE FIRST STEP OF EMPATHY

Before trying to understand the person who has hurt you, let's set the backdrop. Here are some things to consider.

Soft emotions often hide behind hard emotions. Underneath any attack is often a sense of fear, stress, worry and hurt. Attacks are often attempts to achieve goals. When people fear they cannot reach a valued goal, they get angry. They might use anger to bluff others into meeting their goals. They might use anger to drive others away. They might attack because they do not feel powerful enough to achieve goals without using force or intimidation.

So when a person attacks me, I usually picture the person not as a powerful, strong intimidator but rather as a person who is needy, afraid or weak. Seeing the soft, needy side underneath the attack helps me to understand that this person might need what I can offer—understanding and perhaps forgiveness.

People are influenced by situations. People react strongly to situations. Most people are familiar with Stanley Milgram's classic set of experiments in the late 1960s and early 1970s concerning obedience.[3] Milgram told participants he was studying the effect of punishment on learning, but he was really studying participants' obedience to authority.

A white-coated "experimenter" directed a "teacher" (the true participant) to deliver increasingly strong electric shocks to a "learner" (really a confederate of the experimenter). The "experimenter" could only mildly coax the "teacher" to deliver shocks. He said things like, "The experiment requires you to continue." (Of course, no real shocks were delivered.)

Even when the "teacher" heard the "learner" yell in pain and beg to stop, the "teacher" still usually knuckled under to the "experimenter's" coaxing. In over half of the cases, the "teacher" shocked the suffering "learner" even when the caption beneath the switches read "XXX Danger XXX."

Milgram found that, regardless of the "teacher's" personality traits, race, intelligence, nationality, profession, religion or any of the host of other characteristics, people zapped the victim. It might sound as if people must be naturally cruel. Not so. Milgrim concluded that people were not wolves; rather, they were sheep. That is, they were not evil at heart. They were sensitive to social pressure.

Understanding that people react strongly to situations can help us forgive. We usually think of people who have hurt us as evil. We see them in black capes, intent on inflicting pain and perhaps chuckling evilly. In most cases, though, people are simply caught up in the situation. They are swept along, unable to resist, as were Milgram's participants.

People are hard-wired for survival. People react automatically to some stimuli. For example, a man lounging in a chair on a tropical island may never have seen a tarantula. If he notices a quick wiggling and a dark shape on his sleeve, he will slap at it. He might dive to the sand, heart pounding. Whether the "tarantula" was really a spider or a dark leaf doesn't matter. The automatic reaction is fear. Our brains are hard-wired for survival. Fear and anger are natural responses when we feel threat. So when people hurt or offend me, I should consider whether they feel I have threatened them—whether I have really done so or not.

People are conditioned by past experiences. Sometimes people have become conditioned by their pasts to react in fear and anger. One only has to think of the child whose parent strikes him or her occasionally. If the parent moves his or her arm quickly and the child flinches, we can easily see how the child has been conditioned. The child doesn't think. The child reacts. The same is often true with adults. They may have learned that the best defense against fear is a good offense against the person who frightens them. People who hurt or offend us often do so because they have been conditioned by their past. It is easier to understand attacks when I consider how quickly people can be conditioned.

People don't think things through when they're hurt. When people are hurt or offended, they want to lash back. Those feelings can be a cue to think empathically. See the following suggestions about what we might do. For example, I might think, *Why might the person have hurt me? Is he or she covering vulnerability, responding to the situation, trying to survive or reacting to a painful past?*

What to do when you feel attacked
- Don't react. Instead of letting your own feelings rule, *think*.
- Question why this might have happened.
  - Could the person's fear, stress, worry or hurt have provoked the attack?
  - Is the person caught up in the punch and counterpunch of the situation?
  - Is the person feeling that you are somehow threatening his or her survival?
  - Is the person reacting more to his or her own painful past than to you?
- If you have already lashed back, can you do anything to lessen the tension?
  - Can you apologize quickly before things get out of hand?
  - At a minimum, even if you believe the attack was not provoked, can you say, "I am not trying to make you angry—I don't want us to argue"?
  - Before you respond with your own side of the argument, can you listen thoroughly to the person and summarize his or her point of view?

Perhaps the person is reacting. He or she didn't plan to hurt me. It's just punch and counterpunch. In the midst of an argument, a friend might say something that deeply hurts or offends. *Give her a break,* I might think. *I act without thinking at times too.*

If the offense seems more deliberate, try to get into the offender's mind. Most people want to get along more than they want to fight. Therefore when someone seems to pick a fight or hurt you intentionally, usually it's because he or she feels unable to get along with you. Ask yourself, *Why is this person acting this way?* That question is the beginning of empathy—as well as of sympathy, compassion and agape love.

Sometimes we can ask people tactfully what they are experiencing. We might say, "When you yelled at me, I felt like I had made you angry. Did I do something that made you angry?" Getting the other person's perspective directly can help you forgive.

Consider who you are as a Christian. Survival demands that humans have mechanisms that repair relationships. Individuals who are lone wolves have difficulty succeeding. Squabbles are part of life. People compete for time, attention and resources. Relationships rupture. If people leave a trail of relational carnage in their wake, they will not thrive. Relationships must, on most occasions where problems occur, be repaired. So all people have some empathic capacity and the ability to be attuned with others. That empathic capacity is part of being human—part of common grace. Not all people are equally good at using their ability.

But Christians are both charged with special responsibilities and armed with special resources for relationship repair. First, we are told through Scripture to put off activities that are relationship-toxic—slander, malice, gossip, anger, wrath, foul talk, covetousness, evil desires and hatred (Gal 5:19-21; Col 3:8). We are told to put on kindness, tenderheartedness, compassion and love (Eph 4:31-32; Gal 5:22-24). Paul said, "Therefore, as God's chosen people, holy and dearly loved, clothe yourselves with compassion, kindness, humility, gentleness and patience. Bear with each other and forgive whatever grievances you may have against one another. Forgive as the Lord forgave you. And over all these virtues put on love, which binds them all together in perfect unity" (Col 3:12-14).

Second, we are not left to do this under our own steam. We have been transformed (2 Cor 5:17), and we continue to be transformed (Rom 12:2). We have God's nature within us (1 Jn 3:9). We have the mind of Christ (Rom 8:10; Col 3:3-4). We have the Holy Spirit (Rom 8:11), and we are led by the Holy Spirit (Gal 5:18). With these resources, Peter can confidently say to all Christians, "Finally, all of you, live in harmony with one another; be sympathetic, love as brothers, be compassionate and humble. Do not repay evil with evil or insult with insult, but with blessing, because to this you were called so that you may inherit a blessing" (1 Pet 3:8-9).

How to Empathize

A general understanding of people takes us only to the threshold of empathy. To empathize, we must discern why *this person* has hurt *me* in this way. I have provided below some exercises we have found to help. But first, something essential must be done.

Pray for a gift of empathy. It is hard for us to empathize with one who has hurt us. While we might empathize easily with a person who is like-minded, it is harder to attune our thoughts and feelings with someone who has not had our best interests at heart. In fact, we usually feel that a transgressor—especially one who has harmed us severely, deliberately, remorselessly and without an apparent reason—has set out to defeat our best interests. Almost no one can, in his or her own strength, exert the self-control to empathize with an enemy. We need to agree with God to activate empathy and ask him to work actively within us to bring about more empathy, even if it is against our natural desires. We agree with God through prayer. Prayer can open the door to permit some exercises to help stimulate empathy—and, we hope, also stimulate sympathy, compassion and unselfish love. If you are working through this book with particular transgressions in mind, I invite you to pray before doing these exercises.

Write a descriptive letter. Write a letter as if you were the person who hurt you. Explain your offender's motives, thoughts and feelings. Sure, you might be guessing. You can't know exactly why he or she hurt you. Or the person might have revealed only a part of what he or she was experiencing.

You know how strong situational pressures can be. (Remember Stanley Milgram's studies.) So pay careful attention to what the person saw or might have seen or heard. What did you do that could have been misperceived?

Remember, write the letter as if you were the transgressor. Letter writing was suggested by my son Jonathan who was giving advice to his sister Becca.

"Why do you think Joanie was gossiping about you?" he asked.

"I don't know. I can't understand how she could stab a friend in the back."

"Have you tried to understand?"

"No."

"Why don't you pretend to be Joanie and write yourself a letter. Explain yourself as Joanie. Maybe you can figure how to talk to Joanie if you can understand what might have made her gossip."

Becca scribbled some notes. She and Joanie patched up the break. It worked!

Here is another example. Suppose Louise, a coworker, has offended Ralph by criticizing Ralph's work to the boss. Ralph has been struggling all week to forgive Louise. He decides to write the letter as a way to understand Louise. He writes this:

Dear Ralph,

I wanted to help you understand why I criticized your portfolio to the boss. I hope this will help you to eventually forgive me. I know there is no excuse for putting down your work, so I'm not trying to make light of my actions or justify myself. I just want to tell you how I experienced things.

The boss came in looking for you on Tuesday. He was holding your portfolio. He seemed excited. "Isn't this great?!" he said.

"Yes, it is," I replied. "Ralph did a good job of collecting all the facts and organizing them."

"I'm really glad that *somebody* around here is on the ball," he said. I suppose I felt criticized when he said that. Anyway, a few minutes later, at my earliest opportunity, I mentioned the project I put together last week. He sort of waved his hand like he was brushing away a pest and said, "Yes, but this job of Ralph's was superb."

I was so put out, I blurted out without thinking, "Well, I don't think he included the Sanchez or the Mendel figures."

The boss looked down at the report and flipped through some pages. He turned and went back to his office.

I felt bad about pointing out the omissions. I did not mean to get you in trouble. I suppose my own ego was hurt, and I was trying to show him how smart I was. I really wasn't aiming to get you in trouble at all. I was horrified when the boss criticized you and you got so angry with me.

I'm really sorry.

Louise

Remember, Louise didn't really write the letter. In fact, she might actually have had more sinister motives than Ralph gave her credit for. By trying to get into Louise's head, though, Ralph forced himself to see other motives than he had been thinking about.

Write a letter of apology. In our workshops, we ask people to write an empathic letter from the viewpoint of the offender. However, sometimes we get this: "I am so sorry for hurting you. I'm such a jerk for calling you names. I am scum. I deserve to be less than chewing gum on the bottom of your shoe. Dirty gum. I want to eat worms and live in a cave as the punishment that I deserve, as dung, for having offended you."

This is an apology, not a letter of empathy. The overdramatized apology is a kind of harmless justice. People imagine the offender lowering himself or herself. That balances the scales of justice a bit. It closes the injustice gap, and it reduces unforgiveness. So it makes forgiving easier. In our workshops, we want people to write only an empathic letter, but when people do write a letter of apology, we don't correct them, because the letter of apology will help a little.

The I-am-scum letter works for another reason. The letter of fantasized apology helps change the mood. It is hard to write the I-am-scum letter without bringing humor to the situation. Recall, forgiveness is replacing the unforgiving emotions with other emotions. Humor works. People lighten up. Forgiveness can begin.

Make an audiotape. Some people have a hard time writing letters. We ask those people to audiotape a letter about the motives, thoughts, feelings and situation of the transgressor. Once they narrate the letter, they play it back. In listening, the person feels empathy. Sometimes, even if they cannot feel empathic, they can confront the bitterness and resentment revealed by the audiotape.

Empathy for techies. People who believe they cannot write letters will often write thirty e-mails a day. (Sometimes I feel like a professional e-mail processor, averaging about seventy-five a day.) They can write an empathic e-mail to themselves as if they were the transgressor. If you feel like a professional e-mail processor, sit at your computer and compose. Then delete the email.

For the poetic. Some people write expressive poems. They reveal deep feelings in unrhymed verse. Instead of writing about their own feelings, they can write from the point of view of the transgressor. Is expressive poetry for you? Try it.

Talk to a friend. If you love to talk, grab a close friend and have a cup of coffee. Explain that you want to understand the person who hurt you by getting into his or her head. Then talk with your friend as if you were the transgressor. You will not have quite as much control as narrating an audiotape or writing a letter, e-mail or poem. Sometimes, though, a friend can be a great sounding board to bounce your reflections from, which can promote empathy.

Create your own empty-chair therapy room. Maybe you want to be your own therapist. Remember Les Greenberg's empty-chair conversation. Set up two chairs in a private place. Pretend that one chair is occupied by the person who hurt you. Sit in the other chair. By switching chairs and talking for each person, you might become more understanding, empathic and soft.

Listen to the transgressor's story. You can develop empathy for the person who hurt you if you really listen to the other person's story of hurts. Erwin Straub had people in Rwanda share their stories of pain and hurt. Hutus and Tutsis were brought together. Even years after the massacres, most were not ready to even *hear* the word *reconcile,* much less *forgive.* But when they listened to each other, they developed empathy. Empathy begins with understanding one other person's story, then two people's, then the other group's. In South Africa, the Truth and Reconciliation Commission used the same principle. Victims of apartheid-inspired or rebellion-inspired violence wanted to tell their stories of victimization. Thousands of tearful stories were told at the Human Rights hearings. Victims also wanted to hear the perpetrators' stories. Many wanted to see perpetrators of violence brought to justice. Many just wanted to hear the words, "I'm sorry." As testimonies unfolded from perpetrators during the amnesty hearings, two styles seemed to emerge. Some defiantly confessed their deeds, yet, like the Nazis long ago during the Nuremberg trials, they denied responsibility. Others confessed and said those healing words, "I'm sorry." When regret was sincere, many victims rushed to forgive. Forgiving started with hearing one story, then two, then more.

Rosalie Gerut is a Jewish adult child of a Holocaust survivor. She grew up in a home full of stress. Her mother had survived one of the camps in which six million Jews, more than three million Russians, and people from numerous other groups (such as Gypsies, the infirm and the elderly) were slaughtered under the orders of the SS. Rosalie's insight was to realize how much families of SS soldiers suffered. She found them riddled with guilt and shame. Children of SS soldiers were horrified at what their fathers had done. Rosalie cofounded an organization named One-by-One. She brings first-generation family members of Holocaust victims or survivors together with first-generation family members of Nazis, so that they can hear each other's stories. They empathize one by one.

Meetings are risky for both sides. When people are vulnerable, they can be hurt easily. If they can get past being defensive and listen—really listen— they can feel empathy. One by one they can begin to consider forgiveness.

If you listen as the person who hurt you talks about his or her own hurts, you may begin to feel empathy for the person. This, of course, is the most risky of all the attempts to empathize. It assumes that you will not be further victimized, that you can listen without being provoked, and that you can control your urge to strike back or be defensive. Not easy tasks.

Symbolize your tender feelings toward the transgressor. These exercises have been aimed at helping people experience positive emotions that replace unforgiveness. In the Philippines, I taught a graduate level course in forgiveness at Alliance Biblical Seminary. As part of the course, the students conducted a forgiveness group. After helping people in the group empathize, sympathize, feel compassion for or experience agape love for the one who harmed them, students helped group members symbolize their success. They asked group members to discuss how successfully they felt tenderhearted emotions toward the transgressor. After having group members express themselves in words, the leaders handed out three pieces of construction paper taped together. A gold sheet was sandwiched between two black sheets. The combined papers were cut into the shape of a heart.

Group members stared at the dark exterior and thought about their judgment toward the person who hurt them. They pondered the times they had wished that person ill. They reflected on Jesus' command to love their enemies. They meditated on Jesus' kindness toward them. Finally, they thought about being more empathic toward the person who harmed them. They examined their heart and determined prayerfully whether they could feel any compassion and agape love for the transgressor. When they felt empathy, sympathy, compassion or agape love toward the transgressor, they stripped away the two black layers of paper and revealed the golden heart within. Thus, they symbolized their changed hearts. You can follow that same outline to symbolize your changed heart as well.

THE IMPORTANCE OF EMPATHY

Empathy is important in order for forgiveness to take place. The movie *Regarding Henry,* starring Harrison Ford as Henry, is about a hard-driving, obnoxious, self-interested lawyer. One night Henry went to the store. He blundered in on a robbery and was shot in the head. The head trauma didn't kill Henry, but it changed him to a less aggressive, gentler person.

Henry tried to adjust to his new life, but he had no memory of his past. Learning to live with his wife again was a challenge. While she remembered the old Henry, he didn't remember her. His love for her re-bloomed. Then he discovered that she had been unfaithful to him before his head injury. Henry was devastated, wounded, betrayed. He was utterly unforgiving toward her.

Then he found out that he himself had had an affair. By discovering his own weakness, he finally empathized with his wife's weakness. Only then did he forgive her infidelity. Empathy did not make him forgive. Forgiveness came only with the humility of knowing he and she were the same under the skin. They cried the same tears, felt the same regret, mourned as they felt that love was sliding between their fingers. But they also could work together in an alchemy that would produce pure gold of the soul. In chapter six, I will discuss the humility needed to move up the Pyramid Model to REACH Forgiveness.

CAN YOU APPLY WHAT YOU HAVE LEARNED?

Earlier you selected several transgressions you wanted to try to forgive. I hope that you've been applying what you are learning to each of those. If you haven't already, I would invite you to do so now, before moving on to the next chapter. Can you write an empathic letter, make a tape or talk to an empty chair for each transgression? If you can, it will help you forgive.

When I snuggle down to read a book, I get into a flow. I become The Amazing Page-Processor Man. Being asked to write a letter (much less several letters!) breaks my flow. I have a lot of empathy for the bind I am placing you in by encouraging you to write a letter, make a tape or set up an empty-chair do-it-yourself Freud situation.

You will learn whether you can forgive those hard-to-handle hurts only if you spend the time empathizing, sympathizing and seeking to feel true compassion and agape love for the person who hurt you. Whether you empathize right now, or tomorrow before work, or before little feet begin to scurry around the house is unimportant. That you commit to do this thinking, writing and *feeling* is crucial.

So if you have the time, turn the book back to the sections on how to empathize. Think of the examples you picked in the introduction to part two (or peek back at what you wrote). Then commit yourself to empathizing. Think seriously about when you can set aside time to reflect and empathize. Then press on to the third step up the Pyramid Model to REACH Forgiveness: how to give that altruistic gift that is for giving.

DISCUSSION QUESTIONS

1. Describe the three levels of empathy.

2. The author described Stanley Milgram's obedience experiments. What was the main point he was making?

3. Do you think that understanding that Stanley Milgram showed that people—even good people—are capable of evil if the situational pressures are strong enough helps you gain any understanding or empathy for someone who has hurt you deeply?

4. The section "How to Empathize" describes eight ways to empathize. Summarize two that you think would be most likely to work for you if you were empathizing with someone who had hurt you.

5. Can you think of a time when you experienced empathy for someone who hurt you and found it helped you forgive the person?

6. Can you think of a time when you actually experienced love for an enemy? Jesus said that we are to love our enemies, pray for our enemies and do good to those who use and abuse us. What do you think would happen if we actually practiced this with all of our enemies at work, in politics, in society? What if we interpret our enemies as being people who seek to injure or humiliate or disrespect us? Do we really pray for such enemies? When was the last time you prayed for someone who had made himself or herself your enemy by personally trying to hurt or offend you?

6

A: Altruistic Gift of Forgiveness

Of some thoughts one stands perplexed—especially at the sight of men's sin—
and wonders whether one should use force or humble love. Always decide to use
humble love. If you resolve on that, once and for all, you may subdue the whole
world. Loving humility is marvelously strong, the strongest of all things, and
there is nothing like it.

FYODOR DOSTOYEVSKY

Just because I understood the murderer's impulses and motives did not automatically mean that I would forgive him. I could understand someone perfectly and still think that he or she might have committed an unforgivable act. Something more was needed if I was to forgive.

WHAT WE FOUND THROUGH SCIENCE

In chapter one, I told you about our studies that compared empathy-based forgiveness with self-benefit forgiveness and an untreated condition. People in the eight-hour empathy-based condition were able to forgive more deeply and hold on to forgiveness longer than were the people in the forgiveness-for-self-benefit group (though that group was much better than no group at all).

Even more interesting, we analyzed individuals within both groups. People who forgave more and whose forgiveness lasted longer were those, *regardless of which group they were in,* who felt empathy for the perpetrator. People who did not generate empathy or compassion toward the perpetrator did not forgive, regardless of which group they were in. Even people in the control group forgave if they were able to feel a sense of empathy for the perpetrator. From that study and others we concluded that if a person did not feel empathy, he or she probably would not forgive.

Another puzzle arose from our data. Even some people who felt empathy did not forgive. Empathy is helpful for people to forgive, but it isn't sufficient. We can understand and empathize with a person who has robbed us, but we still may harbor a desire for vengeance. Jason found this out in a victim-offender reconciliation program when he met with the man accused of mugging him. The mugger said, "I'm sorry," but his gaze slid to the side like butter melting on a hot pan. Jason learned that the man had been raised in a broken home. He had been abused by his stepfather, who would drink heavily and then take out his anger on him, his younger brother and his mother. Jason listened to the man's story and halfhearted apology. He felt bad for the man and empathized with him. Yet he wasn't ready to forgive.

Empathy, sympathy, compassion and love take us partway to forgiveness. What else is needed?

Humility

The answer was brought home dramatically as I recalled that night of forgiveness. I could empathize with my mother's murderer. I could understand how he could feel that his freedom would end because he had been seen while committing robbery. I could even see how a youth who already had an impulse-control problem might strike with the crowbar without thinking. Late at night, as I pictured him striking my mom, suddenly my mind flashed back to hours earlier. I had stood with my brother and sister in my brother's back room. I had pointed to a baseball bat and said, "I wish whoever did this were here. I would beat his brains out."

I had just imagined the scene of gory violence and pain that came from a youth beating my mother with a crowbar. When I remembered how I had wished to do the exact same thing, even to someone who had done such evil, I knew I had myself done wrong. True, I had not carried out the act. But what if the youth had stood in front of me in my moment of rage? I might have taken the baseball bat and killed him. Maybe I wouldn't have really hit him. But maybe I would.

The sad truth was the uncovering of bloodlust in my heart. I knew that I was no better than the murderer.

In fact, in some ways I knew I was even worse than he. The youth's plans to quick riches had been suddenly interrupted by my mother's appearance. His response was a knee-jerk reaction. On the other hand, I had contemplated my hatred on a seven-hour trip to Tennessee. All day, as we listened to the detectives unfold the story of the murder, I plotted murder in a vengeful heart. I thought for a long time about the youth's violence. I could not plead impulsiveness. I still was willing to do violence to him in retribution for what he had done to my mother.

I felt embarrassed, ashamed and guilty. That guilt was compounded because I'm a Christian. I didn't want to do things or even have motives that dishonored Jesus. I could truly sense my kinship with the youth who had done the terrible crime to my mother. We were blood brothers. I was capable of wanting to murder.

I became very aware of the ways I was failing God. I held anger and hate in my heart (Mt 5:21-22), was willing to commit murder (Mt 15:19; Mk 7:21; 1 Jn 4:20), was judging the youth (Mt 7:1) and was unwilling to forgive (Mt 6:14-15).

I found that I could be empathic and still judge. When we are wronged, it is easy to feel morally superior. To forgive I needed to go beyond empathy. I did that when I was able to see myself as not so different from the murderer.

It's easier to condemn someone who is different from me than someone who is similar to me. That is why warring enemies emphasize their differences. That's why we dehumanize people that we wish to hurt. We treat them as objects. We think of them as vermin. We want to exact revenge without seeing similarity.

By seeing my own vengeful heart, I experienced humility. I was able to not feel so superior to the one who wronged me. I could see, in humility, my kinship to him.

However, it would not have been helpful to simply stew in my guilt and self-condemnation. By feeling miserable about my own imperfections, I would not automatically forgive.

I needed God's forgiveness. My guilt immediately triggered the Christian thoughts that I had practiced for years: when we truly feel guilty, rather than condemn ourselves, we can take our guilt to God, who will forgive. God's love and mercy were the basis of forgiveness. Like Christians worldwide and throughout history, I knew that I could confess my wrongdoing with sincere regret. God was kind to forgive.

But would I confess? Sensing our own guilt can shame us. When we are ashamed, our natural reaction is to hide our sin. This goes back to the Garden of Eden, with Adam and Eve trying to hide from God, and trying to hide their nakedness from God behind inadequate fig leaves. Kirby has a wonderful picture that captures our natural tendencies. Christians produce fruit. When we sin, we produce bad fruit. Our natural reaction is to pluck the low-hanging, easy-to-see bad fruit and bury it where we think no one will see it. Yet the fruit we buried will burst from the ground as a group of fruit trees, each of which will produce bushels of bad fruit.

Instead of hiding our bad fruit, we should gather all the bad fruit we can—the easy-to-see and the fruit hidden from others behind healthy-looking leaves. Then we must take the fruit to God, who will burn it up. Our fruit trees will then be cleansed and free of bad fruit.

So I prayed to be forgiven of my darkened heart and bloodlust toward the youth. I felt God's forgiveness for my hatred and murderous intent. When that happened, I was flooded with gratitude toward a merciful and loving God. It made me want to give to others something precious because I had been given something precious.

We can recall others' forgiveness. My sense of being forgiven was a religious experience. We have found in our research that the same psychological impact occurs when people recall other times when they were forgiven—by humans.

By now, over two thousand people have gone through our Pyramid Model to REACH Forgiveness. Every one has been able to recall a time when he or she hurt or offended someone who then forgave. One group member, Lauren, said, "I rebelled against my parents during high school and college. I told them I was at a friend's house. Instead I shot up with heroin. They trusted me. I told them I was visiting a different church from the one where I grew up. Instead I got high. They trusted me. I told them I was a virgin. I lost it one night at a party when I was drunk. They trusted me. I was living a lie. I hated to be at home because my parents were trusting me.

"In my junior year of college I told my dad. He was shocked. It was harder to tell my mom because I knew she would judge me. But I couldn't keep living the lies.

"My mom was disappointed. She cried. My dad had been disappointed, too, I guess. He seemed to know I didn't need his judgment. He was more accepting of me even though he was hurt.

"For a month, I expected to be disowned. I waited for the angry judgmental confrontation from my mom. After a month, she drove four hours to my school and was waiting for me on the steps of my apartment when I came back from class. When I saw her sitting there, I almost ran away to hide.

"We went inside. Her first words were, 'Honey, I love you so much. You are still my daughter. I forgive you.' We talked for hours.

"I still sometimes get drunk, but at least now I'm not living a lie. My mom and dad both forgave me for lying to them and for disappointing them. The day I knew they forgave me and still loved me was probably the happiest day of my life."

Lauren used the memory of her gratitude after receiving her mother's forgiveness to motivate her to give the gift of forgiveness to the young man who had taken her virginity when she was passed out at a party. That young man needed the forgiveness that only she could give.

So, like Lauren, I felt someone's forgiveness—for me it was God's forgiveness—of my hatred and murderous intent. When that happened, I was flooded with gratitude.

Actually, we have found over the years that Christians in our groups usually do better if they do *not* use the divine forgiveness they have experienced from God as the basis of knowing that they are forgivable. True, God's forgiveness is perhaps the greatest gift that a person can obtain. Yet, paradoxically, because God is so loving, so forgiving, so completely accepting, so divine, some people do not benefit by thinking about their salvation. They benefit at first, but then the reasoning kicks in: *Of course God can forgive these big transgressions. God is God. But I'm just a poor fallible human. I can't possibly forgive like God does.* They squirm off the hook.

So we usually encourage Christians to be grateful for how much God has indeed forgiven them. But we also ask them to think of some human who forgave them. Then they can see that forgiveness is achievable even in their human state. And they can feel real gratitude to a person for having granted that forgiveness.

THE GIFT OF FORGIVENESS

When I had confronted my own dark motives and received the freedom of forgiveness, I came to an inescapable conclusion: If I could be forgiven for wanting to kill someone (Acts 8:22), couldn't this needy young man also benefit if I forgave him? If I could be forgiven for having a darker heart than he, then who was I to withhold my forgiveness from him? I could not tell the young man I had forgiven him. Probably he'll never know because the perpetrator has never been brought to justice. However, in my imagination I could extend the gift of forgiveness to him.

He had damaged my family. He had taken my mother's life. I could not undo those losses by hating. He had hurt me by his act; I could do something about that. I knew that youth *needed* forgiveness. I could not withhold what he needed. I forgave. Since then, I have felt peace.

Skeptics can ask whether my act of forgiving would benefit a person who might not know I had done so. Cynics might think I am playing word games in claiming that my forgiveness was altruistic. "It is meaningless if the perpetrator never knows," they might say. For the Christian, this is a mystery. Jesus appeared to his disciples after his resurrection (Jn 20:21-23) and said, "Peace be with you! As the Father has sent me, I am sending you." John's account continues, "And with that he breathed on them and said, 'Receive the Holy Spirit. If you forgive anyone his sins, they are forgiven; if you do not forgive them, they are not forgiven.'" The meaning of this connection between humans granting earthly forgiveness for sins and divine forgiveness is uncertain. There may be the implication here that the impact of forgiving a transgressor on earth will someday be experienced by the transgressor—perhaps in the eternal.

THE SURPRISE OF FORGIVING

All our positive emotions, such as love, affection, empathy, compassion, pity and sympathy, are in a tug of war with the negative emotions of unforgiveness. It is as if we are contesting on a plateau on a mountaintop. When we yield to unforgiveness, it can drag us over one edge of a cliff into a free fall of bitterness, resentment and hatred. To win the tug of war requires hard emotional work. We also cannot see how close we are to the precipice of forgiving. If we step over the other edge, though, our momentum pulls those hot negative emotions into a cool bath of forgiveness. We are surprised by joy and love.

When we're tortured by unforgiveness and are finally able to grant forgiveness, a transforming surprise occurs. Forgiving is like a flood of light at sunrise. Darkness has covered the sky. Then the sun suddenly peeks over the horizon, illuminating giant clouds that stretch from the horizon to miles above it. Billowy clouds are lit with orange, red and purple. The sky is afire with colors. Such is the relief of forgiveness after wrestling with unforgiveness.

ALTRUISM

Altruism is unselfish regard for another person. Altruism is giving the other person something simply for his or her own good. We feel good when we act altruistically, but we do not act altruistically to feel good. We act altruistically because it is the right thing to do.

O. Henry wrote the brilliant short story "The Gift of the Magi." A husband and wife, deeply in love, gave up their most prized possessions to purchase Christmas gifts for each other. The husband sold his treasured watch to purchase beautiful combs for the never-cut hair of his bride. The wife cut off her hair and sold it to purchase a beautiful chain for her husband's watch. Both people gave self-sacrificially and altruistically to bless the other person.

Martin Sheen and Alan Arkin starred in another beautiful story of altruism, *The Fourth Wise Man*, based on Henry van Dyke's novella, "The Story of the Other Wise Man." Martin Sheen portrayed a rich man, one of four magi (wise men), who sought to be present at the birth of the Christ child. While he was converting his entire fortune into three precious jewels, the other three wise men set out by camel to follow the star that would eventually lead them to Bethlehem.

The fourth wise man (Martin Sheen), accompanied by a whiny attendant (Alan Arkin), sold one of his three jewels to purchase what was needed to make the journey. He came into Bethlehem as Herod's troops were slaughtering children. He purchased the life of one child with the second of his three jewels.

Sheen and Arkin stumbled into a leper colony. The fourth wise man agreed to stay, using his medical training to help the lepers, "just for one day." One day turned to two, which turned to years. Still the fourth wise man hoped someday to see Jesus to give him the final jewel.

When the existence of the colony was threatened, Sheen offered to trade his final jewel for seeds to sustain the colony, but his friends refused his sacrifice. Later, he used the final jewel to purchase freedom for a friend's daughter who was being taken to be a slave. He had given away his fortune. Thirty or so years from the story's start, the fourth wise man had spent his fortune and health on unselfish service to others.

One day, word arrived: Jesus, the Christ, had come to Jerusalem. A blind friend of the wise man had been healed. "Come, let's go see him!" said the friend.

In the most poignant moment of the film, the fourth wise man looked at his destitute surroundings, felt his weak, work-worn heart, and—having poured out his life for others—said in true humility, "But I have nothing to give him."

Altruism is other-oriented love. Often, altruism is thought to be tainted if it is not self-sacrificial, or if the giver derives some benefit from an act. But benefits that flow from loving acts are inevitable. Love occurs between two people. Love given is love returned. Altruism is not giving without getting anything in return. It simply is giving for the benefit of the other person.

Jean Valjean in Les Misérables could forgive throughout his lifetime because he recalled the way Monsignor Bienvenue had forgiven Valjean, purchasing his soul for God, as the Monsignor said. Valjean knew what it felt like to be on the receiving end of forgiveness. He was quick to forgive others and pass along this altruistic love.

As Christians, we have been forgiven much by God. We can find times when we have been forgiven by others. Can we pass along this blessing by giving that altruistic gift to our transgressors, who don't deserve to be forgiven any more than we deserved it?

Helping people give an altruistic gift of forgiveness to one who has harmed them consists of three distinct acts: guilt, gratitude and gift.

THREE PARTS TO THE ALTRUISTIC GIFT OF FORGIVENESS

Guilt. In our research, we ask people to recall an incident in which they did something they knew ahead of time to be wrong, yet the person whom they wronged forgave them. At first people may recall trivial times when they were forgiven. When I began to think of times in my past that I had wronged someone and had been forgiven, I first recalled a night in which my brother and I were doing the dinner dishes. Mike was washing, I was drying, and we were teasing each other as we often did. As I would walk over to pick up the dishes, Mike would flick soapy water on my face. I would snap him with the dishtowel. We continued this bantering, but I tired of it before Mike did. I warned him. When he flicked water one time too many, something snapped (not my towel). I had been sipping Coke from a bottle. (Those were the days—five cents per bottle.) I simply turned the Coke bottle upside down in his pocket. As the Coke ran down his leg, the shock on his face was extremely gratifying (for me).

But I had acted out of proportion to the transgression. I felt guilty and also worried. Mike could have held a grudge. He could have poured Coke on me after I went to sleep that night. He did neither. He forgave, and the War of the Coke Bottle ended quickly. I was grateful for his forgiveness.

As we reflect on our growing-up years, numerous examples of receiving forgiveness come to mind. In fact, in our research studies we have never found a person who could not eventually come up with several examples of times when they wronged someone and were forgiven. Even recalling a trivial example like the War of the Coke Bottle can trigger memories of dozens of other incidents.

More serious than the War of the Coke Bottle was the way I hurt and worried my father by my behavior on a summer job. After my sophomore year in college, I got a job driving a truck at night. I delivered newspaper bundles to carriers throughout East Tennessee. Honestly, I was a terrible driver. I promised my father that I would drive carefully. (I would have told him I would fly if it convinced him to let me take the job.) As soon as I was behind the wheel, predictably, I put the pedal to the metal.

One morning I was late getting home. I was just outside of Athens, Tennessee, about sixty miles away from Knoxville. I was standing on the accelerator. I was probably making about 80 miles per hour when I entered a curve. I could barely hold the truck on the road. Tires were squealing. I was fighting the steering wheel when I glanced out the window at an oncoming car. It was a black 1959 Ford—the kind that my father drove. I muscled my way out of the other car's lane. My speed had fallen to 75. As the other car went past, I saw the upturned face of my father staring at me. Dread overcame me. I immediately slowed to 55 miles per hour. All the way home, I anticipated a stern lecture when he next saw me. My best hope was that he would not force me to quit the job. I fully expected to be grounded until I received my first Social Security check.

That night, sitting at the table, he spoke as I poured myself a soda. "That looked a lot like you in that delivery truck early this morning."

"Yes, I was finished with work and heading home," I said.

"You seemed to be struggling to hold the truck on the road."

"I guess I was going a little too fast."

"Your mom and I would both be very sad if you were killed in an acci-dent."

"It wouldn't exactly make my day either," I said.

"I won't say anything to your mom. It might worry her. But be careful, will you?"

"I will."

I turned away absolutely stunned. He had not even been critical. My re-lief was almost a physical release. I had known I was in trouble, but sud-denly, I was free.

Cokes in the pocket are mild offenses. Reckless driving is more serious. My bloodlust to kill the youth who murdered my mother was dead seri-ous. I knew my attitude was opposed to Scripture and a disappointment to God. Yet I knew that God would forgive much—far more than my brother and father had.

Gratitude. Simply recalling events in which we were forgiven, though, is not enough to make us yearn to grant the gift of forgiveness to one who has offended us. In our groups, we ask people to describe their feelings af-ter they knew they had been forgiven. People's responses are remarkably similar.

"When I knew I had been forgiven, I felt as if a giant weight had been taken off my shoulders."

"I felt free."

"I felt that the chains that had imprisoned me in hatred were cut."

"I was deeply happy."

These are the feelings of gratitude. Gratitude lifts us.

Gratitude or thanksgiving can be simple or complex. Simple gratitude is that feeling of freedom from having received a no-strings-attached gift. If you want to forgive, try to recall a time when you were forgiven as a gift—no strings attached.

Sometimes gratitude is more complicated. If you feel that a gift is given grudgingly, it does not set you free. It binds. If you feel that a gift is given insincerely or to manipulate, it does not free. It ties you up in knots of an-ger.

Try to remember when you received forgiveness as a simple gift. And when you grant forgiveness, treat it as giving a gift from your heart.

Gift. In our groups, we then invite forgiveness. "You can empathize with the one who hurt you. Maybe you can feel sympathy, compassion or even agape love for that person. You probably feel less angry and resentful, and you probably also have turned loose some or all of your desires to get revenge or even avoid the person. Also, you've recalled that you have hurt others and have received a gift of forgiveness. You have benefited by the gift of forgiveness from God, but also from flawed humans. Would you now like to give such a gift of forgiveness to the one who hurt you? That gift would consist of a further release of negative emotions and motivations, and perhaps even wishing some blessing on that person who hurt you. Would you like to give that gift now?"

Some people look us right in the eye and say, "I don't think so. Not today."

We ask, "If not all, then how much of your unforgiveness can you overcome with the gift of forgiveness? Perhaps 75 percent? 50 percent? How much?"

When people have empathized, sympathized, sought to feel compassion for and sought to love the person who wronged them, when they have remembered what they felt like when someone forgave them, almost every person is willing to give up all or part of their unforgiveness and replace it with forgiveness.

Amy was unhappy with her boss. He had been assigned to write a technical report on the feasibility of a new product line, but because he was busy, he threw Amy the project. "He pestered me daily to get the report done," Amy said, "but he never lifted a finger to help." When the report was finished, he submitted it to the vice presidents. They not only liked the analysis but promoted him to head the production team for the new product!

"All he did was complain about the things he didn't like with the report. Now no one knows that I did the report, and he's off at a new location. I got no credit, only grief. And no one will ever know, because he's gone."

The turning point that allowed Amy's forgiveness came when the president of her community recreation association thanked her for a report she had submitted on repaving the parking lot. She realized that she had received the accolades for the report, yet she had worked closely with her best friend to compile the report. And Amy had not acknowledged her friend's help. Oops.

Immediately she phoned her friend and apologized. "No problem," her

friend assured her. Then Amy phoned the president of the recreation association to give credit where credit was due. Surprisingly to her, that
event helped her to see her former boss as less manipulative and self-serving. She began to forgive him for not giving her credit for the report into
which she had poured so much labor.

What if you don't want to (or can't) give the gift? People don't always
wish to give a gift of forgiveness to one who harmed them. I would never
want to coerce or manipulate anyone into forgiving. Only if you give forgiveness freely will it have its best effect on you and perhaps on the one
you forgive.

Most people who use the Pyramid Model to REACH Forgiveness are
people who want to forgive but can't. If the person is not ready to forgive,
or if he or she is willing to forgive only part of the transgression, then we
typically invite the person to take two actions.

First, he or she should consider what the barriers are to forgiving fully.
Does the offended person want a full apology? restitution? to see the transgressor humiliated? Is the offended person holding out for something that
he or she knows is highly likely never to take place? Sometimes an honest
examination of the barriers to full forgiveness can help the person hurdle
those barriers.

Second, if the person still really wants to forgive, we invite him or her
to reconsider the steps of empathy, sympathy, compassion and love. Can
the person find new insights by trying to elaborate on the previous exercises to promote empathy? Can prayerful reflection stimulate more compassion and love? The person might consider the commands of Jesus, who
said, "But I tell you who hear me: Love your enemies, do good to those
who hate you, bless those who curse you, pray for those who mistreat you.
If someone strikes you on one cheek, turn to him the other also. If someone takes your cloak, do not stop him from taking your tunic. Give to everyone who asks you, and if anyone takes what belongs to you, do not
demand it back. Do to others as you would have them do to you" (Lk 6:27-
31; see also Prov 25:21; Mt 5:44-47; Rom 12:20). Can the person reflect
on kindness that has been offered to him or her throughout life?

If one hurt is too difficult to forgive, try forgiving an easier one. Put the
hard one aside until later. Try again tomorrow.

When we try any new skill, it feels awkward. When I began to play com-
petitive volleyball, I felt like a klutz. For a year. Let's face it, I *was* a klutz.

But I kept showing up to practice and to games. (Perhaps I'm a slow learner.) One day I hit an actual spike—one that went down instead of against the back wall. The second spike was easier. The tenth was easy. The key was to ignore my feelings of incompetence and keep practicing. If you want to forgive but can't, keep practicing until forgiving happens.

HUMILITY AND GRATITUDE

Humility and gratitude are at the center of the A-step (altruistic gift of forgiveness) in the Pyramid Model to REACH Forgiveness. "Humility," theologian Andrew Murray once said, "is not thinking less of oneself than one ought. It is not thinking of oneself at all."[1] Humility is an other-oriented emotion that elevates the other person. Paul tells us to have the humility of Jesus, who gave up his equality with God to become a sacrifice for us (Phil 2:3-11). Paul identifies humility with altruism. Similarly, Peter encourages us, "Finally, all of you, live in harmony with one another; be sympathetic, love as brothers, be compassionate and humble. Do not repay evil with evil or insult with insult, but with blessing, because to this you were called so that you may inherit a blessing" (1 Pet 3:8-9). Peter's locating humility within the context of blessing instead of reviling or avenging suggests how closely humility is related to forgiveness.

Humility arises from and reinforces a person's sense of empathy. Empathy is also important to feeling gratitude. Gratitude is a feeling of thanksgiving at having received a gift perceived to be altruistic. Gratitude is an extremely complex emotion because it demands sensitivity and empathy from both the gift-giver and the gift-receiver.

In order to feel gratitude, the receiver must perceive the gift as given altruistically. That requires empathy. The receiver must place himself or herself in the shoes of the gift-giver and conclude that the gift-giver is acting unselfishly. The complications to feeling grateful that I mentioned earlier are due to perceiving ulterior motives.

On the other hand, the gift-giver must also be empathic. He or she must understand the needs of the receiver to avoid offending the receiver by offering an unwanted gift.

Therefore, the transaction of giving and receiving gifts resembles a mating dance of porcupines. The two try to get close enough to have contact, yet possibilities of prickles pop up at every twist and turn.

Humility and gratitude are intimately joined. A humble person is aware of his or her gifts and talents and accepts them. Yet the humble person does not believe that those gifts and talents make him or her a better person than others. In fact, the truly humble person rarely compares himself or herself to others. Humility is other-oriented, not self-oriented. Being oriented toward others, a humble person is grateful for what others have done. He or she is grateful to God, to parents, to mentors, to friends—grateful for the many people who have forgiven him or her. That gratitude is a steam engine that powers a drive to reach out in altruistic love to forgive someone who has caused pain.

Father Elias Chacour sat beside me at a dinner one night. He is one of the most humble people I have ever met. As president of a university, he still finds the time to be a parish priest. Father Chacour is a Palestinian Christian. As a member of two minorities in Israel, he has ample grounds for feeling victimized. Instead he strives to promote reconciliation because he believes that is the right thing to do. He has turned his beliefs into action to bring people together. To promote practical reconciliation, he founded a university in Palestine with students and faculty who are Christian, Jewish and Muslim.

When an Israeli terrorist opened fire on Muslims prostrated in worship, spilling the blood of innocent people, Father Chacour wrote to the Israeli government in protest. Soon afterward, a Palestinian terrorist strapped a bomb to his back and set it off in a marketplace, killing or wounding over eighty people, mostly Israeli Jews. Father Chacour wrote another letter of protest to the Israeli government.

His students were not satisfied with his response. He described the incident in a talk at the State of the World Forum in New York in 2000.

> My students came to me. "Have you become an American?" they accused me.
>
> "When Americans are upset, they write a letter to their congressman. They think they have solved the problem. That is not enough," my students said.
>
> My students wanted to show the love that expressed itself in action. I asked, "What should we do?"
>
> "We want to give our blood to help the injured Jews," said the mostly Palestinian students.
>
> So I phoned the Israeli government with my request, and they sent

fifteen nurses. I was afraid that only fifteen or twenty students would show up, embarrassing the school. I need not have worried. For six solid hours, fifteen nurses pumped the blood of Christian, Muslim, and Jewish students and faculty. Palestinians gave their blood for the Jews.

"We became blood brothers," said Father Chacour, who wrote a book by that name.[2] "We were not born Jew, Christian or Muslim," he said. "We were born *babies*."

When we understand—as Father Chacour simply but eloquently said—that we are born babies, that we all bleed blood, and that we experience the same pains and joys, then we have the basis of the empathy and humility we need to be able to forgive.

People are precious. They are not precious because they are dressed like us or have the same color of skin as we do. They are precious because they are people of potential. Because I am a Christian, I believe (as do the other two major religions that sprang from Abraham—Judaism and Islam) that the value of humans derives from being born in the image of God.

At that same World Forum, Stephen Huang, speaking on behalf of Cheng Yen, founder of the Buddhist Compassion Relief Tzi-Chi Foundation in Taiwan, agreed that people are valuable. "If I had a new thousand-dollar bill, would you want it?" he asked. "What if I wadded it up? What if I threw it on the floor? What if I stepped on it and scuffed dirt from my feet on it? Would you still want it?"

Everyone at his talk still wanted the thousand dollars. "Just because the bill gets dirty and stains any hand it contacts does not affect its inherent value," he said. "People are valuable. They need and deserve our compassionate love."

Religion can divide, but it seems that on this point many agree—as do many who embrace no religion. Our empathy, humility and gratitude somehow ennoble us. In so doing, they inspire us to step beyond our own self-interest and give altruistic gifts of love to those in need.

Giving those altruistic gifts elevates the giver as well as the receiver. Even more surprising, those gifts elevate those who observe.

At the same forum, Marty Seligman, a psychologist of great vision who has served as president of the American Psychological Association, described a course he taught at the University of Pennsylvania. It was on positive psychology. He assigned students to do two tasks: do something fun and do something nice for others.

"One woman was driving her friends home one snowy night," said Seligman. "She said, 'I saw an old woman whose car was stuck in the snow. She was trying to shovel it free. Down the road, one of my friends asked to be let out. I thought he knew a shorter way home. I watched in the rearview mirror as he walked back. When he picked up the shovel, I began to cry.' The woman went on to say," said Seligman, " 'When I had fun, I felt good for a while, but just seeing him help the old woman has made me feel *proud to be a person* all week.' "

There is an ancient Chinese saying:

> If you want to be happy . . .
> for an hour, take a nap
> for a day, go fishing
> for a month, get married
> for a year, get an inheritance
> for a lifetime, help someone.

Forgiving is an altruistic gift you can give to someone who *needs* forgiveness. You do not even need to tell the person you have forgiven. Just change your actions to reflect the altruistic gift you have bestowed.

APPLYING THE ALTRUISTIC GIFT OF FORGIVING

If you have been applying what you have read to several of your own relationships that might require forgiveness, pause here. Identify at least three incidents where you have been forgiven. Write about each incident.

Think about how you felt when you knew you had done wrong. Imagine the guilt, embarrassment and perhaps shame you felt. Recall how concerned you were over the consequences. Remember how you tried (if you did) to justify your acts even though you knew deep down that you had done wrong. Write about what happened.

Then recall your feelings and thoughts when you were granted forgiveness. What were they? Write them down.

What if the person you hurt made you feel guilty? What if you felt manipulated? Did you want to make the person who hurt you feel guilty or manipulated? How could you avoid making him or her feel badly? Try to come up with and write about at least three incidents in your life where you received forgiveness.

Now you are armed with three incidents where you could be grateful for having been forgiven. Return to the several incidents where you were hurt and want to forgive. Pick one. Think it through again. Recall the hurt. Don't see yourself as a victim. Don't see yourself as the avenger.

Now empathize with the person who hurt you. Get inside his or her head, and feel what he or she might have felt. Sense your common humanity with the person.

Then recall a time when you were forgiven. Tell yourself that you can rise above hurt and revenge. You can give a gift of forgiveness to the person who hurt you. You can love the person who made himself or herself your enemy by harming you. You can bless, not curse. You can forgive. It's your gift to the person regardless of whether you ever tell him or her that you have given that gift. Would you like to do that?

DISCUSSION QUESTIONS

1. Describe each of the three parts to the altruistic gift of forgiveness.

2. Define *humility* according to Andrew Murray. Do you agree with that definition? If not, do you have a different understanding? What is it?

3. Would you tell the group about a time when you did something altruistic for someone who was needy? How did you feel when you did the altruistic act? How long did your good feelings last? Compare that with the last "success" you had at work or in your family. In which case did the good memories and feelings last longer and give you more deep-seated satisfaction?

4. Is it possible to do anything that is truly altruistic? Do we gain good feelings and perhaps other benefits from doing something altruistic? Does our gaining benefits make our act nonaltruistic?

5. Should you feel guilty about doing something nice for someone and deriving benefits from it?

6. Summarize Father Chacour's students' response to terrorism. What responses have you had to acts of terrorism you have witnessed?

C: Commit Publicly to Forgive

I am ashamed that my tongue cannot live up to my heart.
Augustine

Have you ever struggled to forgive someone and finally emerged from your struggles believing that you had granted forgiveness—only to doubt that forgiveness later? For most people, such self-doubts about the reality of forgiveness are common.

I was no different from most people. On the night I forgave the murderer, God transformed me emotionally. I profoundly *knew* that I had forgiven.

Later, though, I would occasionally flash back to the imagined scenes of violence that I could not seem to shake. I would feel the pain. *Maybe I didn't fully forgive,* I would think. The loss of my mother brought a sense of darkness and emptiness. Did that mean my forgiveness was bogus? Did God not act? Was my forgiveness merely self-deception?

Doubt would steal in like an intruder seeking to rob me of my peace. Growing weary of self-doubt, I decided to combat that doubt by using some of the methods we had developed in our workshops.

When Do We Doubt Our Forgiveness?

Doubt was my enemy. To defeat the enemy I had to understand what led to it. Let's assume you've struggled to forgive an acquaintance, Bob, who betrayed a trust. You haven't seen Bob for years. You believe you have forgiven him. When are you likely to doubt that your forgiveness is real?

First, you may doubt your forgiveness if you see Bob again. Seeing him reminds you of the hurt. Memories are linked to the emotions of fear and anger, which are stored in your brain and body. This is especially true if you don't see Bob often, or if you meet him unexpectedly without having the chance to prepare yourself.

Second, you may doubt your forgiveness if you are hurt similarly by someone else. If someone else—let's call her Natalie—betrays your trust in the same way Bob did, then you might think, *That's the same way Bob hurt me*, and the new hurt by Natalie triggers a re-experience of the old hurt by Bob. Because you feel the hurt from Bob again, you might think that you haven't fully forgiven Bob.

Third, you may doubt you've forgiven if you're under stress. When you're stressed, old hurts can resurface. You might suddenly recall how Bob hurt you because the stress creates emotions in your body that arouse memories and feelings of old hurts.

Fourth, you may doubt your forgiveness if you are hurt by the same person again. For example, even if you have forgiven Bob for a past betrayal, if he insults you tomorrow, you will probably remember how he betrayed your trust previously.

Let's be good Scouts. Life is full of unexpected meetings. No matter how hard we might try to avoid a person, we bump into her, hear her name, see her friend who reminds us of her.

Life is also full of rejections. If I flash back to a painful memory every time someone rejects or disappoints me, I might as well not go to work, not marry and not have children. Life is full of reminders of past hurts.

Life is full of stress. For most of us, life is not only filled with stress but overflowing with it. E-mails, express mail, faxes and phone calls demand attention *now*. Change is everywhere, clamoring for action. Jobs, bosses, friends and even leisure activities pull at us from all directions. If stress can trigger the memory of old wounds, I had better learn to deal with the memory, because stress is a given.

Life is full of other encounters with people who have wounded us. In fact, once I am wounded, the wound can feel like a chewed place inside my cheek. Every time I move my mouth, it brings me back into contact with the teeth that bit me.

The point is, I will surely recall the wounding. Many times. So, if I can't avoid recalling the wounding, at least I can adopt the Scout motto: Be prepared.

Calvin and Hobbes have a unique relationship. Hobbes sometimes puts

Calvin down. Calvin, unsuspecting (and, like me, a bit oblivious), lets it pass. Then, in the dead of night, Calvin suddenly sits up in bed with a puzzled look and says, "What the . . . ?" Let's not be like Calvin. Let's anticipate that those wounds, which are already forgiven, will still hurt us at times.

Don't just treasure forgiveness in your heart. Assume that you've granted decisional forgiveness and that you've moved through the first three steps to the Pyramid Model to REACH Forgiveness. You R, recalled the hurt. You E, empathized with the person who hurt you. You gave an A, altruistic gift of forgiveness, which has made a definite change in your emotional forgiveness. When you forgave, you forgave from the heart. You knew you forgave, but you did not make a public statement of the forgiveness. You did not grant decisional forgiveness aloud. Doubts will happen. Did you *really* forgive?

HAD I FORGIVEN MY FATHER?

My father had a drinking problem. He grew up in a coal-mining town in the East Tennessee mountains during the Depression. He was the son of a railroad man who was killed when my dad was less than three years old. His mother was blind, left with three living children.

Times were tough. So was my dad. Life encouraged him to be hard and cynical, and he cooperated. He fought. He drank. He cussed. He kept a lot of his background from us children while we were young. He succeeded so well that when, as a schoolkid, I overheard him talking to my mother about a "down payment," I misunderstood, thinking he was saying "damn payment." I was scandalized that he was swearing.

When I entered junior high, Dad began to drink a lot. (I hope it wasn't my entry into adolescence that provoked the drinking.) With drinking came its brothers—swearing, anger and simple, mean-spirited hurtfulness directed at us children or Mama.

When Dad was not drinking, he was kind. But the moments of kindness got rarer as I got older.

I was blessed. I could escape into extracurricular activities: tournament tennis, working math problems while shut away in our cold back room, or running around town with my friends. My brother (four years younger) and sister (nine years younger) were not as mobile as I. They received the lion's share of the fallout from Dad's drinking. While I accumulated many of my own wounds from Dad beginning in my junior high years and lasting until I moved out after college, it was the wounds I saw inflicted on my brother, sister and mother that led to the core of my unforgiveness toward Dad.

I began to do focused research on forgiveness in 1990, which was the year Dad died of cancer. As he saw the approach of his death, he mellowed. Seeing him deal with the ravages of advancing cancer helped me feel more tenderhearted toward him.

I was able to think back through the years, recall some of my biggest hurts and eventually forgive. I do not believe I fully forgave until the year after he had died. Shortly after his death, I told others that I forgave. I made a decision to forgive. But I heard the bitterness in my voice when I recalled my dad or talked about his death. That bitter sound pushed me toward trying to experience emotional forgiveness. I worked hard to emotionally forgive, and I finally felt the ocean breeze of forgiveness freshen my bitterness. I felt free of the venom that had soured me for years. I hoped to remain free.

But too many things reminded me of my dad. A conflict at work: scenes of conflict with my dad would intrude into my memory. A disappointment from one of my children: I would remember a similar time when my dad had scolded me.

I had forgiven him . . . hadn't I?

HARD-WIRED TO REMEMBER

Yes, I had fought through to hard-won forgiveness. When I was reminded of past hurts, I no longer felt the resentment, bitterness, hostility, hatred or anger that I used to feel. When I recalled specific events, I remembered the pain. But hurt is not unforgiveness.

Remember in chapter two I defined unforgiveness as the delayed emotions that arise out of vengeful rumination. I was careful to point out that *forgiveness does not replace hurtful memories; it replaces the negative emotions attached to those memories.*

We are literally hard-wired to remember serious hurts or offenses. The first time we touch a stove as a child, it burns us. We never are tempted to rest our hand on a red-hot stove again. The memory of pain is burned into our brain.

The same thing happens when people hurt or offend us. The hurt is burned into our brain. It becomes part of our wiring. The sight of the person's face, the sound of his or her voice, images of the acts of harm, the angry and fearful emotions of our immediate reactions, and the memories of subsequent events are recorded. It isn't really like storing a program in a computer; it's more like changing the circuitry of the computer. The biochemistry of our brain changes. Neurotransmitters, the chemicals that are released into the space between neurons to create pathways for memories, are coded to be released when we are reminded of a hurtful event. Electrical and chemical signals in our brain run a familiar route. They move through the emotional centers of our brain, not merely through the cortex. In fact, sometimes we have *only* a feeling of pain and can't remember why. At other times, we have a memory complete with attached emotions.

When we forgive, we can't stop the memory of the hurt with its attached immediate fear and anger. We shouldn't want to stop them. They keep us from recklessly trusting where trust might not be deserved. What forgiveness has replaced is the second set of emotions that formed due to our rumination. We are freed to experience empathy, love, sympathy and compassion instead of being bound to hatred and bitterness.

I summarize this in figure 7.1. A reminder event triggers the hard-wired "Transgression Loop." Before we forgave, we would have been caught in an "Unforgiveness Loop." After emotional replacement of the unforgiving emotions, we can move to a "Forgiveness Loop."

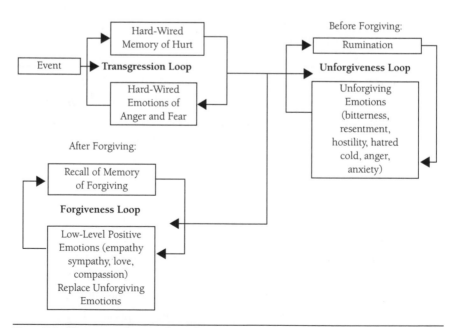

Figure 7.1. The two responses to being hurt

Today, I can remember my father's cruel acts. I can even feel the anger and fear again. But if I do not indulge the Unforgiveness Loop, I can hold on to the forgiveness I worked to experience.

WHEN FORGIVENESS IS JUST IN MY HEART

Forgiveness can be delicate. Decisional forgiveness without an accompanying amount of emotional forgiveness can make us feel hypocritical. That is why we work through the Pyramid Model to REACH emotional forgiveness. Emotional forgiveness, however, can also be fragile. That forgiveness replaces negative emotions. If I confine my experience to private feelings, forgiveness will be vulnerable to assaults by doubt. If I wall hard-won forgiveness inside my heart by confining it to a private experience, then doubts can creep in. But if I do or say something to indicate that I have forgiven, those acts add bodily experiences that announce to my brain that I have forgiven. My words and actions become a public record that I have forgiven. It becomes harder for me to doubt that my forgiveness was real.

Scripture tells us how important it is not only to treasure good feelings in our hearts but also to make them concrete. James tells us not merely to say to the needy person, "Go, I wish you well; keep warm and well fed," but instead to clothe and feed the person (Jas 2:15). James's message is applicable here too. Don't merely tell yourself that you have forgiven; also make it more public. Do something about it!

To make forgiveness permanent, I want to involve as much of my body and my environment in forgiving as possible. I can do this in five ways. I can erect the forms of forgiveness, be my own behavior therapist, symbolize my forgiveness, write about forgiveness and tell someone about forgiveness.

ERECT THE FORMS OF FORGIVENESS

When a builder pours concrete, the builder doesn't just dump it on the ground and hope it will spontaneously become a sidewalk. Instead, the builder constructs forms in the shape of a sidewalk, into which the concrete is poured. Similarly, to build permanent forgiveness, sometimes we must construct "forms" in the shape of behavior that is consistent with already having forgiven. We must act *as if* we have forgiven as we wait for God to complete emotional forgiveness within us.

If my dad were still alive, this would mean that I would try to act toward him exactly as if I had never been hurt by him. If my emotional forgiveness was half achieved, I would try to act as if it were fully complete. In time, the Lord would pour the concrete of complete forgiveness into my heart. In the meantime, the "forms"—my accepting and loving behaviors toward my dad—would be a public indication of my commitment to the forgiveness both experienced and anticipated.

BE YOUR OWN BEHAVIOR THERAPIST

Decondition yourself. I had forgiven my dad for many of his offenses, but I kept replaying the unforgiving tape. It was like the "I Love You" computer virus that fouled computers worldwide in the winter of 2000. Annoying messages replicated out of control. Similarly, my recollections of hurt were intrusive. I needed to do something. I decided to decondition myself.

I sat in my chair and looked at my father's picture. I thought about forgiving rather than condemning him. I repeated this several times daily for a week. Call it boredom or deconditioning. Whatever happened, my feelings about Dad changed.

Discipline yourself not to criticize. I thought critically of my dad less often after I had deconditioned myself. When I started talking about the past, though, old habits kicked in. I would quickly fall into negative talk, whether to my wife or within my head, in that nattering chatter that sometimes passes for thinking. To change, I consciously ordered myself not to criticize. As soon as I would mention my dad, I would try to think, *Don't find fault.*

Old habits, such as speaking critically of Dad, which I had indulged in my family of origin and my marriage, died kicking and screaming in my head. Sometimes I would actually put my hand over my mouth as a reminder not to criticize. Within a year, those habits of a critical tongue were broken. You can stop these thoughts too. If you catch yourself ruminating, tell yourself, "Let it go," "Don't find fault," "Stop the blame," and change the mental subject. Ask your spouse or a close friend to help you stop those critical thoughts and words.

Describe the positive. There was a lot of good in my father. He and Mama raised three responsible and moral children. He must have been doing some things right. I set a goal to replace criticism with thoughts and words of praise.

Even though Dad came from harsh circumstances, he was responsible.

Unable to afford to go to college, he worked long hours as a railroad brakeman and, later, freight conductor. He earned a correspondence degree in accounting, even though he never worked as an accountant. He showed self-discipline in pursuing a degree.

Dad was kind to children. The neighbors' children loved him. I could see that he gave Mike, Kathy and me a loving foundation, and he passed along an excitement for learning and an ethic of hard work.

When I decided to rid myself of criticism, I wrote a list of Dad's strengths—much longer than the one above. Then I intentionally practiced thinking the positive. I knew, of course, that Dad had weaknesses as well as strengths. I had rehearsed those for forty-five years. I figured that even if I lived to be ninety, I need not be concerned that I had painted too rosy a picture overall. Besides, memories of hurts still were sometimes triggered. You can create your own list: a concrete reminder to focus on the positive.

SYMBOLIZE YOUR FORGIVENESS

Washing our hands of judgment. Even before you decide to forgive, you might want to stop judging the other person. Here is an exercise to symbolize that decision. Write a brief summary of the transgression on your palm. Then go to the sink and wash your hands repeatedly. Even with several washings, the transgression will still be visible. But each washing will weaken the image. After many washings and other activities, finally every trace of ink will be washed away.

This is the way emotional forgiveness usually happens. Rarely does forgiveness yield to a single time up the Pyramid Model to REACH Forgiveness. But after several repetitions, one day we notice that the negative emotions are gone.

Rock and roll. Psychologist Rick Marks developed an exercise to help promote public forgiveness.[1] It was based on the biblical story in which town elders caught a woman in adultery. They were about to stone her (the usual punishment for adultery then). Jesus challenged them by writing in the dust and then saying, "If any one of you is without sin, let him be the first to throw a stone at her" (Jn 8:7).

Marks engraved a smooth rock "First Stone." He invites people to respond to those who have hurt them by physically laying down the "First Stone." Try this yourself. Go outside and get a large rock. Pick one of the hurts that you identified at the end of chapter three. As you think about that hurt, hold the rock in your outstretched hand. Now, while holding it out, think about the weight of your desire for revenge. Feel the stress and pain that holding the rock of unforgiveness causes you. When the weight of the desire for revenge becomes so great that you don't want to hold it any longer, you can let the rock fall from your hand as a symbol of your forgiveness. Either let the rock clunk to the floor or deliberately set it down. Feel the relief in your body. That is like the relief of forgiving.

Burning to forgive. In our groups, we also invite participants to symbolize their forgiveness in a way that dramatically illustrates forgiveness. They write a brief description of the transgression. Then they burn it and scatter the ashes.

Cross out unforgiveness. The cross is a powerful symbol of forgiveness. At the cross, God's justice and forgiveness intersected. The cross is our most powerful symbol of Jesus' self-sacrificial giving. It shows that forgiveness is sometimes painful. At a marriage retreat Kirby and I conducted, we borrowed a rugged wooden cross from our pastor, Doug McMurry. We spent a day on forgiveness and reconciliation in marriage. In the afternoon, we gave people thirty minutes to write summaries of transgressions their spouse had committed. We invited them to come to the cross, kneel (if they wished) and offer their forgiveness in a prayer. Then, to symbolize their forgiveness, they pinned the written account to the cross.

You don't need a big wooden cross to do the same thing. Write out a grudge you are holding. Then as you forgive, symbolize that gift of forgiving by imagining placing it at the foot of the cross. Pray that your forgiveness will be apparent by your actions toward the person who harmed or offended you. Pray that Jesus' blood will cover those sins. Then leave your grudge at the cross and destroy the written account of it.

Use a handout for forgiveness. I know you realize that forgiving is so difficult that it can never really be fully accomplished without receiving grace from God. Extend your hands, palms up, and imagine receiving from God the gift of being able to forgive.

When you forgave, you gave an altruistic gift of forgiveness. Symbolize having given your gift by imagining handing a gift to the person you forgave. Extend your hands with the imagined gift clutched inside. Then open your hands to symbolize giving the altruistic gift of forgiveness to the person.

WRITE YOUR FORGIVENESS

Putting our feelings and commitments on paper can be very useful. Here are some ways to do that.

Certificate of Forgiveness. When people in our groups forgive, they create a certificate stating the day and time. Sometimes they decorate it. We encourage them to post it on a bulletin board. If the transgression is more sensitive, they can post it inside a drawer.

Below is an example of a Certificate of Forgiveness (see figure 7.2). Later, if you doubt whether you have forgiven, you can pull out the certificate and look at it to assure yourself that you did.

Certificate of Forgiveness

On <u>October 16, 2003</u>, after experiencing a change of heart from God's agape love working through me, I emotionally forgave my ex-husband Bill for the years of neglect and the ugly arguments he provoked as we were headed toward divorce. I believe my motives for his welfare are stronger than any negative motives.

I acknowledge that I behaved poorly toward him as well. I hope that someday I might be able to talk with him calmly, express my regret for my part and ask his forgiveness.

For now, though, I hereby declare that I forgive Bill, and I lay down the weight of my unforgiveness forever, to the best of my ability. I ask God the Father, Jesus my Savior and the Holy Spirit to work in me and through me to preserve the work they have done.

Jean Hruska
Jean Hruska

Figure 7.2. Sample Certificate of Forgiveness

Letter. Write a letter to the offender. Express your forgiveness for the transgression. Of course, you might not want to send the letter, especially if the person doesn't realize that he or she has done anything to hurt or offend you. Receiving a letter of forgiveness out of the blue for having offended a friend is not likely to enhance the relationship.

Under conditions of confidentiality, you can read the letter aloud to a close friend or your spouse. As you read, listen to your own voice proclaiming forgiveness.

If you have reconciled and have already talked thoroughly with a friend about the forgiveness, you might actually send the letter. But we'll talk more of reconciliation in the third part of this book.

Journal. If you keep a private journal, write an entry describing your forgiveness. Expressing yourself in a journal can help you deal with difficult events. It also can make you healthier, as research by James Pennebaker has shown.[2] Pennebaker asks people to journal daily for several weeks. They write in order to express their emotion—positive or negative—but also to understand more about their experiences. Even though they pour their hearts out on paper instead of to personal friends, the benefits of writing from the heart are great. People heal faster and get ill less often.

Poem or song. If you are creative, write a poem about your experience of forgiveness. Perhaps you play an instrument. Put your thoughts and feelings to music.

TELL SOMEONE ABOUT YOUR FORGIVENESS

Saying something out loud can help actualize it. It gives us an answer to the nagging question, *Have I just thought about doing this, or have I really done it?*

Tell God. As you release negative feelings and replace them with love, empathy, sympathy and compassion, tell the Lord in prayer what you have done. Find a place where you can say it aloud to him. The Holy Spirit encourages, convicts, comforts and prompts you to forgive. Acknowledge that gratefully. Go beyond being grateful for the blessings you have received by forgiving. Pray a blessing on the one who hurt or offended you. As we know, it is better to give than to receive (Acts 20:35). If you have been blessed by freedom from unforgiveness and by receiving grace from the Lord to be able to grant forgiveness, then just imagine how much better to give the blessing of prayer to your transgressor!

Tell yourself. Say aloud that you have forgiven the person for a particular offense. Just hearing yourself say the words adds another pathway for forgiveness in your brain and body.

Tell a trusted friend. Talk with a trusted friend or family member about having forgiven the person who hurt you. Resolve to maintain that forgiveness. Talking about your forgiveness with a loved one or partner not only can solidify your resolve to hold on to that forgiveness but also can reassure you that you have forgiven.

The night when I forgave my mother's killer was extremely emotional. My experiences were private. I was sad over the loss and traumatized by the violence. But I felt free of unforgiveness. The pain of the loss was too great to talk about forgiveness during the week after her death. A week later, when the funeral service was over, my mother's body buried and affairs of the estate put into motion, I returned to Richmond. After arriving home, I began to talk about the murder with my wife, Kirby. I trusted her to understand my initial struggle with rage and my forgiveness of that youth. I knew that she would understand that I thought I could honor my mother's life more by forgiving, as Mom had taught me, than by holding a grudge, which she had taught me not to do. I knew too that Kirby knew me well enough to believe that I sincerely felt a kinship with that young murderer, even though that was painful for me to admit. I trusted Kirby with my experiences, and she helped me make those experiences an essential part of my life. I felt at peace.

Saying that I felt peace after forgiving is not the same thing as saying that I didn't have pain over the loss or that I didn't grieve the hurt. In fact, the pain of the loss was the most wrenching pain I have ever felt. The suddenness and the violence with which my mother was killed was a traumatic loss. I grieved. Talking with Kirby speeded the grief, strengthened my forgiveness and prevented many doubts I might have had about whether I *really* had forgiven.

ANALYSIS

Forgiveness is a complex, primarily emotional event. It's not just a change in the beliefs that we *should* forgive. Forgiveness doesn't make the crime less awful than we know it to be. It is not merely a change in attitude or an act primarily of the will apart from our feelings.

I did not start that night willing to forgive. I started the night skeptically doubting the results of our own research, wondering if it was for me, wondering if our method really made a difference in the big hurts. The power of the emotions made me doubt research that I had poured thousands of hours of my life into. I wanted to put that research to the practical test, not as an intellectual exercise but as an act of emotional desperation to deal with my overpowering emotions.

When I forgave from the heart, my bodily emotions—including my thinking, bodily reactions, behavior and feelings—were changed. I associated the traumatic scenes of harm, offense and transgression with the healing scenes of empathy, humility, gratitude and an altruistic offering of the gift of forgiveness. My motives to make the perpetrator suffer were also changed. After emotionally forgiving, I still wanted to see the youth incarcerated. I did not want him to hurt someone else's mother or someone else's child. But I sincerely wished him well. I wanted the Lord to redeem his life. Even though my emotions and motivations were different than they had been before, I knew that eventually I had to make my forgiveness more public.

Public forgiveness was not just acting in a forgiving way. It was not simply saying that I had forgiven the perpetrator. It was not the same as decisional forgiveness, which actually could be a decision to forgive even though I might never go public with it. Public forgiveness was not simply making a certificate or dropping a stone. It was not merely changing my behavior to be less vengeful. While those things eventually happened, those changes in my behavior took a while to show up.

Public forgiveness is like watching a hurricane approach for days. As the hurricane moves across the water and gains power, you see its power and destructiveness on television. You watch the Weather Channel, which draws a giant red triangle that extends from the eye of the hurricane to where it is expected to hit the United States. The hurricane moves closer hour by hour, day by day, and the red triangle zeroes in on the place where you live. The triangle narrows. Then, just as the hurricane is about to reach the shore, it stalls just offshore, turns north up the coast and then swings out to sea and dies. It leaves a fresh, clear sky. It is nature's broom, sweeping away the pollution. Public forgiveness clears away the condemnation, criticism and complaining. It leaves our conscience clean.

SARAH'S STORY

Sarah had struggled to forgive the relatives who refused to support her during her time of financial strain. She worked through several self-help programs of forgiveness, saw her pastor for two sessions of counseling and even went to twelve weeks of psychotherapy with a Christian counselor. After each experience, she felt as if she had forgiven her relatives. But later, the pain of rejection would return and haunt her, until she found herself just as bitter, resentful and hostile toward her relatives as she had been before. Sarah could forgive, but she could not hold on to her forgiveness.

Then she attended one of our workshops on forgiveness, and near the end she received a revelation.

"Once forgiveness has been granted in one's heart and mind, it is always subject to doubt unless the commitment to forgive has been made public," said the workshop leader. Sarah constructed a Certificate of Forgiveness, which she displayed on her wall. When she doubted whether the forgiveness she had granted was real, she examined the Certificate of Forgiveness and reassured herself.

She also wrote a letter of forgiveness to each of her relatives. Even though she did not send them because her relatives might have responded negatively, merely writing the letters made her forgiveness seem more real. Finally, she read each letter aloud to another member in the group. Hearing herself read the letter of forgiveness provided yet another piece of tangible evidence that she had indeed forgiven.

APPLY WHAT YOU'VE LEARNED

If you've practiced forgiving the events you identified in the introduction to part two, you've probably made some progress. By now, you may have fully forgiven one or two of the events. Perhaps your unforgiveness of the others has lessened. It's time to consolidate your gains.

You may still feel some of the remembered anger or fear, yet forgiveness eliminates the bitterness, resentment, hostility and hatred. If you truly feel that you have forgiven, decide how to make a more public commitment.

- Erect the "forms" of forgiveness.

- Decondition yourself to the person by systematically recalling hurtful events without the attached emotion.

- Symbolize your forgiveness through using the First Stone, burning an account of the transgression, washing your hands of judgment, crossing out unforgiveness or otherwise using a meaningful symbolic act.

- Write about your forgiveness in a certificate, letter, poem, song or journal entry.

- Tell someone you trust, even if it is only yourself. Also tell the Lord, who loves you and wants to know that you forgive from your heart.

In the following chapter, we'll consider ways to hold on to your forgiveness.

Discussion Questions

1. Have you ever had an experience in which you thought you had forgiven, but you later experienced negative feelings and interpreted those as meaning that you really had not forgiven?

2. The author argues that we are hard-wired to remember hurts and offenses and re-experience the "hot emotions" of pain, sadness, fear and anger. Why does he think we are "hard-wired" to remember those? Remember, from chapter two, that he treats emotions as experiences in our whole body. He treats feelings as the fleeting ways we label our emotions. Does thinking of emotions as complex embodied experiences help you understand this "hard-wiring"?

3. Using the Transgression Loop, explain how memories and emotions are hard-wired for remembering.

4. Choose one of the three ways to "be your own behavior therapist," and apply it to a situation in your own life. (If you do not wish to reveal a real situation, make one up.)

5. Can you recall a person who hurt you in your past and then think of three truly good things about that person? Do you think doing this will help you at all?

6. Do you keep a journal? If so, would you be willing to discuss the things you write in your journal (not the specifics, just the types of things) and how they help you, so that others can get an idea of the benefits of journaling?

H: Hold On to Forgiveness

Nothing great is created suddenly, any more than a bunch of grapes
or a fig. I answer you that there must be time.
Let it first blossom, then bear fruit, then ripen.

EPICTETUS

Even though Sarah, from the previous chapter, had created a certificate stating how she forgave her relatives who did not support her, she needed to take one more step. Sarah used another bit of knowledge that helped her through the H-step of the Pyramid Model to REACH Forgiveness—holding on to forgiveness. When people have worked through the past to reach forgiveness, they often think (irrationally) that they will never re-member the hurt again. If they do recall the hurt and re-experience pain, they think that their forgiveness was a fraud. Not so. For instance, consider Kindra.

On their honeymoon, Ronnie had wanted them to rent motor bikes and see Nassau. Kindra said it was too dangerous. When Kindra developed a fever and diarrhea, Ronnie settled her in and then headed for the beach. At least that's what he said. Instead, he headed for a motor bike rental shop and took off on a jaunt.

He didn't see the car, and the driver didn't see him. Ronnie slammed into the turning vehicle, and his head smacked the pavement.

Kindra had "forgiven" Ronnie countless times for the way he betrayed their relationship. But his traumatic head injury had been a constant source of friction between them. *It's so frustrating to live with someone with a brain injury,* Kindra thought for perhaps the thousandth time. *But what can I do?* Ronnie's moods were unpredictable. His memory was impaired.

Sometimes he was just plain nasty to be around. Because he had been so sweet before the injury, Kindra knew that Ronnie's injury had changed his personality. *The frustrating part is that he can't even remember going bike riding,* she thought.

Finally, she worked through forgiveness using the Pyramid Model to REACH Forgiveness. In the last step, she said aloud to the group she was attending that she had, this time, truly forgiven. The leader asked her to say it aloud individually to every person in the group. As she did so, her tear ducts were relief valves for years of unforgiveness. Dealing with the frustration of Ronnie's problems would, she knew, always bother her. Yet she knew that she would believe herself this time. She really had forgiven him.

FLASHBACK TO THE MURDER SCENE

Two pools of blood stained the carpet in the house where I grew up. Even today, more than six years after the day I saw that blood, the mere thought of it triggers upsetting mental images. The two pools of blood on the carpet—beneath the head and hips, each about the size of a dinner plate—are soaked into my memory. They trigger vile images that I can only partially block. The blood splattered on the walls and door speaks of force and violence. I do not want to see these things, but the images insist.

Over time, I flash back less often, but no less vividly. Each time I remember, I have to talk to myself about forgiveness, not listen to my chatter about my loss and pain. I had empathized with the youth who had murdered my mom, and I had forgiven him. I had told the story of forgiveness often. But how do you keep forgiveness from slipping away when traumatic images keep forcing their way into consciousness? How do you maintain forgiveness when people ask you searching questions about the event? How do you hold on to forgiveness when you think about a murderer who might be at large?

Simply knowing that *hurt does not equal unforgiveness* is important. To avoid being re-trapped in the Unforgiveness Loop, though, you must be active.

HOLDING ON IS DIFFICULT

All we have to do is stop unwanted thoughts. Simple, right? Except for one tiny problem. It doesn't work.

Psychologist Daniel Wegner has conducted research on how to stop unwanted thoughts. He has people try *not* to think about white bears.[1] You try it. Close this book and resolve in your mind that you will *not* remember the shape of the black nose, the softness of the bear or the color of the fur. Resolve not to think of its paws. Try as hard as you can for one minute not to think about the white bear. If you slip and think of the bear, tap the closed book with the palm of your hand, every time. Let's pause for a minute. Now remember, *don't* think about white bears.

■   ■   ■

How did you do? If you are like me, you thought a lot about white bears. You may have even beaten the book to a pulp. (Is that where pulp fiction got its name?)

White bears climb into our minds, they crawl across the white walls in our office, nose around the black shoe in the corner and claw their way onto the tines of our forks. When we are actively trying to suppress a thought, everything seems to trigger it.

Perhaps you were successful at *not* thinking about white bears. If you were able to keep the bears at bay, it was probably because you filled your mind with something captivating. Maybe you thought about a recent movie. Maybe you tried to sing a popular song or visualize a music video. Perhaps you contemplated the intricate relationships among quantum physics, general relativity and emerging complexity at the edge of chaos. (Well, different things distract different people.) The point is, to keep from being mentally overrun with white bears, you must be active.

Walter Mischel, another personality psychologist, placed children alone in a room with marshmallows and pretzels.[2] Mischel told each of them they could have two marshmallows if they waited until Mischel returned or they could have one pretzel if they couldn't wait. Regardless, they had to stay seated at the table. The forbidden marshmallows lay in plain sight. The pretzel whispered saltily, "Eat me now. Put me out of my misery."

Mischel waited behind a one-way mirror recording the children's behavior. Sometimes the kid had the pretzel in his or her mouth almost before Mischel got the camera rolling. Sometimes Mischel got fifteen minutes of tape, and the child never gave in.

Those children who waited distracted themselves vigorously. They sang. They looked around. They talked to themselves. Maybe they thought about nuclear physics. Who knows? One child even went to sleep.

Self-control takes effort. Social psychologist Roy Baumeister asked Case Western Reserve University students to skip lunch and arrive at his lab hungry.[3] Meanwhile, he and his research assistants baked chocolate chip cookies. Sweet smells wafted through the lab and filled the building. Graduate students from bioengineering were reportedly walking across campus to beg for cookies. When students who were research participants arrived, half were allowed to eat cookies. The others met a crueler fate.

Baumeister's associates asked the student's name. After consulting a list, the experimenter sadly announced, "Oh, I'm sorry. You are in the radish condition." The radish condition? Surrounded by sights and smells of fresh chocolate chip cookies, those students had to eat a bowl of radishes. (It makes one wonder whether psychologists have a bit of a mean streak, doesn't it?)

Resisting the temptation to scarf up stray chocolate chip cookies and perhaps do bodily injury to the research scientists in the process took its toll. Students who had to resist temptation exerted less self-control in a subsequent physical-exertion test. They were less willing to exert effort in a test of their grip strength. (Come to think of it, the "radish condition" looks like a great new way to create unforgiveness in the laboratory.)

Does Baumeister's study remind you of working out at a spa? Baumeister says that self-control is like a moral muscle. If we work hard to control ourselves on an important task, we might be at a disadvantage for controlling ourselves on another task in short order. It is like doing a set of sit-ups. If I max out, I cannot do as many sit-ups in a second set unless I allow time for recovery.

Does that mean we should not practice self-control? Will small efforts at self-control wear us out and leave us unable to cope with important temptations? Baumeister found that students who practiced regular self-control on one task—something like attending to posture, flossing daily or trying to think nice things about people—did better on other tests of self-control. Like a moral muscle, self-control gets stronger as we use it, but two back-to-back tests might fatigue the moral muscle.

Practicing forgiveness whenever we recall the transgression is an act of self-control. Look back at figure 7.1. When we forgive, we disconnect the Unforgiveness Loop from the Transgression Loop, and we connect a Forgiveness Loop to the transgression. That act is an act of self-control. If we ruminate again, we can undo our hard work.

Even after we have forgiven, it's not easy to resist unforgiveness. For many people, unforgiveness is the low point to which they automatically roll if left alone. Holding on to forgiveness requires an uphill fight.

SIX WAYS TO HOLD ON TO FORGIVENESS

There are six things you can do to hold on to forgiveness.

1. Realize that the pain of a remembered hurt is not unforgiveness. Remind yourself that feeling pain or anger when you remember a hurt is not the same thing as feeling unforgiveness. Unforgiveness requires rumination. Don't give in to vengeful rumination.

2. Don't dwell on negative emotions. It's natural to feel emotions when you recall being hurt. You could re-experience anger or fear in a milder form. But if you don't dwell on the emotions, then unforgiveness won't regrow. Remember Daniel Wegner's white bears. Actively distract yourself rather than merely instructing yourself not to dwell on the emotions.

3. Remind yourself that you have forgiven the person. Recall the times when you talked to a trusted friend, pastor or spouse about having forgiven the person. Remember that you said aloud that you have forgiven. Say it again.

4. Seek reassurance from a partner or a friend. You may have talked with a partner or friend about having forgiven the person. Your partner or friend should be able to remind you of that.

5. Use the documents that you created. Read your Certificate of Forgiveness. Read the letter that you wrote describing your forgiveness.

6. Look at the Pyramid Model to REACH Forgiveness (see figure A on page 73), and think through the steps again. If, by now, you simply don't believe that you have completely forgiven, maybe you haven't. Trust your feelings if they persist. Perhaps there are actually things you haven't forgiven even though there are many things you have forgiven. Work through the REACH steps with other transgressions. This will help you deal with whatever might still be unforgiven.

BECOMING A MORE FORGIVING PERSON

You won't suddenly become a more forgiving person. Dispositional forgivingness will grow like fruit in your life if the plant from which it is to grow is nurtured. Being a forgiving person is one of the fruits of loving the Lord.

Unforgiveness is like a tree in the winter. The buds are taut and closed. But when the warmth of a springtime of positive emotions arrives, the blossoms of forgiveness replace the buds of unforgiveness.

Becoming a more forgiving person can mean becoming a person who values more strongly what I earlier called the warmth-based virtues—empathy, love, compassion, humility and gratitude—as character dispositions. Yet not everyone can be naturally drawn to the warmth-based virtues. Some Christians gravitate to the conscientiousness-based virtues—responsibility, honesty, accountability, hard work and self-control. We can see from research by Wegner, Baumeister and Mischel that forgiveness can be brought about by self-control and the exercise of our moral muscles. We can conscientiously attempt to destroy the negative emotions comprising unforgiveness with the positive other-oriented emotions that neutralize and replace it. We can hold ourselves accountable for not giving up on emotional forgiveness. We can exert self-control to reach forgiveness.

Self-control is part of the fruit of the Holy Spirit (Gal 5:23). So we do not need to exert self-control by gut-it-out effort. We can anticipate that the Lord wants to produce self-control in us, so he will be motivated to help us.

Can unforgiveness be a character disposition? In Clint Eastwood's Academy Award-winning movie *Unforgiven,* Eastwood plays a retired gunfighter named Will Munny. The Schofield Kid, an itinerant young gunfighter, comes by Will's farm to see if Will will join him in collecting a bounty. Two cowboys in Whiskey Flat, Montana, cut the face of a prostitute in the town, and the prostitute's friends collected money to offer a bounty to have the two men killed. So the Schofield Kid attempts to persuade Will to share the bounty with him.

Will claims he has changed. He has given up gunfighting and bounty chasing. Since his wife died, he has been doing his best to rear his children. He is responsibly eking out a living farming the hard ground of Kansas. He turns down the Schofield Kid and refuses to seek the bounty.

After the Kid leaves, though, Will changes his mind. He tries to get back in the saddle to catch up with the Kid, but he keeps falling off his horse. It isn't easy, but eventually he fights his way back into his lifestyle of hate and violence.

Will and the Schofield Kid are joined by a friend, Ned. They ride to

Whiskey Flat. Will shoots one of the perpetrators in the stomach. It takes him a long time to die. Disgusted, Ned heads back to Kansas, having no stomach for bounty hunting.

The next morning the Schofield Kid kills the second perpetrator. Later, as they discuss the Kid's murder of the outlaw, the Kid admits that the killing is his first. He vows to head home.

A prostitute arrives with the money for the bounty. She also brings news that Ned has been captured by the sheriff and died under interrogation.

Will is outraged. He begins to drink heavily to numb himself to what he is about to do. Will vows to exact vengeance on the town for Ned's murder. Loaded with bullets and booze, he heads into Whiskey Flat, Montana.

Will enters the saloon and shoots the sheriff and five men. The sheriff, while dying, says to Will, "I don't deserve this."

"Nobody does," says Will, who shoots the sheriff again. As Will rides out of town, he yells, "You give my friend a decent burial, you hear. Or I'll come back and kill you all."

Unforgiven is not just a shoot-'em-up Western. It is a serious movie about people's character. In that movie, virtually everyone seems to be unforgiving, unforgiven and unredeemable. The movie raises questions about whether unforgiveness is a terminal character trait that is endemic to humanity.

Although an act of hurt and offense (hearing that Ned had been tortured to death) enraged Will, the movie asks whether that event or other horrid circumstances make people unforgiving, or whether Will or people in general are unforgiving at the core, simply waiting on an event to justify vengeful violence. That's a good question, and it deserves a Christian response.

Although people are fallen, they have within them the image of God. They are redeemable by appropriating the work of Jesus (satisfying demands of justice) and God the Father's forgiveness (satisfying demands of grace and mercy). Some people will disagree with me about the message of *Unforgiven*, but I claim that the movie does not cast us into a nihilistic cavern of despair. For twelve years, Will had been responsible and self-controlled. Was that period a thin veneer of civility due to the positive restraints imposed by having a wife and children? Was he unforgiving at heart, so that, with the slightest motivation and provocation, he chucked aside the self-restraint of a virtuous life and resumed his (true) unforgiven ways?

I don't think so. Certainly the movie does not portray humans as, at root, forgiving and peace-loving. Even though Will was the soul of peace for twelve years, he was lured to vice relatively easily. Yet we can see the spark of good in the characters at times. Ned refused to participate in violence. The Kid was morally sickened by having murdered. An endnote to the movie says that Will later resumed his peaceful life in San Francisco.

Are people *by nature* unforgiving or forgiving? Our answer probably resides more in our preference for theology or philosophy than in facts and evidence. People will probably never agree. We can agree, though, that people make choices that lead to the development of long-lasting dispositions that persist for years. And even if that disposition is unforgiveness, people can be redeemed.

Some people are characterized by a disposition of unforgiveness. Across time and situations, they seem habitually unforgiving. Anger is never far beneath the surface. Fear of hurt or offense lurks within the psyche. They have been wounded so deeply or so often, or have ruminated so much, that they seem to have radar for rejection. They are targets waiting expectantly for the arrows of offense to prick them in sensitive spots. Resentment and bitterness sharpen their tone of voice to an aggrieved whine.

I recently talked with such a friend. I'll call her Janet. I hadn't seen her for twelve years. She dropped by my office after work with her husband and children.

"Have you been in town long?" I asked.

"Nah," she said. "We had to come by to sign papers on some rental property we just sold. Besides, I really didn't want to see any of the old gang."

"Why not?"

"I've fallen out of contact with most of 'em. Myra—you remember her, don't you?—wrote me for a few years, but even she stopped writing. I have no use for them."

"What about Emma?" I knew that she and Emma had been best friends when they attended graduate school.

"We had a falling out. I gave and gave to her when we roomed together. Then, right before we graduated, I asked her to run a simple errand for me. She refused! Her boyfriend was coming to town, and she was afraid that he wouldn't want to spend the couple of hours it might take to drive to Williamsburg and back. Once she unfurled her true colors, I saw that she didn't really care about me."

"That's too bad. I know you were good friends."

"No big loss. I cared more than she did."

Janet chatted awhile longer. Then with a final bitter comment, she and her husband left to sign papers on the rental property.

Can we have a character that is both unforgiving and forgiving? Some people with unforgiving characters also have forgiving characters. It sounds weird but it happens. They are unforgiving at the drop of a hat, but they usually come around quickly to forgive.

They seem to get hurt easily. They seem sensitive and reactive. They ruminate about hurts and develop strong grudges. They are unforgiving of almost every transgression. They have an unforgiving character.

After a while, though, they forgive almost every transgression. The same sensitivity that makes them prone to grudges makes them empathic, emotional and fervent forgivers. They have a forgiving character. While they always seem to have a backlog of grudges, the grudges are usually a fresh crop.

Most of us seem to gravitate more to one character trait than the other. We can lean toward bitterness (and be bitterly unforgiving of ourselves for our bitterness). Or we can lean toward forgiveness.

What kind of character do you want to have? Few people aspire to be unforgiven and unforgiving, like Will Munny. Instead, we want to be like Jean Valjean in Victor Hugo's novel *Les Misérables*, which many have seen performed as a play or movie. Valjean stole some silverware from Monsignor Bienvenue, a church official who had provided food and shelter for a destitute Valjean.

The next morning, Valjean was caught and faced prison. The Monsignor said, "My friend, you forgot the silver candlesticks that I said you could have." When the police left, a grateful Valjean tried to return the silverware and candlesticks, but the Monsignor was earnest about the gifts. Valjean fell to his knees in front of the Monsignor, a forgiven and, from that moment, a forgiving man.

In the Broadway play, Javert (Valjean's nemesis) sang, "A man like you can never change." Yet Valjean did change. Javert, on the other hand, was an unchanging hound of justice, and one day it drove him to drown himself.

Did Will Munny change? He was a bounty hunter, then a family man, then a bounty hunter and finally a family man again. I believe people can change. Long ago I heard a brief poem.

> Two natures beat within my breast.
> One is cursed, and one is blessed.
> One I love, and one I hate.
> The one I feed will dominate.
> *Anonymous*

Whether our theology is more Calvinist or Arminian, we can still acknowledge our dual nature. We each have within us Valjean and Javert. We need justice and forgiveness. Either can get out of balance. The virtue of the love of justice can easily turn to pursuit of revenge. Forgiveness is more difficult to corrupt, but it can become a disdain for justice in extreme cases. Whether we feed the new nature because we are predestined to do so or are freely choosing to do so, we can agree that, as Christians, we want to feed the new nature and starve the old, corrupted nature. We want to put on the new as we put off the old. In this we reflect God's nature, glorify him, and yield to his work in and through us. To God be the glory.

TWELVE STEPS TO BECOMING A MORE FORGIVING PERSON

Below I describe twelve steps that you might take over time to help you become a more forgiving person. If you apply these steps, you'll have a challenge that can occupy you for a lifetime, and I believe it is worthy of a lifetime.

Table 8.1. Twelve Steps to Becoming a More Forgiving Person

1. Reflect on why you want to be more forgiving.
2. Identify your greatest wounds from the past.
3. Forgive one wound at a time.
4. Identify heroes of forgiveness.
5. Examine yourself.
6. Reduce negative traits; cultivate virtue.
7. Change your experience of the past.
8. Plan your self-improvement strategy.
9. Practice forgiving under imagined conditions.
10. Practice forgiving day to day.
11. Seek help from someone you trust.
12. Start a campaign to love your enemies.

1. Reflect on why you want to be more forgiving. Humans are not simple, and we could probably drive ourselves crazy trying to discern our "real" motives for wanting to be more forgiving. There may be dark motives, such as wishing to be seen as a spiritual giant. Or we might want to use guilt to manipulate others. *If I forgive her*, we might think, *she'll owe me big time.*

Our motives may fall into the gray area. We may want to forgive because unforgiveness makes us feel angry, fearful or sad. Or we may want to forgive because we believe that a grudge is harming our physical, mental or relational health. There is nothing wrong with those motives unless they are our dominant or only motives. God wants us to be to count others better than ourselves (Phil 2:3). That is, God wants us to be other-oriented more than self-oriented. It isn't possible to have no self-interest. Caring about ourselves is part of being human and is often a motive that is invoked in Scripture (Phil 3:14; Col 3:15).

Some motives are more preferred. We might forgive out of obedience, responsibility and self-control. Or we might forgive in spontaneous gratitude for Christ's redemptive work, out of love for God, compassion or agape love for needy people.

Why do you want to be more forgiving? Can you ask the Lord to search your heart and know you (Ps 139:23)? Trust him to purify your heart (Ps 51:10; Prov 3:5-6).

2. Identify your greatest wounds from the past. To be a more forgiving person, you must forgive more past transgressions, which will allow you to succeed at forgiving wounds that will arise in the future. You cannot predict which wounds will arise. Those will be your character tests. Remember the wounds from your past, and try to forgive them. Then learn from them. Refer to the hurts you recalled in the introduction to part two. That is a start; add to your list.

3. Forgive one wound at a time. We forgive one event at a time. We can change our motives—like Jean Valjean—and decide we want to be more forgiving in the future. But to forgive, we must tackle hurts one at a time. Strive for both decisional and emotional forgiveness for each.

For each event, work carefully through the Pyramid Model to REACH Forgiveness. As you forgive, check off your events to show yourself that you are making progress. Don't feel that you must forgive perfectly. Move toward forgiving along a broad front.

4. Identify heroes of forgiveness. Our heroes can act as models who inspire us to forgive. With the cynicism of the 1960s, 1970s and 1980s, people rarely identified their heroes. My generation (adolescents in the 1960s) and those following us often didn't believe that there were heroes. Today, few people have heroes.

Whom do you want to be like? Examine your past and determine whom you admire. Why? Do they forgive quickly and easily? Here are some of my heroes.

Eric Liddell came to most people's attention as a result of the movie *Chariots of Fire*. The movie dramatized Liddell's moral stance toward the British Olympic authorities. But that event was merely one event in a virtuous life. After the games, Liddell went to China as a missionary. When World War II broke out, almost twenty years after the Olympic Games that were shown in *Chariots of Fire*, Liddell was imprisoned. In a prison camp, he sacrificed to help other prisoners stay alive. He stood up for his faith. He forgave the people who abused him and the other prisoners. Eventually, Liddell died in that prison camp. His life was a testimony to love and forgiveness.

Another paragon of forgiveness is Aleksandr Solzhenitsyn. Solzhenitsyn spent much of his adult life in the Russian gulag, the Soviet prison camp system. Despite his suffering, when he was released, he wrote books of compassion, empathy and understanding of the people who had imprisoned him. Nonetheless, he firmly decried the system that imprisoned people. Solzhenitsyn is a wonderful blend of justice and forgiveness.

Mohandas Gandhi was firm in his resolve to conquer prejudice and oppressive treatment in his native India through nonviolent protest. Despite being the object of violence numerous times, Gandhi persistently forgave. His was a blend of nonviolent social justice and forgiveness.

In the United States, Martin Luther King Jr. fought the injustices of bigotry and prejudice. He walked the line of nonviolent social justice. He combined justice and mercy and became a hero to people of all ethnicities.

Jesus is the cornerstone of Christianity, which is built on forgiveness. The central narrative of Christianity is that Jesus gave his life to take the sin of all people, who were sinners against God and other humans. Justice demanded death as payment for sin. Jesus voluntarily took the punishment. God granted forgiveness. In his life on earth, Jesus was abused, persecuted and finally tortured. Yet as his life drew to an end, he prayed that

God would forgive those who did evil against him, which showed his own forgiving heart toward those people.

It is helpful to measure your life against your models of forgiveness. Your hero might be a religious figure, a historical person, a contemporary hero like Nelson Mandela or Desmond Tutu, a public figure who seems forgiving (such as Oprah, Diane Sawyer or Peter Jennings), or a person you have known who is an excellent forgiver. Setting your sights upward on a model lifts your head. It focuses you on others, not yourself.

In measuring your life against a model, though, do not fall into a shame trap. We all fall short of our ideals. We all feel guilty because our lives lack virtue. I hope that looking to models of forgiveness will motivate us to live more virtuous lives, not shame us into self-condemnation.

5. Examine yourself. If you're like me, it is sobering to see how many unforgiven events clog up your free flow of love. Although I forgave the murderer, I have seen repeatedly, not just that first night, how often I do the very things I have vowed not to do. Novelist Frank Peretti wrote an unforgettable book called *The Oath*. In that book a dark, gooey stain oozed from the heart of anyone who practiced evil. As evil became etched into a person's character, the stain spread from the invisible heart to the visible chest and clothes. Sooner or later, the person infected with the stain would embrace evil and would be devoured by a beast. Unforgiveness is like that dark stain. Once it gets a beachhead, it spreads.

Practicing unforgiveness is a trap. We start into the trap of unforgiveness by thinking it's a safe place to be. We worm our way inside inch by inch. We pass sharp wires that face the center of the trap. When we are inside, practicing habitual unforgiveness, we do not want to go back. To forgive, we must face the jabs of confronting our unforgiving character traits and the stabs of trying to change. We can wallow miserably in guilt and self-condemnation. Or we can face the jabs.

The good news is this: When we meet unforgiveness head-on and forgive, we start a character reaction—like a chemical reaction that titrates the dark stain of unforgiveness. When we practice forgiveness, we can be "trapped" by empathy, compassion and a heart full of love and mercy.

If you wish to become more forgiving, examine yourself. Be (first) honest and (second) gentle with yourself. Ironically, when unforgiveness of others is a habit, it's easy to turn the same condemnation on yourself.

Some people are ruminators. They think, worry, and stew over events.

Others, called dissipators, seem to let troubles roll off of them. Ruminators experience more depression, anxiety, fear and hostility than do dissipators. They also are more often unforgiving. That doesn't mean that dissipators are immune to unforgiveness. While they may not stew about transgressions, the stain of unforgiveness can be just as wide, just as messy. The flip side is that ruminators are often more aware of their struggles than are dissipators. So they are often primed to do something about their unforgiveness. They tend to ponder empathically more than do dissipators.

After my mother's murder, I experienced forgiveness that helped heal my trauma. Even better, though, my self-examination helped me to become aware that I needed a "heart transplant." I found that unforgiveness was more of a struggle for me than I ever thought it could be. Solzhenitsyn in the gulag was able to say, "Thank you prison camp for bringing this illumination into my life, which otherwise I would have lost." I thank God because out of the evil of my mother's murder God brought good. I can honestly say to my mother's murderer, as the Jewish patriarch Joseph said to his brothers, "You intended to harm me, but God intended it for good" (Gen 50:20).

Reflection on painful life events has revealed the stain of unforgiveness in my own heart. As I turned to God, God washed my heart—which had lusted earlier after the blood of the murderer—in the blood Jesus shed at his crucifixion. I was forgiven; I could forgive.

Perhaps you want to examine your life. How unforgiving are you in general? How forgiving? If you are not particularly unforgiving, is that because you forgive quickly or because you simply don't develop much unforgiveness?

6. Reduce negative traits; cultivate virtue. My self-examination has motivated me to try to replace my unforgiveness with virtue. I don't always succeed. Still I try to practice love, mercy, empathy, sympathy and compassion. Those are at the core of forgiveness.

I also try to practice the humility of seeing my similarity to all humans. That includes my capacity to do evil as well as good. When I am favored by someone who does something nice for me and when I can learn from suffering, I also try to practice gratitude. I am grateful for what people can teach me. I can also be grateful to God.

By examining my life, I concluded that I wanted to develop a more virtuous character. You might decide the same. Write a list of personal qualities that you would like to increase. Your list might differ from mine.

For each trait, complete this sentence: "If I were more _____, I would _____ more often." Fill in the first blank with a personal quality and the second with specific behaviors. For instance, "If I were more *loving toward people at work,* I would *compliment them, try to understand them, empathize with them and forgive them* more often." Determine which traits are most important. Plan specific steps to do those behaviors.

Don't phrase your goals in negative terms. For example, do *not* say, "If I were more *loving toward people at work,* I would *not criticize* so often." Instead of saying what you would *not* do, say what you *would* do. If you follow these steps, you have begun a program to cooperate with the Lord to help you become more virtuous. I hope that being more forgiving is one of your goals.

7. Change your experience of the past. If you think you're too unforgiving, you didn't become that way this morning. Freud said, "The child is father to the man." Wounds in your past may have started you along the road that led to frequent unforgiveness.

While you cannot change what actually happened, you can change

- your perception of what happened
- your emotional and mental associations of what happened
- your understanding of the meaning of the event

When you empathize with the person who hurt you, you are adding information that you had not previously perceived. When you recall in humility that you may have provoked your friend, you are changing your perception. When you experience a strong sense of empathy, you change the mental and emotional associations with the event. When you feel guilt over your role in a misunderstanding and gratitude over having been forgiven, you change mental, emotional and motivational associations.

When you set a goal for yourself as wanting to have a forgiving character (step six) and you see unforgiveness as working against that goal, you can change the meaning of the transgressor's acts of revenge or retaliation. When you do forgive, you can see that your forgiveness is more than an isolated event. It is another block in a structure of virtue.

You can also use your visual imagination to change your experience of the past. Imagine that you are going to face the person who wounded you. Now imagine that one of your heroes of forgiveness is with you (see step four). Perhaps it is your mother, a favorite teacher or Jesus. Imagine facing your nemesis and talking about the painful wounds of the past while being encouraged by your hero of forgiveness. Vividly imagine the scene as if it were really happening.

Remember the prejudiced professor of my behavioral psychology class who inflicted a five-dollar wound on me when he gave me a B (see chapter four). I carried that grudge for over ten years. In a prayer service one night, evangelist Joy Dawson spoke on forgiveness. She invited us to recall a hurt and imagine it graphically. I visualized the prejudiced professor. Joy asked us to invite an image of Jesus into the scene. When I saw Jesus comforting the professor, it dislodged my unforgiveness. Since that night, I have never been able to think about that professor without also imagining Jesus. My memory was not replaced. It was redeemed.

You can literally change your experience of the past by such vivid imagery. Memory experts tell us that memories are literally rebuilt each time we call them to consciousness. When you recall past wounds but change things in your mind's eye, you rebuild a more positive past for yourself.

8. Plan your self-improvement strategy. If you fall short of your ideal, decide to do something about it. Take one step at a time. As Lao Tse said, "A journey of a thousand miles begins with a single step." Your self-improvement strategy might involve doing more honest self-evaluation, reading inspirational books or developing a more sincere life of faith. You might simplify your life by building margins. On a trip, I heard a portion of a radio talk that stuck with me (I do not know who gave the talk because I was channel-hopping). The man advised listeners to build margins into their lives. Like the blank spots on the printed page, which frame the content and focus our attention, setting aside times for self-examination, confession, repentance and reflection on our grudges can allow God to more directly melt our hearts. Depending on your experiences, you will design your own strategy that aims you toward being a more forgiving person.

As I have thought and written about forgiving, I have been challenged by my own failures to forgive. It has damaged my self-esteem. But I have found that to be a good thing rather than a bad thing. Recognizing my frequent failures has motivated me to lay aside pride and pursue virtue.

9. Practice forgiving under imagined conditions. To forgive, continually practice forgiveness. Select one of the past events that you have not forgiven. Perhaps this involves a person with whom you often talk. (You will benefit most if you go back to the introduction to part two and select a specific transgression that you are still trying to forgive.) Set aside ten minutes to imagine discussing the event, during which you forgive the person who hurt you. Do this three times. First, imagine that the conversation worked perfectly to produce forgiveness. In psychology, we say you are using yourself as a mastery model. Imagine this now.

Of course, life is rarely perfect. After you have completed your mastery imagery, imagine the same scene again. This time assume that, as you discuss the transgression, the person provokes you. Imagine how you might respond if you were a perfectly forgiving person. Conclude the scene by again imagining that your conversation led to forgiving. Imagine this now.

Imagine your conversation a third time. This time imagine that you tried to talk about being hurt, but got angry and said something you knew you would regret. See yourself apologizing immediately. Change directions and get the conversation back on a positive track. Imagine this now.

If you can imagine yourself under these three conditions—mastery, having been provoked and having lost your temper—you have covered much of the waterfront. By rehearsing, you can make it more likely that you will develop a forgiving character.

10. Practice forgiving day to day. The test of whether you are developing a more forgiving character will come in how you respond to real-life provocations. Maybe you had a recent conflict with your spouse. Maybe your child acted rebelliously. Maybe you were criticized by a coworker or an unreasonable boss. Prepare yourself for the possible challenges you will face in dealing with this person each day. Think about how you might be provoked and imagine yourself forgiving. Then gird yourself for the battle of living out your forgiveness.

11. Seek help from someone you trust. What if you are still unable to forgive? If the unforgiveness emotionally upsets you, then you might want to seek help from someone who can be objective and help you forgive more.

Friends provide emotional support, but often friends are so supportive that they cannot help you move past your current unforgiveness. If you say, "I *want* to forgive him," a loyal friend might respond, "I've seen the way he treats you, and it's shameful." Such statements support you but also keep you stuck in the rut of unforgiveness.

Like friends, spouses can help you work through unforgiveness and develop a more forgiving character. Your spouse often knows more sides of you than do friends. He or she has often seen more of the negative parts of your character. Yet, under the best circumstances, your spouse is committed to remain in a loving relationship with you and is often more capable of being honest and loving at the same time. Of course, not all marriages are the best circumstances.

A professional helper, such as a pastor, counselor or therapist, is trained to be the most objective. He or she can help you examine your relationships without the investment of needing to live with you.

12. Start a campaign to love your enemies. Some of us might have enemies who openly seek to harm or destroy us. For most of us it's not that drastic, yet some people seem to oppose us. Their motivation is not usually hostile to us as much as it is focused on themselves. Regardless, the high calling that Jesus demands and gratitude to God encourage us to love those enemies. We can begin today to wage a campaign in the war to oppose the natural pull to unforgiveness, resentment, avoidance and revenge. We can plan to promote love.

In war, a campaign is a strategic attack on vulnerable and important fronts to achieve a specific objective. If loving our enemies is our objective, then we must (1) identify specific people to love and (2) develop a plan to demonstrate that love. List people to whom you want to show more love. For each, write two ways you can show agape love this week (or the next time you see them). For instance, suppose you have had a conflict with the teacher of your adult Sunday school class. You might show love both by telling him that you appreciate his teaching and by refusing to criticize him to anyone. Suppose you were passed over for promotion at work. Your boss promoted her best friend, who did not seem to be as devoted as you and had been at the company less time than you. You might show love both by refusing to grumble and by noticing at least one thing your boss did well this week. After you identify the people to whom you need to show love and the ways you can do it, put your campaign into effect.

PRAY FOR THEM

Here are some ways to focus your prayers.

• Meditate on God's message of mercy and grace to you.

- Meditate on the forgiving heart of the father in the parable of the prodigal son.

- Meditate on the good Samaritan.

- Meditate on the martyrdom of Stephen.

- Meditate on Christ on the cross.

- Apply your meditations about acting in love to those who have harmed you.

Remember Frodo in J. R. R. Tolkien's *The Lord of the Rings*? Frodo could carry the ring all the way to the top of Mount Doom, but he could not by mere strength of character defeat his sinful flesh. It was only when his enemy Gollum took charge that virtue could occur.

You cannot carry out a campaign to love your enemies with complete success under your own effort and striving. God wants us to act responsibly, but he will win the victory if we yield to him.

APPLYING THE PYRAMID MODEL TO REACH FORGIVENESS

A woman—let's call her Susan—has been unforgiving toward her father for fifteen years. Their relationship was completely severed after Susan's mother's untimely death by cancer four years ago. Susan felt that she had no reason ever to go home again.

Then she learned that her father had prostate cancer. She decided that she should try to reconcile with him. She knew she had to forgive him first.

When Susan was young, her father always seemed to be at work. He was available to everyone but his only daughter. When he was at home, he was gruff. He never seemed to understand her. The event that stuck out in her mind was as vivid as if it had happened yesterday.

Susan began to employ the Pyramid Model to REACH Forgiveness. She vividly recalled a hurt (R). As a teenager, Susan had been looking forward to her first prom. Asked as a sophomore, she was the envy of her friends. The week before the prom, she stayed out with her friends, drinking sodas and eating ice cream at the local Friendly's. They were having a great time. Suddenly, in horror, she looked up and saw her father striding toward her. It was almost an hour past her curfew. Susan was mortified as her father dragged her by the arm from the restaurant. The next day he forbade her to attend the prom.

To empathize (E) with her father seemed beyond her capacity at first, but she was determined to try to forgive. She began to imagine, tentatively at first, what her father might have felt as he and her mother waited at home for her. Tidbits of his angry speech flooded back into her memory. "We were worried sick. We knew that Jennifer [Susan's friend] isn't an experienced driver, and we were afraid something might have happened." Susan imagined the fear that must have passed between her father and mother. (Her mother, she remembered, always seemed to magnify mounds into mountains. Her father always said that her mother's catastrophizing drove him crazy.) Susan fell asleep having sympathy for him.

Two days later, Susan had time to reflect on forgiving again. As she began to see things from her father's point of view, she had to admit to herself that she pushed the envelope when it came to limits. She frustrated her parents by her rebellious attitude. Although Susan still believed that her father's insensitivity was inexcusable, she could see how she had provoked him. She realized he had his own set of pressures. She had moved from sympathizing to empathizing with her father. Her empathic understanding did not make his inexcusable behavior *right*. But it made it more understandable. Understanding, she wanted to forgive.

Susan began to employ the third step, the altruistic gift of forgiveness (A). She recalled several times in her youth when her mother and father had forgiven her. She thought carefully about each incident, but it did not seem to further her forgiveness. She could not seem to get immersed in any of those memories.

The next day, she recalled an incident that had occurred the week before. Susan had offended her boss. Even though the consequences could have been disastrous, her boss dismissed the incident. "No problem," he said, waving his hand. "All is forgiven." Susan left her boss's office with a smile and a light step. It was easy to see how forgiving her father might free him in the same way. For two days, she turned all these memories over in her mind. She knew she should forgive. But she had lived with resentment for fifteen years. It was hard to let go.

A movie pushed her over the edge into forgiveness. Ironically, the movie was a forgettable crime thriller about revenge. After the movie, she lay in bed, rethinking the prom episode. She forgave her father.

Unable to contain herself, she phoned her best friend, Marta, and poured out her experience of finally forgiving her father. "Forgiveness is like drinking hot coffee after being out in the snow for three hours of cross-country skiing," said Susan. "My legs are tired. My feet and toes are cold. My fingers feel as if they are going to fall off. Then I grasp a warm cup of coffee, inhale deeply to breathe in the aroma and feel the warmth of the first gulp of liquid spread out through my entire torso. That's the way I felt when I forgave Dad—flooded with warmth." As Susan and Marta chatted, Susan was practicing the fourth step of the Pyramid Model to REACH Forgiveness, committing publicly to forgive (C).

When she put down the phone, she thought about phoning her father even though she knew he did not keep the same late-night hours that she and Marta kept. As she thought of calling, some of the hurt came back. Old feelings of shame, embarrassment, fear and sadness welled up within her. *I thought if I forgave I'd be finished with those feelings*, she thought. Then she remembered: *Hurt isn't the same thing as unforgiveness. I can accept the reality that my father's actions were truly hurtful, but my unforgiveness is gone as long as I don't dwell on the negative.* By understanding that fundamental difference between remembered hurts and unforgiveness, Susan was practicing the fifth step, holding on to forgiveness (H).

Susan intentionally used the Pyramid Model to REACH Forgiveness. Her forgiveness took place over several days. That's not always the case. Sometimes it happens quickly, even with events that are traumatic, like my mother's murder. Sometimes forgiveness happens only after empathizing repeatedly for hours and attempting to forgive for days or weeks.

Over the years, I have become convinced that there are no easy answers or glib formulas for how to forgive. The Pyramid Model to REACH Forgiveness provides five steps, but don't be disappointed if you employ the steps and unforgiveness does not suddenly disappear. Keep repeating the steps. Keep recycling. Try to feel empathy, then sympathy, then compassion and then love for the person who harmed you. Grant decisional forgiveness at any point, and continue to work up and down the Pyramid to experience emotional forgiveness. Forgiveness may soon break through, and both your emotions and motivations will change.

The five steps are a method God can use to break into your life. They are like morning devotions, attending Sunday school or practicing spiritual disciplines—they are forms into which God pours the concrete that hardens into Christian character.

Forgiveness and the Transformation of Relationships

Forgiving my mother's murderer was a one-time event. Chances are low that I will ever have to forgive the murderer again simply because I don't know for sure who the murderer is, and even if I did, I would not regularly interact with him.

Most of the time, when we struggle to forgive, it is because a person hurts us repeatedly. When that happens, we usually change our tune from talking of specific transgressions to saying, "I can't forgive *him!*" We generalize. Many transgressions coalesce into a person.

When we see the person, stress increases. We feel angry and bitter. Hatred shoots up like a signal flare, alerting us to potential danger. How can we possibly forgive the person? *Forgiving everything he has done to me*, we think, *could take a lifetime.*

Nonetheless, the road to forgiving a person winds its way through forgiving important (symbolic) events that remind you of why you cannot forgive. Work through the Pyramid Model to REACH Forgiveness for each of those events that come to symbolize the person's blameworthy character. Once you forgive those symbolic events, you will possibly find that your animosity has evaporated.

Discussion Questions

1. Explain Daniel Wegner's "white bear" studies in about fifty words.

2. In the Clint Eastwood movie *Unforgiven,* what do you think the main point of the movie is?

3. In *Les Misérables*, tell why you think Jean Valjean has a forgiving personality. (If you think he has an unforgiving personality, tell why.)

4. In the section called "Forgiveness and the Transformation of Relationships," how does the author recommend forgiving someone who has harmed you many times? Do you agree?

5. What are the character traits that you really want to develop in yourself? What is your part? What is God's part? Do other Christians have any part? Is there anyone you want to use as an accountability partner?

6. Who are your heroes of forgiveness? List five. Share with the group one person whom you think everyone would know. Would you like to tell anyone you know that you admire his or her ability to forgive?

How to RECONCILE

In the second part of *Forgiving and Reconciling*, you have learned a five-step method to help you reach the forgiveness that a Christian relationship to the triune God encourages, stimulates and commands. You have practiced each step. You saw how to use the method to help yourself develop a more forgiving character. You saw how to pick symbolic hurts to enable you to forgive a hard-to-forgive person.

In each case, we assumed that the person you are trying to forgive isn't present. When you have to deal with the person, forgiving becomes more complicated. He or she can respond to what you do, referring to his or her own agenda and perspective on the events. The person might believe that *you* are at fault and might hurt you again.

We need to take the next step and consider how our interactions can help or hinder forgiving. Rebuilding trust is the context of seeking, granting and accepting forgiveness. That is the focus of the third part of *Forgiving and Reconciling*. We will walk carefully across a bridge to reconciliation.

9

Decisions

You cannot build a bridge by starting in the middle. Bridge-builders begin from the side they are on.

JOHN PAUL LEDERAC

In our laboratory and clinic, after I had developed the Pyramid Model to REACH Forgiveness, my students and I began to apply it. Jennifer Ripley helped groups of couples from Richmond who were seeking marital enrichment.[1] Near the end of the group, we had partners talk to each other about past unforgiven transgressions. Imagine the scene. Five couples were scattered around a room. One group leader tried to monitor those conversations.

When the group leader was nearby, most couples talked calmly. But the leader was always facing away from several couples. Voices began to rise. The group leader would drift toward the rising voices. Under the leader's attention, the partners could calm down. Meanwhile, though, two other arguments might erupt. The group leader was like a pinball, bouncing back and forth among the couples. No group leader could control five conversations. Some wounds were healed, but other wounds surfaced. We had not taught partners how to talk about the transgression itself. Some talked harshly with each other. They sometimes hurt each other anew.

By looking hard at our study's weaknesses, Jennifer and I saw ways to correct them. The scientific method had worked. We had new ideas. We just hope those first groups of couples forgave us.

We realized that forgiving was more complex when people had to go nose to nose with another person than when individuals were forgiving an absent person. (This might seem like a "duh" insight, but we had not taken it seriously prior to Jennifer's study.)

We began to think about forgiveness within the context of reconciliation. In this third part of the book, I will describe how to forgive and perhaps reconcile when you are still in a relationship with someone who hurt you. As with forgiving, so also empathy, sympathy, compassion and agape love are at the core of reconciling.

DIFFERENCES IN FORGIVENESS AND RECONCILIATION

People can forgive a person who is absent, like a parent who has been long dead. They can also learn to forgive someone who must be faced daily. When you have to interact with a person, two roads open up if you discuss the hurt. You can resolve or dissolve the relationship.

The other person can talk back, bring up times when you inflicted hurt, push your buttons and provoke you to blind rage. But the other person can also be accommodating, contrite, remorseful and loving. How you both interact will determine the future of the relationship. Will you tick each other off or tackle the problem? Will you jerk each other's chains or link your hearts closer together?

What's the difference between forgiving and reconciling? When people interact, we are no longer considering mere forgiveness. We are talking reconciliation. *Reconciliation is restoring trust in a relationship in which trust has been damaged.* Reconciliation requires both people to be trustworthy.

Forgiveness and reconciliation are often confused with each other (see table 9.1). Forgiveness is internal. I replace negative emotions or grant forgiveness as a gift. Reconciliation is interpersonal. It is not granted but earned. It occurs within a relationship.

Reconciliation and forgiveness are related to each other but are not joined at the hip. We can forgive and not reconcile. For instance, I can forgive my father for ways he hurt me when he was alive. Yet we cannot reconcile because he is dead.

We can reconcile and not forgive. Think of all those office squabbles. If we had to go to the mat and explicitly forgive every small breach of trust, we would never get any work done. We would spend many days tromping up and down the Pyramid. Yet because we must work together, we find ways to rebuild trust.

Table 9.1. A Quick Comparison of Forgiveness and Reconciliation

	Forgiveness	Reconciliation
Who?	One person	Two or more people
What?	Gift granted	Earned, not granted
How?	Emotional replacement	Behavioral replacement
Where?	Within your body	Within your relationship
How to?	Pyramid Model to REACH Forgiveness	Bridge to reconciliation

Feeling forgiveness can motivate reconciliation. Even though forgiveness and reconciliation are not joined, they are clearly related. When we forgive, we are often moved to pursue reconciliation. Let me go back to shortly after my mother's death for an illustration.

After I returned from Tennessee and my mother's funeral, I talked about my feelings only to my family. I was emotional whenever the subject of her death came up, so I tried not to talk publicly about the murder. I passed along the basic information to my friends and colleagues and accepted their condolence. Then I changed the topic fast.

Only with Kirby could I really let my hair down. I could talk safely about the pain that I felt. We spent many hours on long walks, with her listening, me trying to make sense of the murder. How did it fit into my world? What would it mean not to have Mama alive?

Almost four full months after the murder, I spoke about it publicly for the first time. I was to receive an award for teaching. I was slated to speak to about five hundred students, parents and university faculty.

I talked about the noble privilege of the teacher. "Character," I said, "is often more difficult to develop and to maintain than is an inquiring mind. As teachers, we have the noble yet often humbling task of helping students develop positive character traits." I talked of how my own character had been tested by the death of my mother, and I described the events of her murder. I shared from the heart how I reacted: first with rage, then with the lust for murder and finally with peaceful forgiveness of the murderer. I concluded, "Life often throws a sudden test of character before us. Will our students, and will we (as students of life), be able to pass our tests of character?"

At the end of the night's award program, at least fifteen people moved forward and shook my hand. Most shared their own struggles at forgiving people. Several made a passionate vow to find the person who had hurt or offended them to make things right—to reconcile.

I was amazed. I had hoped to help teachers want to teach positive values. Yet the effects of sharing that I could forgive my mom's murderer extended far beyond my hoped-for effect on teachers. Teachers, parents, students and administrators were moved to try once again to enter into the difficult task of forgiving those whom they had tried to forgive many times before. Even more, several wanted to reconcile with those who had hurt them. They wanted to restore their friendship. Hearing about forgiveness had unleashed a desire in them to restore trust in a trust-scarred relationship.

Encouraged, a month later I talked again about forgiving the murderer. This time I was speaking to a conference of professional counselors. At the end of that talk, people again moved forward and shared their personal struggles and stories of forgiveness. They wanted to know how I forgave. They wanted to test their character with a challenge to forgive. Again, knowing that I could forgive a tragic murder helped them want to make things right with people they had hurt and with those who had hurt them.

Yet sometimes, despite a desire on each side to reconcile, the trust gap widens like the earth opening up during an earthquake. An innocent remark ignites an explosion. A not-so-innocent jibe exposes an angry fire that has been smoldering beneath the surface. Talking about forgiveness and seeking to reconcile are risky. We've all tried to reconcile with people, only to have the conversation blow up in our face. If only there were a foolproof way to restore trust.

WHAT SCRIPTURE SAYS ABOUT RECONCILIATION

Remarkably, Scripture gives us almost no direct guidance about reconciliation. The Hebrew Scriptures have zero references that use the word. The New Testament isn't much more complete. The primary passage dealing with reconciliation is about reconciliation of humans with God—which is the main thrust of scriptural guidance about reconciliation. In 2 Corinthians 5:17-21, we find the main passage on reconciliation.

Therefore [because Christ, who died for all, showed a love that compels us (v. 14)], if anyone is in Christ, he is a new creation; the old has gone, the new has come! All this is from God, who reconciled us to himself through Christ and gave us the ministry of reconciliation: that God was reconciling the world to himself in Christ, not counting men's sins against them. And he has committed to us the message of reconciliation. We are therefore Christ's ambassadors, as though God were making his appeal through us. We implore you on Christ's behalf: Be reconciled to God. God made him who had no sin to be sin for us, so that in him we might become the righteousness of God.

That passage is completely focused on human reconciliation with God and on the way that people are called to help reconcile others with God.

We find the same emphasis in Colossians 1:19-20 ("For God was pleased to have all his fullness dwell in him [Jesus], and through him to reconcile to himself all things"), Romans 5:10 ("For if, when we were God's enemies, we were reconciled to him [God] through the death of his Son, how much more, having been reconciled, shall we be saved through his life!"; see also Rom 5:11) and Romans 11:15 ("For if their [Jews'] rejection is the reconciliation of the world, what will their acceptance be but life from the dead?"). The primary concern in the New Testament is reconciliation of people to God.

Interpersonal reconciliation—of people to each other—is seen in only three passages. In Ephesians 2:16 ("and in this one body to reconcile both of them to God"), Paul argues that Gentiles and Jews have historically seen themselves as two separate people. However, when people become Christians, the two people are joined in Christ into a single reconciled people—reconciled with God and with each other. In 1 Corinthians 7:10, Paul mentions that a woman who becomes separated from her husband must be reconciled to her husband or remain unmarried.

The main teaching on interpersonal reconciliation is in Matthew 5. In Jesus' Sermon on the Mount, Jesus presented the Beatitudes. He then claimed to fulfill, not abolish, the law. He gave applications of his fulfillment of the law. He cautioned against being angry with one's brother, not just against murder (as had traditionally been the law). "Therefore," he said, "if you are offering your gift at the altar and there remember that your brother has something against you, leave your gift there in front of the altar. First go and be reconciled to your brother; then come and offer your gift. Settle matters quickly with your adversary who is taking you to court. Do it while you are still with him on the way, or he may hand you over to the judge, and the judge may hand you over to the officer, and you may be thrown into prison. I tell you the truth, you will not get out until you have paid the last penny" (Mt 5:23-26).

At the beginning of the passage (vv. 23-24), the emphasis is on taking the initiative to reconcile with someone whom you have harmed. In the last two verses, the emphasis is on taking the initiative to reconcile with someone to whom you owe a debt. Our lesson: when we are wrongdoers, we are to *take the initiative* to try to make things right.

In one of the passages on church discipline (Mt 18:15-17; see also 2 Cor 13:1-3), we are told how to confront in love a church member who is committing wrong against us. We are to go to the person and tell our concern. If the person does not listen and change, then we are to go with others. Importantly, we are told to take the initiative rather than simply to wait for the other person to change. We are to confront, if necessary, in love.

In another passage, 2 Corinthians 2:5-11, Paul urges members of the church not to continue to punish a wrongdoer, but instead to "forgive and comfort him" (v. 7) and to "reaffirm your love for him" (v. 8). They are told that if they forgive anyone, Paul also forgives him. (Paul is probably talking of decisional forgiveness—granting freedom from revenge and avoidance—rather than emotional forgiveness, which cannot be "granted" but must be experienced through changed emotions.) Therefore, in these passages that pertain to reconciliation, we see that we are to take the initiative to reconcile—regardless of whether we were the wrongdoer or were wronged.

Because there are few passages from which to derive explicit teaching about reconciliation, we must use the message from Scripture globally to infer a theology of reconciliation. In chapter three, I described the roles of the triune God in forgiveness. However, I did not consider a Christian anthropology.

Humans are born to be in relationship, which mirrors the Trinity. God is three beings in continual interaction within the Trinity. God's nature is just and loving. In Romans 11:22, Paul says, "Consider therefore the kindness and sternness of God." We have needs for significance and intimacy, which mirror the character of God. We want to make a difference, and we want to experience intimacy. This dual nature is why so many aspects of our relationships throughout life consist of these two dimensions. For example, parenting has been found to depend on both control and support.[2] The interpersonal circle discovered by Timothy Leary, and elaborated by numerous people since Leary, has dimensions of power and affiliation. Our two clusters of virtues—conscientiousness-based and warmth-based virtues—mentioned previously, also fit with those dimensions.

Because humans fell in the Garden of Eden, we always have a longing for relationship but will, by nature, continue to sin against God and against people. We desire to have influence on the other and closeness with the other. We desire relationship.

However, when we experience a disruption of relationship, our being is threatened. We were created for relationships, and transgressions and violations of trust disrupt fulfillment of that need. Therefore, we build walls and create distance between ourselves and the transgressor to protect ourselves from further alienation and estrangement. Life becomes, as theologian Miroslav Volf describes it, a dance between exclusion and embrace.[3] Defensiveness excludes. Reconciliation seeks to reestablish embrace. It seeks to reestablish trust when trust is broken. To do so, people must overcome their sense of self-protective distance and their psychological (aloofness, avoidance, disengagement, revenge that drives the other away) and physical (staying away in different buildings) walls.

Closeness is reestablished while allowing for feelings of significance on both people's parts. Reconciliation involves four events. People make a mutual *decision* to face each other, as theologian LeRon Shults and psychologist Steven Sandage argue.[4] *Discussion* that involves dialogue is needed. Discussion allows people to attune themselves emotionally with each other. Attunement is created through sharing empathy, sympathy, compassion and agape love. Each person transcends essential aloneness by engaging with the other person at a deep emotional level. Through vulnerably interacting with each other, both parties can discover the poison in themselves and the damage done to the relationship. They can thus begin to *detoxify* their own souls through confronting their own sin and through repairing their tendency to maintain self-protective distance and the psychological aloofness, avoidance, disengagement and revenge that drive the other away. They can also begin to detoxify the relationship by taking actions to repair the relationship—to regain intimacy and embrace. With some healing occurring, people can feel safe enough to try to repair a sense of *devotion* to each other.

Reconciliation can obviously happen between people who are not Christians, but Christians do have a unity in being siblings in Christ. That unity can be an additional way by which reconciliation occurs, and an additional reason to reconcile (see Eph 2:16).

THE BRIDGE TO RECONCILIATION

When we have invested our time and much of our life in a relationship, we usually want to reconcile. But how? The emotional terrain seems littered with nasty, hidden mines that spring up and cut you off at the knees or blow your head off. Sometimes it seems easier just to avoid the other person than to step out in an attempt to reconcile.

I began to study reconciliation. To my surprise, I uncovered many fields of study, which included primatology (how nonhuman primates repair conflict),[5] child-child or parent-child conflict,[6] restorative justice,[7] international conflict negotiations, political reconciliation and religious dialogues.[8] Quite a diverse set of bedfellows!

From these very different fields, we began to discern common principles. Like chemists, we spun the elements, distilled them and purified them into four steps. These make up the Bridge to Reconciliation.

To build the Bridge to Reconciliation (figure 9.1), each person offers four planks to join together. Partners are motivated by a mutual desire (though not always equally strong) to make the relationship better rather than let it unravel. Both partners may try to reconcile but be skeptical about the outcome. But if they want to save the relationship, they at least need to make an honest try at reconciliation. The trust gap cannot be leaped. It must be bridged. A bridge does not *poof*—spontaneously appear. It must be built. That requires risk and hard work.

The Bridge to Reconciliation is one way of helping two people build a bridge across the trust gap.[9] Using the principles I described in the Pyramid Model to REACH Forgiveness, the Bridge to Reconciliation adds principles about how to reconcile that I discovered through research and my practical experience as a marital and family counselor. The Bridge to Reconciliation involves four planks. We *decide* whether, how and when to reconcile (plank one). Then we *discuss* the transgressions with "soft attitudes" (plank two). We *detoxify* our relationship of past poisons (plank three). Finally, we *devote* ourselves to building up a relationship of mutual valuing (plank four).

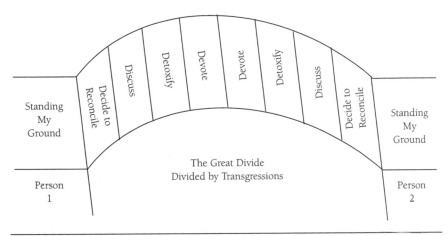

Figure 9.1. The Bridge to Reconciliation

Let's begin to walk across the Bridge to Reconciliation. We will examine each of the three decisions in plank one.

DECIDE WHETHER TO RECONCILE

First comes the yes or no decision of *whether* to reconcile. A component of the "whether" decision is analyzing why you might or might not want to reconcile.

Deciding whether you want to reconcile is not as simple as making up a balance sheet of pros and cons and then measuring the length of the columns. Those rational considerations are needed first steps, but there are also psychological barriers that must be climbed. In addition, false hopes for a magically restored relationship can paralyze us, just as the fantasy that the other person is completely to blame and will recognize his or her guilt can also stop us from seeking reconciliation

Why you might not want to reconcile. When people have become estranged, it's common that at first they might not want to reconcile.

- They might already have a sense of closure about the situation. "It is finished," they say. "I don't want to reopen the relationship."

- The people might like being apart.

- One person might refuse to reconcile. Reconciliation requires movement on *both* sides, so either person can block it.

- Reconciliation involves effort. One or both might not be willing to work hard enough.

- The estimated benefits of reconciling might appear to be less than the costs.

Even when both parties are willing, there are further factors to consider.

Reconciliation entails risk. People put their time, effort and egos on the line when they try to repair trust. We risk being taken advantage of. Even thinking about reconciling is risky. It requires us to consider our own part in a relationship. *What if I'm to blame? What if I confess my part? Do I diffuse the other person's responsibility? Will it let him [or her] off the hook? Will he [or she] seize on this as an admission that I am to blame? If I admit wrongdoing and the other person doesn't, does this lower my bargaining power? Does it make it less likely that the other person will want to reconcile? Do I set myself up to clean toilets for the rest of my life because I am now one down to the other person?* These and many more risks are inherent in seeking reconciliation. It's no wonder that most people let damaged relationships, like sleeping dogs, lie. They might get bitten.

Reconciliation is not always desirable. It might be unhealthy or unsafe to try to reconcile. A woman who has been beaten repeatedly by her husband should not put herself back in harm's way until he has had help and it's safe to return. A child who has been sexually abused should be protected from the abuser. A man who is continually verbally abused by his boss should consider a new job. A student who is abused by a teacher should look for another class or get a person in authority to provide protection.

Reconciliation might also not be desirable if the perpetrator shows no remorse and no intention of changing his or her injurious behavior. Without, at minimum, remorse, it seems likely that trust will be violated repeatedly. Reconciliation isn't safe when it could put one of the members at serious risk for physical or psychological injury.

Reconciliation is almost certainly not desirable if one partner has violated trust repeatedly. One woman told me that her husband had been unfaithful not once but six times. Each time, she had listened to his confession, wiped away sincere tears, heard his well-intentioned promises never to stray again. Each time he fell. After the sixth time, she decided not to take him back. She wanted my assurance that this was the right choice.

She had to decide for herself. Every person has a different threshold for attempting reconciliation. I probably would have tried a "tough love" approach earlier than betrayal number six, but each person must make a decision based on the circumstances.

Reconciliation may not be possible. A person may not be available. Maybe the person who inflicted the hurt or offense is dead, has moved far away, is in jail, is very ill or can't be contacted.

Reconciliation may not be prudent. Even when it may be safe and possible, reconciliation is often difficult and painful. Simply trying to reopen a relationship risks making ourselves vulnerable. We become uncomfortable and awkward. Many people wish to avoid such discomfort.

In addition, reconciliation might be hard to face because hurt has simply been too deep. Perhaps it is still too fresh or too painful. A person might not have worked through the event enough to want to open the possibility of discussing whether and how to restore trust—at least right now. Perhaps after some time has passed the wounds will scab over. As for now, though, reconciliation might not be wise.

This litany of warnings, reasons, risks and costs makes us think, *Why would anyone ever want to reconcile?* Let's listen to the countermelody.

Why you might want to reconcile. *People reconcile because they do not like to accept failed relationships.* They might feel lonely or alone. They hope that reconciliation will fill the hole of loneliness in their hearts. They can treat reconciliation like a bandage that covers a giant wound. Usually such efforts at patching up pain without pursuing the work of healing are ill-fated. On the other hand, people can allow the wound to heal itself. Empathy is the antiseptic. Forgiveness is the bandage keeping away threats of infection. Love is the heart pump of healing, bringing the lifeblood to nourish the relationship and absorb germs.

People reconcile because they value the other person and the relationship. They do not want to lose touch with a valued person or give up a once rewarding relationship. They will work, fight, cry and sacrifice for the smallest chance of recovering a precious relationship. I have seen this often in marriages in which one spouse has an affair. The wounded partner is often hurt and angry. Yet in spite of the pain, the person wants to hold on to the love that they had (and often still have) and is willing to forgive. Sometimes the wounding partner recognizes his or her error and comes begging for forgiveness. Even if a blizzard of cold rejection threatens to freeze him or her out, he or she persists, fighting for love. Watching partners who have been driven apart by an affair has always wrenched my heart. They struggle to bail a boatload of tears from a flood of emotions. Sometimes they sink. But sometimes they restore a seaworthy relationship.

People reconcile because they have invested in the relationship, the other person and the children. While they might value the relationship and the person for their own sake, they also do not want to lose their investment. I have seen couples hang through some very conflictual times for the sake of their children. They care about their family so they work through their differences, give up pet desires and sacrifice for the love they have invested in their children. If they emerge miserable, it might make one question the wisdom of their decision. But the investment in the children can be the capital that prevents marital bankruptcy.

People reconcile because they are not willing to return to the status quo. They believe that reconciliation will lead to a stronger relationship than existed prior to the breach of trust. *Bones heal stronger in the mended places*, they think.

People reconcile because they know that doing nothing spells disaster. It is not as if relationships get better on their own when hurts are not dealt with. They usually get worse. People who are hurt are prickly. They tend to be sensitive to new prickles. Sometimes they feel the prickles even when none were intended. (That's the prickle pickle.) In most cases, pursuing forgiveness and reconciliation is likely to have more positive outcomes than doing nothing.

Climbing the psychological barriers to seeking reconciliation. The barriers to deciding whether to reconcile are often our own thoughts, worries and fears.[10] Whether we are innocent victims, evil perpetrators, or (as is almost always true) both receiver and giver of hurts, our thought patterns can erect barriers that seem insurmountable.

Often these fears arise because we are not settled before the Lord on what we should do. Prayer is the first step. Seek closeness to the Lord. Guidance will often come spontaneously when you get close. But if not, don't hesitate to ask for guidance. "You do not have, because you do not ask God" (Jas 4:2). If you feel guilty over your wrongdoing in a relationship, be quick to confess to the other person (Jas 5:16). As we know, the Lord is eager to "forgive us our sins and purify us from all unrighteousness" (1 Jn 1:9).

Once we have taken steps to restore our relationship with the Lord, we are able to tackle our own psychological barriers with God's help. We usually listen to the fear-producing chatter in our heads. Now it's time to talk back! As a young boy, I always wanted to talk back to authorities, but somehow it never seemed like the smart thing to do. Now it is.

We must scale the unreasonable barriers that prevent us from seeking to restore redeemable relationships. We scale those barriers by identifying the negative and fear-producing thoughts, then arguing back at them.

In tables 9.2 and 9.3, I identify seven barriers to seeking reconciliation if you are the wounded one (table 9.2), and eight barriers to seeking reconciliation if you dished out more hurt than you received (table 9.3). In each table, I list ways you can talk back.

Table 9.2. Are Any of These Barriers Holding You Back from Seeking Reconciliation After You Have Been Hurt?

Barriers	How to Climb the Barriers
I haven't prayed about whether or how to reconcile.	Pray.
I don't want to give up my right to see him or her suffer.	Ask yourself, *Do I really have a right to see him or her suffer? Will seeing him or her in pain lessen my own pain, or might it add to my own pain?*
I don't want to give up my right to punish him or her.	Ask yourself, *Will I really feel better if I hurt him or her? Or will that lower me to his or her standards or below?*
I feel morally superior. I don't want to give that up.	Ask yourself, *Is feeling morally superior helping to restore the relationship? Could I relate better by admitting that I also make mistakes? Do I really want to continue keeping score?"*
I feel vulnerable to being hurt or rejected again.	Assess the likelihood. Do not put yourself in danger. But realize that love does not happen without risk. It is taking the risk and finding the other person trustworthy that makes love special.
I'm afraid that I won't be holding him or her accountable.	Ask yourself, *Did holding him or her accountable prevent the previous transgression?* Forgiveness this time does not mean that repeated transgressions have no consequences.
I'm still in too much pain. I need time to heal.	How much time do you need? We all need time to heal, but we cannot let that prevent us from ever trying to reconcile. Set a time that you think will be sufficient, and revisit the decision after that time has elapsed.

Table 9.3. Are Any of These Barriers Holding You Back from Seeking Reconciliation After You Hurt Another Person?

Barriers	How to Climb the Barriers
I haven't admitted to God my wrongdoing.	Confess in prayer. Consider whether to confess to some other person (such as your pastor, prayer partner, family member or friend; Jas 5:16).
I don't want to admit, even to myself, that I am capable of doing such acts.	It is difficult to admit we're human. We all do things we are not proud of, even downright ashamed of. Admitting you are capable of harming others is the first step in harming others less often.
It is embarrassing to admit to him or her that I did wrong.	Can you admit to yourself that you are embarrassed at not facing up to your acts? You'll be embarrassed either way. If you face up to your acts, at least you can face yourself in the mirror.
I know I was justified in my acts.	Believing you were completely justified in your acts may make you feel self-righteous, but it usually overlooks the truth that there are two sides to every story. Remember that we all make self-serving misperceptions.
I can't say, "I was wrong." It shows I'm weak.	Realize this: If you're having a hard time saying you were wrong, then saying you are wrong takes more courage and strength than if you keep it to yourself.
What if he or she refuses to forgive?	That will be difficult. But that reflects badly on the other person, not on you. You cannot control the other person's behavior. If you sincerely sought forgiveness, you did the right thing. Consider the scriptural pattern: We are usually supposed to initiate reconciliation if we have decided that reconciliation is the right thing to do.
The other person might use my admission of guilt against me later.	True. The other person might use your wrong behavior against you later. Usually, a sincere apology coupled with an effort to "make things right" can head off angry reprisals, but this is a risk you must judge knowing the people involved.
The other person might extract some horrid restitution because I harmed him or her.	While you will want to do whatever is reasonable to make things right, you need not accept being degraded as a person. If the other person suggests an act of atonement that you simply cannot do, you can make a counter-offer.

Check out each list. See whether each thought sounds familiar. If it does, read my suggestion for talking back. Even better, make up counter-arguments yourself. See yourself as a defense attorney defending yourself from the evil prosecutor who wants to see you remain alone and estranged.

Often that accuser is Satan, trying to set you up for alienation and depression.

Don't let false hopes stop you from deciding to reconcile. Get over the fiction that if you get justice it will lead to reconciliation. When misunderstandings, offenses or injustices have occurred, a natural response is to seek justice—to restore the balance that was upset. But achieving justice is no guarantee that reconciliation will occur. For example, in the book *A Time to Kill* by John Grisham, and in the movie made from it, a town was enraged by the vicious rape and attempted murder of a pre-adolescent African American girl by two adult white men. The girl's father felt certain that justice would not be done because the town was primarily white. He doubted whether a jury would convict the two perpetrators. He took justice into his own hands.

As the rapists were taken into the courthouse, the father blasted them with his shotgun in front of a hundred witnesses. He was quickly apprehended without attempting to get away. A trial took place. Clearly the father had killed the rapists. But was he *guilty*? Would convicting him be just or unjust? At that point, the main question was raised: Is there a time to kill? Was true justice served by the father's vigilante justice? Will the criminal justice system recognize this as a just outcome?

The movie unfolded with both sides of the conflict rallying support. In the climactic scene at the end of the movie, the two sides faced off in front of the courthouse awaiting the verdict of the father's trial. Racial tension crackled.

"Not guilty!" said the court. There is a time to kill. Did justice lead to reconciliation? No. Violence erupted into a bloodbath.

Justice rarely leads to reconciliation, even when justice can be achieved (such as with a fair trial). At best it brings an uneasy truce.

In most relationships, justice never really is experienced. When one side believes justice has been done, the other side doesn't. If you want to reconcile, you must *decide*. I have outlined the general reasons to reconcile or not. It's up to you to read those, look the pros and cons squarely in the eye, and decide. You can experience empathy, sympathy, compassion or agape love, follow the Pyramid Model to REACH Forgiveness—and then walk away. Sometimes that's the only sane thing to do. Or you can count the costs and start walking across your side of the Bridge to Reconciliation toward a meeting place somewhere near the center.

The costs of a hard attitude. Because it is difficult either to seek forgiveness if we did wrong or to grant forgiveness if we were wronged, we usually find it easier to avoid forgiveness and reconciliation. We might try to ignore a problem or blame it on our partner. I call this a "hard attitude." We insist that we are right and demand that the other person should see things our way. That hard attitude has costs.

- It makes the other person want to argue back.

- It makes the other person angry.

- It stimulates the other person to try to prove that you are wrong and he or she is right.

- It has an effect opposite to what you wanted, which was to get the other person to see that you were right.

- It creates more distance between you rather than more closeness.

As you read this in a favorite armchair, these costs of a hard attitude seem prohibitive. We can easily see that demanding the other person's sword in surrender will almost never work.

Yet face to face it's a different story. Our wounded pride pushes self-protective buttons. When we feel vulnerable, we hunch our shoulders, ball our fists and pull up a hard shell. When we feel insulted, we defend ourselves. Sometimes the best defense seems like a preemptive strike. Pain and threat activate our primitive drive to survive. We see the person who hurt us as the threat, the enemy.

But we have an equally basic drive—to affiliate with others to achieve a common purpose. We were created by a relational Triune God to be in relationships. People who are threatened draw together and seek strength in numbers. That also is a drive to survive.

Closed fist or outstretched hand? So we have a choice. We can make a fist or make a friend. We can seek revenge or reconciliation.

However, it's not always best to push the affiliation button. Some threats and hurts truly are dangerous and must be defended against by distancing instead of coming together. That is one reason that Scripture does not mandate reconciliation as it does forgiveness. Even God will not reconcile with everyone in the end (Rev 20:10, 15). We need the presence of mind to allow the surge of adrenaline that accompanies conflict to activate our discerning mind instead of pushing our button to attack, avoid or affiliate.

DECIDE *HOW* TO RECONCILE

Most reconciliation takes place implicitly rather than explicitly. If we had to discuss every little slight, offense or insult that occurred, productive social interaction would likely come to a halt. Talk about reconciliation would be the center of most conversations. We usually reconcile without talking about it. This is called *implicit reconciliation*. It occurs in several ways.

Stop hostilities. We can realize that conflict, anger and revenge are counterproductive, and we can adopt a strategy of peaceful coexistence. We can agree to disagree. By deliberate choice we decide to get along. We bury the hatchet (not in the other person's face). Similarly, without thinking much about it, we might lose the hatchet. We talk and work with the person; then one day we realize that the hurt and anger are less. We can also make a principled decision to reconcile because reconciliation is consonant with our social philosophy, religious beliefs and values. Maybe we decide to reconcile because we simply believe that reconciliation is the right thing to do and remaining estranged is the wrong thing to do.

Come together. We can also work together on a common task. Meeting challenges and working toward common goals help people rebuild trust. In a closely related way, we can reconcile through doing pleasing activities together. Parents and children often put aside relationship strains after playing, hiking, watching television or reading together. Spouses sometimes find that making love washes away relationship tension.

One plus one plus one equals two together. Sometimes a third person can help. When siblings conflict, the parent might play with one sibling, invite the second sibling to join, and then exit the situation, leaving the two siblings playing together. Adults can do the equivalent at parties by joining two adults who might be tense with each other, engaging them both in conversation, then moving on.

Recognize we are brothers and sisters in Christ. As Paul urged the Ephesians, we need to understand that we are members of one body. Knowledge of unity in Christ can break down dividing walls between groups or individuals (Eph 2:14-16).

Be positive. We can reconcile through complimenting or stroking, making each other feel good psychologically.

Forgive and reconcile. We can reconcile and thus trust each other again because we have healed our wounds through forgiving.

The trouble with implicit reconciliation is that it can be easily misunderstood. When we don't explicitly say we want to reconcile, the other person might not even realize we are trying. When we *say* we want to reconcile, though, the other person might disagree or might not want to accept our approach. But at least he or she knows our intent. For instance, if you decide to try implicit reconciliation, the other person may not know that you are trying to reconcile. If you offer to work on a task together, you might be hoping that you can repair the relationship, but the other person may believe you are trying to bribe or "guilt" him or her, so reconciliation fizzles. You may initiate sex with your spouse in the hope of reconciling. Your partner might then say, "Thank you very much for the sex. I feel less horny, but I'm outta here." Remember, implicit reconciliation often works. It is often kinder and gentler than explicit reconciliation. But it is more easily misunderstood.

Sometimes it's better to be explicit. The Bridge to Reconciliation—you're almost completely across plank one as you make these decisions—is one method of explicit reconciliation. See table 9.4 for guidelines about deciding.

DECIDE WHEN TO RECONCILE

If you decide to reconcile and you know how you wish to do it, the question of timing still remains. Remember, reconciliation is a process, not an event. Because reconciliation requires rebuilding mutual trust, it takes time. Decisional forgiveness can be granted instantly. Emotional forgiveness sometimes happens quickly. Reconciliation almost always requires a period of time during which people are wary of each other. They walk softly (and often carry a big stick). They hope for a hug but prepare for a punch.

Look for a good time to make a tentative first step toward reconciling. Don't wait for the other person to take the initiative. People who have hurt each other often have wounded pride, which makes them hesitate. You can starve to death emotionally while waiting on an estranged person to feed you. So usually you will want to make the first move. Besides, as we saw based on Scripture, the biblical pattern is for Christians to look for chances to initiate reconciliation if God wants us to reconcile. Wrongdoer or one who feels wronged, Scripture encourages *all* Christians to seek to initiate reconciliation.

Table 9.4. Guidelines for Deciding When to Try Implicit Reconciliation and When to Continue Across the Bridge to Reconciliation

What You Think or Feel	What to Do
I am really, *really* torqued.	Let your adrenaline be a cue for you to think, not act. You may eventually talk about the issue, but first cool off.
The situation does not lend itself to long talks (e.g., at work).	Try avoiding the person until some time passes, burying the hatchet, opting for peaceful co-existence or working on a task together.
The person holds power over me.	Is the person vindictive? Be careful. Proceed across the Bridge with caution. Perhaps you need to try to regain some trust through working peacefully together before you talk.
I am in a position of authority over the other person.	Again walk cautiously. Attempts to force a conversation can be perceived as coercion, regardless of how gentle you are.
We have a history of conflict.	Try implicit reconciliation. If that does not work, move to the Bridge. Emphasize your own vulnerability rather than attacking.
We have a history of being able to forgive and to reconcile.	Proceed across the Bridge to Reconciliation.
We don't seem to be able to read each other's intentions accurately.	Proceed across the Bridge to Reconciliation. Talking about your intentions will help.
I am very hurt.	Soft emotions, like vulnerability and hurt, usually inhibit the other person from strongly attacking. When you feel hurt (but not seething with anger), you often will be more likely to reconcile through crossing the Bridge rather than through sulking.
I am stressed to the limit.	Don't even think about bringing up a transgression.
I'm frustrated. I haven't had my say.	You probably don't really want to discuss. You want to talk. If you move to plank two, discipline yourself before you launch into your own story. If you charge ahead with your story, you'll vent but probably drive the other person away.

Be careful, especially if the other person's pride was wounded. One way in which people restore their own diminished sense of self-esteem is to attack and defeat another person—and you may find yourself on their radar screen. Just as dangerous, you may have impure motives. A Christian worldview, in fact, tells us clearly that our own motives are not as pure as they seem at first glance. Examine your own heart. Have you been hurt? Do you harbor an urge to vindicate yourself? Your desire to "discuss the issue"—ostensibly to reconcile—might be camouflage for attack.

When are you most likely to want to reconcile? Perhaps it's when you feel guilty over some misdeed. Perhaps it's when you think of how bad you feel when disappointment separates you from your spouse, friend or co-worker. Perhaps it's when you see others enjoying close relationships.

Two warning signs signal you to wait on trying to reconcile. When you're extremely stressed, it often doesn't take much of a bump on the track to derail your good intentions. When you're seething and feel you haven't been able to get your say, you are probably fused for a fight. In either case, take a few deep breaths and let things calm down before you move to reconcile.

If you feel that you are on an emotional roller coaster, expect the other person to feel the same way. Use your empathy skills. Ask yourself whether the other person is stressed or furious. Does he or she feel the pull to talk softly, or to pull you by the neck? If the conditions are right, go for it.

TAKING THE PLUNGE

Taking the plunge into explicit reconciliation requires that we talk about the transgression. This is like entering a minefield, especially if both partners are sensitized to the negative. How do you talk about the transgression, forgiveness and reconciliation productively? How do you discuss getting back together in relative safety without an explosion of conflict?

In many ongoing relationships, reconciliation can occur because people forgive. In others, people forgive because they have already reconciled. There is not one single way to reconcile effectively. The Bridge to Reconciliation can help, but it's both difficult and risky. And the hardest and riskiest part is plank two—discussion. This is where the bridge can crumble. Or it can stretch farther across the trust gap.

Do you have one or more trust gaps in your life? Have you decided to attempt to reconcile? Have you decided to address the issues explicitly? If so, before you decide that now is the time, make sure you understand the next plank: discussion.

DISCUSSION QUESTIONS

1. Do you think reconciliation is required by Scripture? Explain why or why not.

2. Explain what you think is meant by the quote from John Paul Lederac at the beginning of the chapter.

3. If you have someone with whom you are not reconciled, what do you think is the main barrier preventing that reconciliation (using the tables in the chapter to aid your analysis)? If you feel that you are reconciled with absolutely everyone in your life, what do you think would be the major barrier to reconciling if you had hurt someone important to you?

4. Explain what implicit reconciliation is. Give an example of a time when you did something that resulted in implicit reconciliation.

5. A hypothetical Christian woman is being struck and injured by her husband once every two or three months. She comes to you and says that she is moving out, and that she will never forgive him. She says she is confused about her responsibilities as a Christian. How will you counsel her?

6. What if you try repeatedly to reconcile with a person? How much should you try before "shaking the dust off your feet"? For example, suppose a woman has repeated affairs. Each time she is remorseful. She repents. She stays faithful for a year or more but falls again. How long should her husband work toward reconciling? How many affairs should he tolerate?

10

Discussion

*The public form of forgiveness is reconciliation. And this is of necessity a much
longer, more complex process. . . . Reconciliation entails several stages:
repentance, contrition, acceptance of responsibility, healing and finally reunion.*

JOHN T. PAWLIKOWSKI

Once upon a time, two people lived together in blissful harmony. They
never said a cross word to each other and were always supportive and loving. They valued each other completely and never devalued each other.
One day, one partner simply hauled off and betrayed the other person.

You undoubtedly recognized right away that the above story is my hal-
lucination (no doubt brought on by too much chunky peanut butter). In
reality, when two people live together, perfection can't exist. People—accidentally or purposefully—hurt each other. Over time, a history of
wounds accumulates, regardless of how good the relationship is. The
number and severity of wounds might be insignificant compared to the
loving acts in the couple's lives, but there is always a backlog of wounds
that have been treated with forbearance, ignored, accepted, forgiven and
often forgotten.

Furthermore, whenever people do hurt each other, they usually don't
inflict the hurt out of the blue, with evil intentions. They may not even
know they have caused pain. They may have felt provoked by the other
person, stressed, frustrated, cranky from lack of sleep or in need of dietary
fiber. Transgressions always have two sides.

Of course transgressions have two sides—except when I'm in the heat
of battle. Then forget it. I'm right! There's only one side: mine. If I acknowledge the other person's point, I feel downright unpatriotic. I feel dis-

loyal to myself in admitting that I might have been partly to blame for a hurt that I received. To protect myself, I harden my attitude. I am right. Period.

Unfortunately, a hard attitude spells disaster for reconciliation. To reconcile, you must create a soft attitude and engage in soft talk about the hurt. Having a soft attitude requires that you admit to yourself that there are two sides to *this* conflict and to *this* hurt. And admitting to yourself the two sides of the conflict is the mere beginning. You then must convey this to your partner.

SOFTEN YOUR ATTITUDE

Many people blame the other person for whatever goes wrong. This is a fact of human nature. People don't explain the causes of events by referring to their own character. They focus on what they see and hear—the other person. For example, if you see "Joey" hit a man, chase him, scream loudly and throw cold water on him, you will probably say that Joey is aggressive and cruel. But if Joey is asked to explain his own behavior, he won't say that he's aggressive and cruel. He'll say, "That guy insulted my wife and children, and I gave him what he deserved." It's natural for people involved in a conflict to explain their actions by referring to what the other person did because the other person's behavior is easier for them to see.

The other person is almost always seen as the perpetrator. Greg Jones, Dean of Divinity at Duke University, says, "In many situations, the possibility of reconciliation has been eliminated because both parties (or all the parties) come prepared to forgive and are completely unprepared to be forgiven."[1] Sometimes we can admit we have done wrong, but usually we feel like victims.

Therefore two self-identified victims are usually found in relationships, both blaming the other. Both "victims" usually believe that they perceive the events correctly. The other person is, thus, wrong (at best) or lying (at worst).

Unfortunately, both are usually equally wrong in their perceptions, as shown in an experiment by psychologists A. M. Stillwell and Roy F. Baumeister in 1997.[2] In that study, three groups of people were read a long story about an offense that took place between a victim and a perpetrator. The situation, offense, reactions, and the consequences for both parties were described. One group was told simply to remember accurately what was said. The second group was told to listen as if they were the perpetrator. The third group was told to listen as if they were the victim. The researchers later tallied and compared the number of errors in factual memory among the groups. The fewest errors were made by people who listened objectively. Surprisingly, people who listened as victim or perpetrator made the same number of errors in memory. However, they made different kinds of errors. "Perpetrators" remembered the victims' provocations. They remembered their own decisions to stop attacking the victim. They minimized the consequences to the victim. When the victim said that the event did not really bother him or her, the perpetrator took that at face value. On the other hand, while "victims" made as many mistakes as perpetrators, victims overlooked their own provocations of the perpetrator. They remembered asking the perpetrator to stop the attacks. They remembered their own pain. So both victim and perpetrator unintentionally distorted their memories in self-serving ways. This tendency of human nature hardens people's attitudes against reconciliation. By understanding this, perhaps we can be more humble. What we perceive and believe to be correct might not be totally accurate.

Soft Attitudes That Help You Talk Softly

Empathy and humility are both vital to forgiving. While forgiving is done by an individual, reconciliation is interpersonal. Think about how you can implement empathy and humility to help you replace a hard retaliation with a soft response.

Empathy. We already know that empathy (as well as sympathy, compassion and agape love) for the one who hurt us will help us forgive the person. We need to feel what the person might have felt if we are to let go of our hatred and replace negative emotions with positive ones.

Empathy is also important if we have hurt or offended someone. We need to put ourselves in the shoes of the victim in order to ask him or her to forgive us. Empathy is just as crucial for seeking forgiveness as for giving it.

A team in our lab, headed by Steve Sandage, studied college students and sought to predict who will and will not tend to seek forgiveness when they have wronged someone.[3] The strongest predictor of unwillingness to seek forgiveness was inability or unwillingness to empathize with others. Unforgiving people often failed to see how much they hurt others. They could not imagine others' suffering, so they could not imagine that they might need to apologize or make things right through making restitution.

Empathy can help us both forgive and seek forgiveness, and it plays another crucial role in reconciliation. If we see that the other person is empathic towards us, we feel understood. That makes us want to patch up a tattered relationship. Let me illustrate the power of feeling understood.

At a conference for counselors in 1996, I spoke on forgiveness. I talked about the death of my mom and how I forgave by empathizing with the murderer. After my talk, several people in the audience began to share with me their stories of giving and getting forgiveness. Out of the corner of my eye, I noticed a woman who held herself apart while others stepped forward to talk. At one point, I looked at the woman, silently giving her the opportunity to speak, but she gave her head a little shake. Someone else filled the gap. Finally, everyone in the room had gone except for that woman.

"I feel new hope," she told me. "When I heard you describe what you thought the boy who murdered your mom might have felt, I cried. My son . . ." She stopped, choked up. A tear tumbled down her cheek. She tried again. "My son broke into a woman's house and killed her. He was convicted of murder. He had just turned eighteen, so he's serving his sentence in adult prison."

Again she struggled to go on. "Adding to my heartsickness, people in our community, and even in our church, could not accept my husband and me. They would see us at church but not speak. They would see us in the grocery store but head down a different aisle. We felt isolated. No friends. Even people at the PTA seemed to shun us." She seemed to be trying for a little humor, but it fell flat.

"Frankly, my husband and I had about given up. We've seriously considered moving to another state where no one has heard of us. No one can understand. No one. People say the most hateful things. They say, 'How could you raise such a monster?' They treat us as if we taught our son to murder."

I made an encouraging murmur. "It feels like nobody cares," I said.

"They don't. They can't understand. He grew up as a good boy. He did the usual adolescent pranks. He wasn't perfect. He was normal. I've been a counselor for almost twenty years. I've seen hundreds of adolescents. He was *normal*."

She paused. It was almost as if she stood at the edge of a diving board, uncertain about whether to leap. "Then the night that ruined his life came. He broke into a house for thrills. But while he and his friends were robbing the house, the woman who lived there came home. He attacked her, and she died.

"Until you talked today, I didn't think that anyone could ever understand what might have been going on in his life when he committed that murder. Hearing you describe your experience with such empathy and compassion changed me. Your understanding of the boy who murdered your mother gave me hope. I now believe that *someone* can understand. If one person can, then others can.

"My husband and I have cut ourselves off from the community and our church since people have given us the cold shoulder. I see that I need to try to forgive those people who have reacted to the horror of the murder. They don't understand what they are doing to my husband and me. Jesus said, 'Forgive them, for they know not what they do.' I've known all along that I should forgive, and I can grant *some* forgiveness, but . . ." She struggled for the words to express her feelings. "But when I heard that you could understand and even forgive, it helped me empathize. It also let me feel a little forgiveness begin deep inside instead of just in my Christian talk. It gave me the courage to try to make things right with people who used to be friends."

One of the difficult parts of being a speaker is that when I meet interesting and courageous people such as this woman, I walk with them for a short way, but I do not get to see the rest of their stories. I, of course, wished her and her family well. My hope is that her story can help others to persevere and to reconcile.

So many people carry enormous pain. We have no idea the load others might be wrestling with. When we choose to empathize, sometimes that can be the key to lift their burden enough so that they can take steps toward seeing and admitting their own unforgiveness. It might even lead to reconciliation.

Remember Rosalie Gerut from chapter five? She is the wonderful, charismatic Jewish woman whose mother survived the Holocaust. Rosalie cofounded the organization One by One. Her organization helps children of Holocaust survivors and children of Nazi soldiers to begin conversations that eventually lead to healing. Her method is based on getting people together in a room. Formerly faceless "enemies" then have human faces.

They can share their own stories with each other. By listening to the stories of the struggles that people from the other side have to tell, a deep sense of empathy can build within the group, and people can become open to being reconciled with others whom they had previously thought badly of. The One by One philosophy can promote reconciliation and healing. It is based on discussion in openness, honesty and empathy. If children of Nazis and Jewish Holocaust survivors can talk and empathize, you can too.

Humility. Pride is a hard attitude that often trips reconciliation at the starting gate. Whenever I begin to feel prideful, I use a vivid story to deflate my swelled head. Unfortunately I have forgotten the source of the story.

A young man was in his college dormitory room lifting weights. He glanced in the mirror and saw that his muscles were bulging from having pumped iron. Feeling like Arnold Schwartzenegger, he decided to head to the student union and "give the women a treat." (Did I mention that humility was not his strong suit?) He slipped his tank top over his torso and headed out the door. At the last moment, as he glanced in the mirror, he thought, *The scholar athlete will be much more impressive than the mere athlete.* He blew the dust off of a few textbooks and tucked the six weightiest under his arm. (He had finally found a use for Gray's *Anatomy.*) Glancing at the mirror again, he noticed that the scholar-athlete look had the side benefit of causing his biceps to bulge.

He swaggered into the student union where he bought an All-American college meal: burger, fries and shake. Balancing the tray with one hand and his six books with the other, he headed toward an open seat across the cafeteria. He knew instinctively that every woman in the room was looking at him. *I'm cool,* he thought.

He noticed several young women that he wanted to impress, so he casually leaned down to drink from his straw . . . and missed. Embarrassed, he lunged at the straw again. It bounced off of his lip. His straining lips and thrusting tongue chased that pesky straw around and around in circles, but it eluded him like a rolling stone. Frustrated and embarrassed, he opened his mouth and lurched at the straw. It bounced off of his lip and lodged in his right nostril. Not cool. He flexed his nose. The straw hung there. He shook his head. He sniffed (bad idea). He blew. Bubbles splattered the milkshake onto his face. In desperation, he jerked his head backward, but the straw came with him. He became The Amazing Man with the Straw in His Nose, a legend in his own time. Swinging his head from side to side, he did a sort of Jackson Pollack-like milkshake splatter-painting of all the people sitting nearby. He was a popular guy.

"Pride goes before a fall," said the writer of Proverbs. Remembering The Amazing Man with the Straw in His Nose has helped me keep my pride under control many times.

Pride is a significant barrier to asking for forgiveness and seeking reconciliation. Even when people know they are in the wrong, it's hard to admit it to someone else.

Developing humility is more than merely defeating pride. At least one psychologist, June Price Tangney, has begun to think scientifically about researching humility.[4] Initial efforts have not been promising. Humility is difficult for psychologists to investigate. Imagine the dilemma. Suppose I ask people, "Are you humble?" If they answer yes, it's almost proof that they aren't humble. If they answer no, they might be truly humble. Then again, they might simply have self-esteem lower than a worm's belly button, or they might be arrogant and know it. So humility is hard to study.

True humility is not defeating pride. It is thinking of the other person. The characteristics of empathy and humility and the absence of pride are thought to be the character traits that most predict being willing to risk seeking forgiveness.

You can cultivate humility by understanding that you might not be as correct as you think you are. It's a simple matter of perception.

How to Keep Your Cool

Here are some specific steps you can take to keep cool when you're discussing hot topics.

Practice forbearance. Forbearance is attempting to keep revenge and avoidance motivations at bay. Instead of lashing out, practice self-control. Shoot a quick arrow prayer for forbearance. Then take some deep breaths. Those breaths calm your body and make it easier to forbear. Before you say anything, think about the consequences. When you think, your mind helps you forbear. If you still find yourself having trouble holding your tongue, before you say anything you will regret, simply ask if you can talk at another time. That will give your spirit a chance to calm and will allow you to consider your response without the heat of the immediate situation. When you can deal with the situation calmly, then practice empathy.

Practice empathy while the other person explains. When the other person explains his or her point of view, try to see things from that point of view. The natural reaction when you disagree is to argue mentally as the other person tries to explain. That is the road to a heated exchange. Instead, stay cool. Try to understand the pressures, stresses and special circumstances that influenced the person to hurt you. That will help you empathize. It keeps the focus off yourself.

Summarize what the other person says. Practice your empathic listening skills, reflecting what the other person says and what his or her feelings are. Let the person know that you accurately understand what he or she is feeling and thinking. This is called active listening.

For instance, Sharon says, "I can't stand being here when you criticize me. It drives me absolutely nuts. I feel violent inside. I want to run away screaming. That's why I left and slammed the door. I was afraid of what I'd do if I stuck around."

Margo replies, "You hear me say something critical, and it hurts you. You feel angry—so angry you have to get away fast. Just a few minutes ago that anger made you leave and slam the door. Am I understanding you?"

Give the person the benefit of the doubt. Few people try to hurt someone they care about. Almost no one tries to hurt or offend strangers, or even rivals. Most hurts are due to misunderstandings, unusual stresses, or striking back in quick anger from a presumed provocation. Instead of assuming that the person who hurt you is the evil chief emissary of the Dark Side of the Force, give him or her the benefit of the doubt. Assume the person had positive motives. Misunderstandings usually happen not because people's motives are evil but because they can't turn their positive motives into positive actions.

For instance, recently Kirby had one of those terrible-horrible-no-good-very-bad days. She was in the backyard shed where we keep our clothes dryer. As she checked to see whether the clothes were dry, she told me of her day. She paused to open the dryer. I stepped into the backyard to pick up a limb that had fallen from the tree.

"Where did you go?" she said, clearly hurt. "I was still talking."

I apologized. "I thought you had finished for now. You said we'd talk more when we went for our walk later."

"I didn't ever stop talking."

"You turned your back. I guess I didn't hear. Sorry."

As we talked further during our walk, I said, "You know I love you, so you know I didn't get up this morning and say, 'I think I'll reject the person I love.'"

"Yes, I do know that. But I didn't feel that," she said. "I felt rejected. Because I know you love me, and because I feel that love now that we're talking about it, I can give you the benefit of the doubt. My head knew you loved me, but my heart didn't know what to do with the feelings."

Be fair in your expectations. You want to be fair, but nature is working against you. You naturally see things from your own point of view, not from the other person's point of view. Therefore, you see the costs that you've incurred more clearly than the costs to the other person.

It takes work to cultivate empathy for the other person. It requires effort to be humble. But it's well worth it. Act with the knowledge that he or she is the same, under the skin, as you are. You might naturally expect the person who hurt you to grovel contritely. Not a humble expectation. Or you might naturally expect that the other person will offer to pay you one million dollars in restitution—not likely to occur. If you examine things from the other person's point of view, you will be able to create a more realistic expectation that will keep you from being disappointed.

Consider forgiving. If the other person has admitted wrongdoing, apologized and offered restitution, then the burden has been placed upon you to consider granting forgiveness. Some people think that the transgressor should be thoroughly repentant before they are obligated to forgive. That is, they believe forgiveness is to be granted only after a person has given evidence that he or she is going to change direction and act positively. As Christians, though, we are admonished to grant decisional forgiveness right away. Don't wait for the offender to repent. If we wait for the other person to thoroughly repent, we probably will never want to grant forgiveness.

The issue is one of humility. Personally, I have found it hard to know my own motives. I know how weak I am. I sincerely *want* to act positively toward someone who might have offended me. But just a moment's thought convinces me not to hold out for the person to repent. I simply think of what I'm like when I have wronged someone else. I'm self-protective and defensive. Before long, a negative thought creeps in, or a critical word, and I "forget" to be nice. All the time, I sincerely want to rise above any tension between us and take the high road. But I can't. Why do I expect more of someone else than I do of myself?

So when I start feeling that I want to see repentance before I forgive, I come up against my own weaknesses, foibles and failures. If I can't expect unfailing repentance from myself, how can I expect it from someone else? Even worse, if I can't even know my own motives, then how can I presume to judge the other person's motives? How can I say to myself *he isn't really sorry for what he did* or *he's just pretending?*

Out of the humility of knowing my own limitations, then, I want to err on the side of forgiving too easily. I want to be quick to forgive. That is the humble thing. Also, forgiveness pleases God.

Decide whether you should give or get forgiveness—or both. Who is responsible for seeking reconciliation if a misunderstanding has occurred? Both people should want to do whatever they can to restore their closeness. And if we are acting biblically, we'll be trying to outdo each other to initiate reconciliation. Even if the other person does not seem to want to act, don't wait for him or her to initiate reconciliation. Relationships are too precious to give up on them easily. Clearly, you don't want to become a doormat by not holding the other person accountable for his or her behavior. On the other hand, giving tit for tat will rarely restore a relationship. You must find your balance, which isn't easy.

Keeping your cool in a two-sided disagreement is very hard to do. It challenges you to employ the virtues you want to build in yourself—even in the face of provocation. Empathize. Look first to understand rather than be understood. Give the other person the benefit of the doubt. Be fair, and be humble. If you can do most of those things most of the time when you feel provoked, you can keep your cool and show forbearance.

EXAMINE YOUR ACTS

Before you launch into a discussion with someone who wounded you, identify clearly what you believe he or she did that wronged you. That sounds obvious, but when we are wronged, we *feel* but do not always *think*. Researcher Pietro Pietrini has studied people using Positron Emission Tomography (P.E.T.).[5] He has found that when people get angry, they shut down most rational thought. Any thinking that occurs is in the service of anger. I know that's the way I am. I usually want to react rather than plan a response. When I do react, though, I'm usually sorry later.

So be sure you can say what was wrong *before* you say it. Practice when you're alone. How does it sound when you say it aloud? Remember, you can say the same thing with vinegar or honey. As long as you're alone, it will also be helpful to think about why the other person might have acted as he or she did. Start the motor of empathy.

Resolve to examine your own part in the hurt before you discuss it. Think about what, if anything, you might have done to provoke the other person. What was the person seeing and hearing? With what background did he or she enter the situation? Was he or she frazzled because of stress at work, driven to distraction by demands from children or friends, attempting to cope with fifty deadlines before lunchtime?

When you understand what was going on for the other person, then examine how you responded to his or her actions. What did you say when he or she hurt you? What did you feel? What did you do? Did you get defensive and lash back with harsh words? Did you throw gasoline on a small fire? Think about how your acts may have made the person feel and how you might have felt if you had been him or her.

Finally, examine what you have done since the incident. Have you retaliated? Sulked? Slammed doors? Ignored the person? Failed to look him or her in the eye—or stared hard in hatred? Sabotaged with passive-aggressive meanness? Have you been accommodating? Maybe you have smiled and let the incident pass, seemingly unperturbed, so that the person has no clue that you're still upset about the hurt. To the other person, your actions might feel mean and hateful. The person might not connect your behavior with the pain caused by that incident.

This self-examination should not be legalistic. It should not be a find-one-thing-that-I-did-wrong-so-I-can-blame-my-partner type of self-examination. Rather, true self-examination tries to create an atmosphere of give-and-take and sees oneself honestly.

TALK ABOUT THE TRANSGRESSION

Now you are ready to talk about the transgression (see figure 10.1). The talk should eventually include three parts: a *reproach* by the person who feels wronged, an *account* by the wrongdoer and a *consideration of forgiveness*. Here are some suggestions for how to do each part.

Make a gentle reproach. When a transgression occurs, the wronged party will usually ask for an explanation, called a *reproach*. You can make a harsh reproach, saying, "You barbarian. You have the sensitivity of gravel. How could you do such a horrid thing to me? Don't you love me?"

Now, color me cynical, but I predict that this approach will not make the relationship flourish. It's just a hunch, mind you.

On the other hand, a gentle reproach might say, "When you insulted me, I was surprised. You're usually very sensitive. Can you tell me what was going on? Help me understand." A gentle reproach affirms the person's positive motives and usual positive behavior. It asks for an explanation from the other person's point of view. It asks for the person's help. It is respectful, and it will usually keep the door open for genuine dialogue.

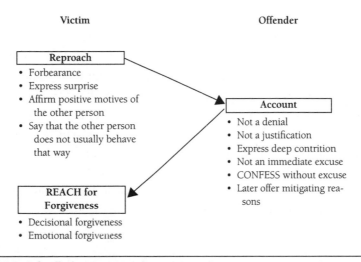

Figure 10.1. Soft talk about transgressions

Give a soft answer. How you reproach the other person will affect the type of explanation you get. Some answers are "hard." Others are "soft."

Let's put the shoe on the other foot for a moment. Suppose you erred. Perhaps you're ashamed. You think desperately for an excuse. You know a reproach is soon to come. You'll soon have to give an account for your behavior. What are your options? There are four types of answers: denials, justifications, excuses and concessions.

You can *deny* that anything was wrong. The person says, "You hurt me." You say, "I didn't." Or you say, "You shouldn't have been hurt by *that*." That's a denial.

Or you could *justify* what was done. You justify yourself when you admit that you did the act and that it was indeed wrong; however, you also say that due to circumstances you were morally allowed to do it. By justifying yourself, you imply, "Anyone would have done as I did." For example, you might say, "Sure, I insulted you, but it was because you insulted me first." That is a justification. It says, "I had a legal and moral right to do wrong to you because you wronged me first, so we're even." When we justify ourselves, it is almost always because we think we are simply responding as any sane person would have responded. We make the first move in the blame game.

The third possibility is to *excuse* yourself for the act. This type of answer says, "I did wrong, but there were compelling reasons for doing wrong." For instance, you might excuse yourself by saying, "Sure, I insulted you, but it was because I was under huge stress. My boss gave me ten jobs to do today. The children were each disciplined at school and sent home. Our dog bit a lawyer's child. The IRS has notified me that I am going to be audited tomorrow, and I had spinach on my front tooth when I talked to the president of the company this afternoon. Therefore, I cannot be held accountable for a little insult." Excuses say, "I was wrong. I should have known better. However, these compelling reasons might at least make my actions understandable."

The fourth type of account is called a *confession.* You confess to wrongdoing and concede that you did wrong. You don't try to justify or excuse your behavior.

A SECOND LOOK AT GIVING HELPFUL ACCOUNTS

Now let's examine each account more closely. Which ones are most effective?

We will feel best if we deny our wrongdoing—assuming we really don't feel that we did anything wrong. If we're trying to cover up, that's a different story. Denial works best for our feelings if we really believe we are innocent. However, denial is tough on our relationships.

If we deny wrongdoing, the other person will usually be livid. By denying, no matter how tactfully, we spit in the person's eye. We say, "I can't believe you're accusing me! You're wrong. In fact, you're stupid for accusing me. Take it back." The other person's options are few: fight or flight. Neither will help the relationship.

What should we do if we truly believe the reproach was incorrect? Assume that the person is feeling hurt or angry for a good reason. Find out why. Instead of denying, say, "You seem angry. What happened? I want to know. Help me understand." Then listen carefully—not to pick holes in the argument but to understand the person's experience.

If we justify ourselves by blaming the other person, we will feel less wrong, but the blame game is a no-win situation. It catapults us into argument. Unless we thrive on conflict, we will probably pay a large price for blaming the other person.

When we say, "I did wrong, but I was justified because you did wrong first," we take a weak moral stance. We are saying, "Two wrongs make a right." Logically, we would never agree to such a position. But arguments seem to use logic only as a blunt instrument to pound the other person with. Emotion seems to be the driving force. By taking the two-wrongs-make-a-right stance, we open ourselves to be pounded as well as to pound. We get nothing but two pounds of pain.

Instead of jumping in by justifying ourselves or blaming the other person, we should listen. Hear the other person out. If we believe the other person provoked us, we would be wise to deal with our own misbehavior *before* we try to correct the other person.

If we truly believe that we have some good excuses for our behavior, we would be wise to share those with the other person. Yet timing is crucial. When we say, "Sure, I insulted you, but . . . " it really doesn't matter what we say next. When the person hears us say *but,* the person turns off. I recall being in a group with an elderly woman who had a hearing aid. Whenever someone said something she did not agree with, she dramatically reached up, turned off her hearing aid, leaned back and smiled. The word *but* is an off switch.

Telling the other person about the pressures we were experiencing can promote empathy and help the person reach forgiveness. Remember, that's precisely what the person needs to do to forgive us—empathize with all the pressures that we were under. Yet the *but* that precedes a litany of excuses is a hot button that clicks off the emotional hearing aid and links that person to an attack program. When we say, "I insulted you but . . . " it says to the person, "I insulted you, but I have no clue how much it hurt you or how angry it made you. All I care about is that you understand *me* and the pressure *I* was under." So if we make immediate excuses, it suggests that we are insensitive and self-focused. It triggers (1) blame, (2) more explanations about how hurt or offended the person was and (3) a hard attitude not receptive to reconciling.

So instead of making excuses, we'll have more success if we make a good confession. After we have admitted our wrongdoing fully (using the following CONFESS approach), then—and only then—we will be able to help the person understand us better.

THE CONFESS APPROACH

George forgot to put money in the checking account. Gwyn wrote a check that bounced. Because George was out of town, Gwyn had to spend an entire morning straightening out their accounts. When she mentioned it, he blew up and left the house, slamming the door. Now he's sorry.

Here are seven steps to a good CONFESSion. Each begins with a letter of the acrostic CONFESS.

C = Confess without excuse. George needs to say, "Honey, I forgot to deposit the money in the checking account." He should make a simple confession. No excuses. No buts. If George is feeling particularly loquacious, he can even add, "I feel terrible. I'm so brain-dead sometimes."

Let's face it. It is hard to admit that we are wrong. We lose face. We can say, "I made a mistake. I messed up." But somehow it's hard to come right out and say, "I was wrong." George needs to say it. "Honey, I was wrong. I don't have an excuse. I blew it."

O = Offer an apology. It is essential that we are sorry for what we did. An apology is one of the best ways to start reconciliation. An apology helps restore personal justice. It reduces the injustice gap. To be effective, an apology must be specific. A general apology like "I'm sorry I hurt you" isn't very effective. A very general apology like "I'm sorry for all the times in the past that I hurt you" is even less effective.

Effective apologies are specific. George said, "I'm also sorry I called you names and stormed out when you were trying to explain yourself. Deep down I knew that would hurt you, and I am really sorry that I hurt you. That was wrong, too."

In our research, we have found that there is nothing magical about the words "I am sorry." Rather, to be effective, an apology must convince the other person that we feel sincere *regret* and *remorse* for doing what we did. If we can get this across, regardless of precisely what we say, we will promote forgiveness and reconciliation. So George needs to add to his apology something like this: "It makes me feel sick that I caused you all that work. I feel so irresponsible, and I'm really ashamed of myself."

Why does an apology help the other person forgive us? It not only disarms the person, but it also stimulates the other person to empathize with us. If we apologize and convince the other person that we are truly remorseful for what we did, it helps the person get into our shoes instead of fighting with us. He or she can see our pain and can be quicker to forgive. (Faking remorse will only damage the situation further.)

N = *Note the other's pain.* "I see by your tears that I have really hurt you badly. When I wound you deeply, you seem to draw inside a protective shell. I know you were counting on my depositing the money in the checking account," said George. "You must be very disappointed with me. I also know that I wasted your time, which made you stressed and angry."

George has let Gwyn know that he has understood what she is feeling. By empathizing with Gwyn, George shows he is connected to her. His empathy lets her know he cares, which makes it easier for her to forgive him.

F = *Forever value.* Love is valuing the other person. George can show that he loves Gwyn by saying, "I know I didn't respect your time. I want to always value you. I'm sorry I acted so irresponsibly. I didn't treat you with the honor that you deserve." George does love Gwyn. He isn't using a "technique," trying to manipulate her or attempting to weasel out of trouble. By expressing his love, he lets her know he still loves her.

E = *Equalize.* Equalizing is making up for the loss that the other person experienced. To offer *restitution* is to equalize the balance of justice. Any hurt or offense causes the person who is hurt to lose something. Perhaps he or she loses self-esteem, self-respect or a tangible benefit (such as if I offend you in front of your boss and you lose a promotion opportunity). So it is an act of kindness for the transgressor to offer to make up for the loss. George can offer to equalize. He should say, "Is there anything I can do to make up for what I have done?"

When the transgressor spontaneously offers restitution, the victim often softens. If the transgressor waits so that the victim must propose the restitution, it is usually more demanding. For example, when George offers to make restitution, if Gwyn is empathic, she will realize that making such an offer costs George something in terms of his self-esteem. Therefore, Gwyn might say no restitution is needed, or she might suggest a small restitution.

However, if George did *not* spontaneously offer restitution, Gwyn might say, "I think you should do something to make up for what you did. Why don't you clean the toilet for the next twenty years?" Gwyn will likely name a restitution that involves more punitive damages because she does not perceive George as having incurred any cost if he doesn't offer to make things right. If he doesn't seem to incur any cost, she might hammer him. In fact, by not offering to make restitution, George is making Gwyn ask for restitution, which increases the amount that she perceives herself as having lost because she is risking further rejection. So she will likely hammer him hard. The bottom line: If we offend, we must see whether we can do something to make up for the transgression. Fast.

S = Say "never again." It will help relational healing if we say that we will *try* not to hurt the other person in the same way again. We cannot absolutely promise we will *never* hurt him or her again. Accidents happen. Events may conspire so that we do hurt people, regardless of how hard we try not to. Having a clear positive intention—and saying it aloud to the other person—is important to building trust. "I am going to do my best," said George, "to always deposit my check on the way home from work. I also don't ever want to get so angry with you and with myself that I storm out without resolving things."

S = Seek forgiveness. George must now ask for forgiveness. He should be specific. He should say something like, "Can you forgive me for insulting you and for not being considerate? I'm so sorry." By asking for forgiveness, he admits clearly that he has done something that deserves condemnation. Many people walk through CONFES and cannot take the last step to the final S. "Can you f—, f—, f—, for— . . . you know, can you?" George needs to look Gwyn right in the eye and say, "Honey, I don't deserve it, but can you forgive me for not respecting your time and then—to make it worse—storming out?"

In the case of mutual offenses, ask forgiveness for your own part regardless of what the other person did to hurt you. If he or she hurt you, that does not justify your hurting him or her. So take responsibility for your own actions. If you hurt the person, ask clearly for forgiveness. In so doing, you also acknowledge that you did wrong and that the other person has the power to forgive you for what you did.

In all of these steps thus far, you are practicing empathy and unselfish agape love. You are seeing things through the eyes of your partner. You are trying to do things that your partner would appreciate. You are demonstrating understanding of, emotional identification with and compassion for your partner, all of which combine to make up sincere empathy. You are laying down your life for the other person, in humility as Christ did (Phil 2). Empathy and love turn out to be the keys in reconciliation, just as they were the keys in forgiveness.

The two hardest parts of CONFESS are usually C (confess without excuse) and the last S (seek forgiveness). Both challenge our egos. Humility is the fraternal twin of empathy. Together they can help the other person want to forgive us.

A TIME FOR REASONS

Offer to explain yourself if the other person wants to hear. After—and only after—we have completely CONFESSed our part of the interaction, we might offer the opportunity for the other person to understand the reasons why we acted as we did. We need to be careful not to justify or excuse what we did. Instead, we provide the reasons that will make our act understandable. We don't want to convey to the person that we're making light of or worming out of our part. We are not trying to excuse our behavior.

Explaining our reasoning can help the other person empathize with us (and perhaps forgive more easily). The difference is in our timing and style. When the person asks for an account for our behavior and we immediately list ten good reasons for what we did, our explanation will be perceived as excusing or justifying our behavior. Instead, we want to think of how the other person must feel. Gwyn wants to know that George has taken clear responsibility for his acts and that he is truly sorry for the pain he caused. Once she believes those two things, she is opened up to understand some of his reasons. After admitting his wrongdoings, George might say, "Would it help you to forgive me to know what was going on with me?"

Offer your reasons without blame. If the other person says, "Yes, I would like to understand your reasons," then we can offer those reasons without suggesting that the other person made us hurt him or her.

Kisha says, "I'm truly sorry I poured ice water on you when you were sleeping. Would you like to know why?"

Lou says, "Yes, I would."

Kisha says, "I did it because you were being such a jerk to me that I couldn't respond any other way."

Needless to say, Kisha and Lou are going to spend the night in separate bedrooms dreaming about ice water. Kisha blamed Lou. That will harden Lou's attitude and undo any positive gains that they might have made.

When Lou asked Kisha what her reasons were for dousing him in ice water, she probably should have said, "I was angry, and I lost my temper." If she stays away from blaming Lou, they might still end up in different beds, but maybe they'll each dream less of ice water.

MAKING THE GOOD CONFESSION

I've developed George's CONFESSion piece by piece above. Now let's put it together and hear how it sounds.

"Honey, I forgot to deposit the money in the checking account. I feel terrible. I'm so brain-dead sometimes. Honey, I was wrong. I don't have an excuse. I blew it. I'm also sorry I called you names and stormed out when you were trying to explain yourself. Deep down I knew that I would hurt you, and I'm really sorry that I hurt you. That was wrong too. It makes me feel sick that I caused you all that work. I feel so irresponsible, and I'm really ashamed of myself.

"I see by your tears that I have really hurt you badly. When I wound you deeply, you seem to draw inside a protective shell. I know you were counting on my depositing the money in the checking account. You must be very disappointed with me. I also know that I wasted your time, which made you stressed and angry. I know I didn't respect your time. I always want to value you. I'm sorry I acted so irresponsibly. I didn't treat you with the honor that you deserve.

"Is there anything I can do to make up for what I've done? (George waits and then deals with Gwyn's answer.)

"I am going to do my best to always deposit my check on the way home from work. I also don't ever want to get so angry with you and with myself that I storm out without resolving things.

"Honey, can you forgive me for insulting you and for not being considerate? I'm so sorry. I don't deserve it, but can you forgive me for not respecting your time and then—to make it worse—storming out?

"Would it help you to forgive me to know what was going on with me?"

COSTLY CONTRITION

In naming the parts of a good CONFESSion, I mentioned apology (O = offer an apology) and restitution (E = equalize). These are crucial steps to promoting forgiveness. Because they are so important, I wanted to give them special attention.

We asked students at VCU, our large state university, to imagine that they had returned to their apartment and found they had been robbed.[6] This was not much of a stretch because about one-third of the students reported that they actually had been robbed in recent years. They were told to imagine that money, identification cards, credit cards and some personal effects had been taken. We assessed their reactions using questionnaires. They were usually highly unforgiving toward the thief.

Then we asked the students to imagine that they received either a weak apology ("I'm sorry I took your stuff; I feel bad"), restitution (all materials returned plus some extra money for the anguish caused by the robbery), both, or neither (a note from the police saying no progress had been made on the investigation).

Students who were informed that no progress was made were equally unforgiving as they had been the day before. Students who received the weak apology divided into two types of reactions. Some granted a little forgiveness, but others got furious. "He's messing with my mind; he's not really sorry," some wrote. "He's taunting me," others wrote. The net result, with some people granting a little forgiveness and others becoming even more unforgiving, was that the average forgiveness score across the whole group who heard the weak apology did not change. When people got restitution, though, they reduced their unforgiveness and granted some forgiveness. Those who got both restitution and a weak apology forgave at about the same rate as those who got only the restitution.

We did the study again, but this time, we had the offender send a note that was positively groveling. The thief went on and on, for about a half page, about how very sorry he was and how bad he felt. That produced a lot of forgiveness in the students—about the same amount of forgiveness as did the restitution. When the strong apology and restitution were both received, the students were highly forgiving.

We did the study a third time, again with the strong apology. This time, we did it in the laboratory run by Charlotte Witvliet at Hope College, a Christian college in Michigan. Charlotte wired the students to instruments that assessed stressfulness (blood pressure, heart rate and sweat) and tension in their facial muscles. Even though almost all of the students there were Christians, the students at Hope College answered the questions very much like the students at VCU, where only around half reported being

Christians. The measures of the students' physiological responses were right in line with their questionnaire responses. Apology (in its sincere, strong form) and fair restitution brought a sense of personal justice into the situation. The injustice gap was reduced. We hypothesized that emotional forgiveness in such a case would be easier to experience. That is exactly what happened. Note that when we assessed students' physical responses, we were actually measuring their emotional forgiveness—not merely decisions to forgive. Apology and restitution actually helped people forgive from the heart. If a wrongdoer is willing to repent, sincerely apologize and make fair restitution for his or her misdeeds, then emotional forgiveness can be stimulated in people who would never otherwise forgive.

COSTLY CONFESSION

Carl Stauffer, a missionary and peace worker in South Africa, passed along a story to me. He had a friend, Elon, now deceased. Elon was a Jewish Christian living in Tel Aviv. One night, he was driving through a Palestinian area. A young deaf child in a Muslim settlement ran out in front of his car. Elon hit the child, and from the impact it was clear that the child was either dead or gravely injured.

This was a volatile area of Palestine. The common wisdom was, if something like this occurs, never, *never* stop the car. Keep driving. The friends and family of the victim will exact swift and brutal justice.

But Elon couldn't just drive away. His Christian beliefs wouldn't permit that. So he got out and tearfully waited for the village to gather to the child, who indeed had died. The Muslim villagers were shocked and grief-stricken. But they were also amazed that anyone would stop. They were so amazed that they did not seek immediate justice. They told Elon to return to the village on a given date to face a Muslim court. This was a huge act of mercy because no one in that village thought Elon would return. Effectively, they were granting mercy, but they were also saving face by insisting that justice was to be served.

As the court date drew near, Elon consulted people about what he should do. If he returned, he almost certainly would be sentenced to death. His friends all agreed. He should accept the merciful release for the gift it was and thank the Lord for it.

But Elon was uneasy. He felt that the Lord was telling him to return for the trial. So he went.

Again the villagers were astonished. Yet justice had to be served. And it was. The trial proceeded, and finally the judge rendered the verdict: Guilty of manslaughter. On trembling knees, Elon awaited the sentence. He was sentenced to be adopted by the dead child's family. Every time he passed through the village, he had to visit them and eat with them.

What a story of reconciliation! In that troubled land, a Jew by birth, adopted into Jesus' family, also became an adopted Muslim. Elon was a one-man reconciliation exemplar. Justice, forgiveness and reconciliation all met.

How to Buy a Little Time

After one person makes the good CONFESSion, the ball bounces to the other side of the net. The other person will be forced to at least consider forgiving. Forgiveness is a gift. It is not required. A grudging, surly "Sure I forgive you" with all the nonverbal signs of hatred will weaken, not strengthen, trust.

Emotional forgiveness is not to be rushed into. If we are the offended party and we feel forgiveness, we would be wise to cut loose and express it. But both people should expect emotional forgiveness to take time. In our studies of forgiving, we found that every event is different. Sometimes we forgive shocking injustices in minutes or hours. Sometimes we nurse a grudge about the tiniest slight for years. But on the average, the longer we spend thinking empathically about the hurt, the more forgiveness we feel. When a friend stretches out her hand with a sincere request for forgiveness, we might rush up the Pyramid to REACH Forgiveness. But most of the time we will need time to walk more deliberately up the steps.

That creates a problem. When a person has made a good CONFESSion, the person has made himself or herself vulnerable. If we do not empathically respect that vulnerability, we can derail the rebuilding of trust.

If we can grant decisional forgiveness truthfully and sincerely, we should do that immediately. We can say, "I forgive you, and I give up any motives for revenge or plans to avoid you." But chances are we will want to add, "It might take my heart longer to change. I still feel upset."

Then we might make sure our partner knows that we respect his or her vulnerability in making a good CONFESSion. To do this, we might say, "I appreciate your admitting that you know you did wrong. It means a lot to me. I know how hard it is for me to say that I made a mistake, so I appreciate your sincere words and feelings. I want us to get past this event. I want to be able to forgive you. Even now I do feel *some* forgiveness because I can see what you have gone through. I know the cost of confessing. For complete heartfelt forgiveness, though, it's going to take me some time. I'm trying hard to empathize and forgive, but it might take me a while. Can you accept my appreciation for your apology and my promise that I won't retaliate—but give me some time to work through the hard feelings of forgiving?"

When we're alone, we can walk in a more leisurely way up the Pyramid. We can recall the hurt objectively, empathize with the person, consider times when we have been forgiven, and perhaps grant the altruistic gift of forgiveness as we appreciate how much we ourselves have been forgiven by God and by others.

If we've been asked for forgiveness, our public commitment to forgive (remember the C step of REACH) can be to tell the person that we have forgiven him or her. We might say, "Last week you asked if I could forgive you for forgetting to come to my retirement party. I appreciated your willingness to ask. I know that was hard. All week I thought about it. I do feel complete forgiveness. I wish I could have expressed it to you before now. Thank you for being willing to patch up our relationship."

In the same way that there is nothing magical about the mere words "I'm sorry," there is also nothing magical about the mere words "I forgive you." What we say is always qualified by how we say it and by the situation.

God found some sacrifices unacceptable because people's hearts were not soft toward him (Ps 51:17; Mt 9:13). In the same way, if we say "I forgive you," but our heart says "I hate you," then merely saying the words is not likely to be effective.

Sometimes people use "I forgive you" as a way to stop conversation and make the other person feel guilty. They fold their arms, scowl and mumble, "I forgive you."

Not surprisingly, when we are on the receiving end of such a communication, we don't feel forgiven. Yet if we say that, then the person will say, "Why can't you let this drop? Why can't you take what I say at face value?" We are shamed by our attempts to reconcile, and we feel that the conversation has been cut off. We have been put in a double bind.

In this case, we must be careful not to accuse the person of negative intentions. Assume (whether you think it's true or not) that he or she wants to repair the relationship. Say, "I see that you care about our friendship. Thank you for forgiving me." By accepting forgiveness as genuine, you allow healing to progress.

If you simply must confront the mixed message, say, "You say that you forgive me. But your face and body language seem to give me a different message. Chances are, I'm misreading your expression. I needed to check—for my peace of mind. I want to understand you. Can you help?"

FORGIVING LEADS TO RECONCILING

When people forgive, it often helps promote reconciliation. In South Africa's Truth and Reconciliation amnesty hearings, two men applied for amnesty for the murder of a local chief. The chief was a despot, favorable to (and favored by) the apartheid regime. He had many tribesmen killed for petty reasons. The two men kidnapped and later murdered the chief. The amnesty hearings occasioned much public attention. As testimonies were winding down, one of the commissioners asked, "Does anyone else want to testify?"

A young man raised his hand. Immediately the room was abuzz with whispers. It was the chief's son. The potential for destruction of the reconciliation process was great. What if he denounced the hearing? What if he called for revolt against the process? The commissioners, committed to hearing the truth, allowed the young man to speak.

He addressed the murderers, saying something like this: "When these hearings began, I wanted to see you both dead. But as I have heard about the horrible things that our father did to our people, I have changed. I wonder whether you could see it in your heart to forgive us on behalf of what our father did? And also, if you would like to ask for our forgiveness for murdering our father, we would be glad to grant it." Instead of the violence that could have occurred if the young man had incited hate, reconciliation within the tribe (and within South Africa) was furthered.

Forgiveness is like the sound of a waterfall midway through a long hike through the arid mountains. The hiking—placing one foot after another, sweating, straining, thirsting—gives way to a splashing, cool waterfall. Yes, there might still be a long hike to come, but forgiveness lets us look forward to the top, not down at the dusty trail.

Reconciliation is finally soaking your feet in the pool on top of the mountain. It is drinking cool, clear water, eating a sweet, juicy apple and enjoying the view.

Forgiveness can help promote reconciliation because it softens attitudes. This is especially true if mutual forgiveness occurs.

SOFT TALK AND HARD ACTS OF RECONCILIATION

To promote reconciliation, we need soft talk about the transgression. To move beyond the Pyramid to REACH Forgiveness, people need to come to three agreements. They need not spell out every word, but they must reach tacit agreement.

Can we agree to focus on changing our own behavior, not the other person's? Reconciliation is restoring trust through mutually trustworthy behavior. We naturally want to hold the other person accountable for his or her behavior. A desire for justice and fairness is built into our character as part of having been created in God's image. Besides that, though, the other person's mistakes are easy to see and, almost, easier to point out. Failures in trustworthiness are taken as evidence that the other person is either unwilling or unable to act trustworthily.

Yet focusing on the other person's behavior won't further reconciliation as fast or as well as focusing on being trustworthy ourselves. Of course, that's the hard part. I know that I try hard yet often fall flat. I cut myself some slack when I blow it. I need to cut the other person some slack too. Even more, I need to focus on my own behavior.

When I say that we naturally focus on the other person's negative acts, I am speaking of the way we secretly feel about the cause of our relational woes. Some people are very direct with their blame. They criticize. They vocalize. They cut the other person down to size. They are ulcer givers.

But other people feel victimized, and that feeling focuses their attention on their own failures and inadequacies. They are ulcer getters. When I recommend that we focus on our own behavior, I do not mean focus on our inadequacies. I mean focus on *changing* our behavior.

Both parties need to explicitly and implicitly agree that they will try to act trustworthily. Each needs to focus on himself or herself, not on keeping score for the other person.

Can we agree on a truce? If reconciliation is to take place, hostilities must cease. We should explicitly agree on a truce. A truce has two parts. One part is not acting in a hostile way toward the other person. The other part is overlooking the other person's minor violations of the truce.

Let's illustrate a truce from a Chinese-American family in which an adolescent daughter was at war with her father. Monica bridled against her father's strict control. "My father is still living as if he was in Taiwan," she told her friends. "He's been in the United States more than twenty years but can't make the adjustment." She was upset because Mr. Han had grounded her for the third time in one semester.

She complained also to her mother: "It's not like I'm into drugs or sex. I just missed a curfew, that's all! He interprets everything I do as dishonoring him. He's driving me to dishonor him even more."

Monica's mother became the truce broker. She talked privately with her husband and convinced him to listen to Monica while trying to refrain from correcting her. Their talk led to a truce. Mr. Han agreed to be slower to use grounding as a punishment if Monica would try exceptionally hard to show honor to her father and not disrespect him. Mrs. Han assumed the role of recognizing and commenting on Monica's attempts to honor her father and on Mr. Han's instances of conscious restraint. The truce allowed the hostilities to cool down.

In another example, after Stanley and Steven had a disagreement at work, their supervisor called both into her office and encouraged them to reconcile. Neither felt conciliatory, but they agreed to a truce and, specifically, to try to overlook minor provocations by the other. That agreement restored some peace within the office.

Putting the two parts of the truce together involves not acting in a hostile way and overlooking minor truce violations. For example, if Irish Protestants and Catholics sign a truce and then a young Catholic child throws rocks at a Protestant child, that isn't severe enough to invalidate the truce. In the same way, partners must agree to overlook small violations of the truce. Give the other person the benefit of the doubt.

Can we agree on a plan to restore the relationship? Stopping hostilities is not the same thing as rebuilding the relationship. If trust has been damaged, trust must be rebuilt. First, stop the slide downhill. If a relationship is tumbling downhill at dizzying speed and partners put on the brakes, they can't expect an instant turnaround. At first the slide downhill will slow, then stop. Briefly, it is motionless. Then the wheels begin to move, perhaps slipping a bit at first. At last they catch and the relationship moves uphill.

As we restore a relationship, we must be realistic. Despite our best intentions, we will almost certainly at times fail to maintain a truce. We will fail to progress toward reconciliation. We must therefore make a plan of how to deal with failure.

It's easy to lose hope when we don't see progress occurring. Hang in there. If both people stay positive, the relationship will change. Trust will grow.

Besides arresting the downward descent, starting the relationship back uphill and making a plan for dealing with failure, partners need to at least begin to rebuild a positive relationship by detoxifying the relationship and building devotion. These steps are the last planks of the Bridge of Reconciliation.

DISCUSSION QUESTIONS

1. Explain what Rosalie Gerut's One by One organization is. How do the hurts you've experienced throughout your life compare to those experienced by people in the One by One group?

2. Give the wording you might use to make a gentle reproach to a loved one who forgot your birthday. When should such a reproach be made? When would you not want to make such a reproach?

3. What do each of the letters of CONFESS stand for? Apply them to a particular incident. The group might set up a hypothetical situation in which an offense occurs. Can each person construct a CONFESSion that would use the CONFESS model? Several people might want to read theirs, or someone might want to role play with another group member playing the offended or hurt person.

4. When you have done something wrong, when (if ever) is it useful to tell the other person about any pressures or circumstances that affected you?

5. Just because a person asks you to forgive, do you need to forgive? If the person asks you to forgive, is the person asking for decisional forgiveness or emotional forgiveness? If you grant decisional forgiveness, do you have the right to sulk or to hold it over the other person's head? Do you have the right to expect accountability from the person who harmed you? What does it mean that you have forgiven? If you forgive, is mention of the transgression totally off limits under all circumstances forever?

6. When both people have committed transgressions, what is your responsibility in reconciling the relationship? Who should initiate the reconciliation? Whose behavior should you focus on—yours or the other person's?

11

Detoxification

*Forgiveness, as an act of love, is felt, not achieved. It can be given, but it may
not always be received. It cannot be bestowed as either a triumph over
another person, or as the means to secure their humiliation or acquiescence.
It is most healing, most profound when it grows out of humility and
realism, a hard-won sense that, whether you are entirely to blame in
these events and I am blameless, there is in each of us insufficiencies and
imperfections that can be our greatest teachers.*

STEPHANIE DOURICK

It was a beautiful gold pocket watch, passed down three generations.
When the top was clicked open, the face still gleamed white with black numerals. The problem with the watch, from Hans's point of view, was that
it rested on Johann's mantel.

The watch was more a symbol of the Kruger family history than it was
a valuable timepiece. Both Hans and Johann recalled many hours when
their grandfather had told stories about coming to the United States with
only that watch in his pocket. When Grandfather passed away, the stories
were retold by Hans and Johann's father. Now he too had passed away.

Hans, the older brother, by rights should have had that watch. He was
in line to inherit it, and the fact that his father had not mentioned the
watch in the will was irrelevant. Johann shouldn't have gotten the watch.
Yet Johann had anticipated the uncertainty and had gone into the house at
night, before his father was even buried, and had taken the watch. Now
the watch mocked Hans from Johann's mantel.

After the funeral, the brothers had argued bitterly about the watch.
They shouted. They swore. Hans went to Johann's house that night and

continued the argument. When Johann asked Hans to leave, Hans slipped the watch into his pocket and walked out with it. Before he got out of the driveway, Johann gave chase. But Hans sped off. Johann called the police and reported Hans had stolen the watch. The police came to Hans's house, arrested him and took him to the police station. Hans returned the watch with the understanding that Johann wouldn't prosecute him.

The War of the Watch was not over. Hans threatened to take the matter to court. He vowed to press his claim as the rightful owner of the watch and charge Johann with violating the estate prior to probate.

As the lawyer fees mounted, Johann and Hans became angrier and more bitter. The cost became so oppressive that Hans dropped the suit rather than continue to pour money into legal fees.

An uncomfortable truce settled in. For twenty years neither brother visited the other. Neither acknowledged the other's existence. Although they lived less than two miles from each other, they never spoke. When they met in the neighborhood or at the local supermarket, they simply walked past each other.

WALKING THE BRIDGE TO RECONCILIATION

Maybe the uneasy truce in the War of the Watch would have lasted for the rest of their lives had not their children met in college. As amazing as it seems, two cousins living two miles apart had never met before they had a course together in the large state university. Annamarie had heard her father Johann talk many times about Hans's theft of the watch from their mantel. Fred had heard often about Johann's nighttime raid before their father's body was laid to rest. Never having met, Annamarie and Fred were not as emotionally invested in the conflict as were their fathers. They struck up a conversation and became fast friends during the semester.

When Annamarie brought up her budding friendship with Fred, Johann forbade her from seeing Fred any more. Annamarie wanted to honor her father, but Fred sat near her in class. They continued to talk. Perhaps Annamarie was going through a rebellious time, or perhaps she simply did not want to carry on the family feud. For whatever reason, Fred and she became even closer. Near the end of the semester, Annamarie talked with her father again. She was forthright in admitting that she had continued to talk with Fred. At first Johann was furious. As she talked more about Fred's positive qualities, though, Johann grudgingly admitted that he seemed to share some of Hans's good traits.

Shortly after that, Hans bumped into Johann as they both stood in line to renew their driver's licenses. Both felt trapped, but waiting in long lines seems part of the shared experience of modern humanity. Johann mentioned the class that Annamarie and Fred shared. To his surprise, Hans responded. It was their first talk in twenty years. Both avoided any reference to the War of the Watch.

As they neared the front of the line, one of the brothers mentioned that they had waited for a long time. The mere mention of time triggered bad memories. Their conversation petered out after some harsh words, then lapsed into silence.

That night when Johann described the incident to his wife, Johann recounted several criticisms that Hans had levied against him. Johann's daughter Annamarie overheard and asked Johann directly whether the criticisms were true. Johann pondered the question longer than he had intended and hesitatingly admitted that there was some truth to some of them. Admitting that to his daughter made him reconsider things he had said against Hans. He wasn't proud of his constant criticism. So he determined to stop criticizing Hans so much to his family. For several weeks, he did not make a critical statement, despite Annamarie's continuing to talk about her friendship with Fred.

Johann wanted the War to be over. On an impulse one night, he called Hans and asked if they could get together on neutral ground. They met for dinner at a local steakhouse. To Johann's surprise, they had a pleasant time during the evening. Two weeks later, Hans called Johann to arrange lunch. Their second meeting again turned out fine, and their boyhood friendship began to be rekindled.

Johann decided to take the plunge. He invited Hans to his home for dinner. Hans accepted. The evening went well until, near the end, Hans insulted Johann. Every family member waited for the explosion. Johann, after a pause, continued the conversation as if the insult had not happened. Everyone exhaled.

Over time Johann and Hans met regularly. Their relationship grew strong again. But Johann still had the watch.

Three years after the relationship between Johann and Hans began to mend, Fred graduated from college. Johann and Annamarie together gave him a graduation present—the watch.

Fred was flabbergasted. He turned to Annamarie, and she said, "Dad and I did this together. I have no use for a pocket watch, and we thought it should be passed to a man within our family." She reached inside the collar of her blouse and looped her finger around the chain that had always hung from the watch, now made into a necklace. "Now we both have a memento of our heritage," she said.

Hans and Johann stood by, watching the reconciliation of the families. Johann faced Hans and said, "Brother, I was wrong ever to have taken the watch from the house. Can you ever forgive me?"

They hugged. "No problem. It wasn't all one-sided," said Hans. "I tried to steal it back, and that was wrong, too. Can you forgive me?"

"Long ago," said Johann and gave Hans another big bear hug.

THE FINAL PLANKS IN THE BRIDGE TO RECONCILIATION

If you've considered whether, how and when to reconcile (plank one, decisions) and talked with each other about the transgressions (plank two, discussion), then the hard work of restoration of the relationship has begun in earnest.

Now you have to step on two more planks. You must reverse the downhill slide and remove the poison from the relationship (plank three, detoxification), and you must try to rebuild love (plank four, devotion). I'll discuss detoxification in the present chapter and devotion in the final chapter. First, let's tackle the hard job: looking honestly into the mirror, not just to see our acts, as we have done before, but to see into our hearts.

FOLLOWING THE HARD WAY

When treasured trust has been violated and bad blood exists between us and other person, we usually want to restore trust if we can. We long to detoxify that bad blood. If only we could run the bad blood of both parties through relationship dialysis! If only we could remove the vile poisons from our interactions! Unfortunately, it's not just the poison in the other person's heart, or even the poison in our relationship, that needs detoxification. Sometimes there's poison in our own soul as well.

I lived my first twenty-two years in the house where my mother was later murdered. After I left home, I visited several times a year. When my children were in high school, we walked the roads I had walked when I was growing up, and I shared memories of boyhood adventures.

After the murder, I went back to the house several times that first week. We toured the house with police officers. They were trying to learn what might have been stolen during the burglary. We entered through the back door. The broken windowpane, which had been used for the initial entry, was boarded shut. Secure, but too late.

Stepping through the back door into the kitchen, I felt that I had been transported into the remnant of an earthquake. The toaster had been thrown through the microwave. The refrigerator had been pulled away from the wall. Black fingerprint dust smeared its front and side. Palm prints stood out, smudged with dust. Debris was scattered across the kitchen. We tiptoed between cracked dishes and canisters sitting askew on cones of flour. The search for valuables had been as violent as it was violating.

As I stepped into the hallway, I looked down the hall at the blood-spattered walls and the gray carpet. My eyes were drawn to two pools of still-gooey blood at the end of the hall near the bedroom door. Each pool was the size of a kitchen plate. One was where Mama's head would have lain. The other, where her hips would have rested.

As I looked at those pools of blood, I thought, *At least she couldn't have suffered long. She doesn't seem to have bled much before her heart stopped beating.* That was something of a comfort.

To get to every room in the main part of the house, we had to keep walking through the hallway. Each step back in the hall assaulted me with images of blood. Each assault was a shot in the gut.

I left with the scene of violence burned into my brain. In our culture, we have almost become numb to violence. We watch murders on television. We plunk down money to see slasher movies. We read novels about bloody killings without batting an eye. We see violence on the news.

I had been involved in a little violence myself. In junior high school, I blundered into the bathroom as a gang fight broke out. I saw a boy whipped with a chain while a gang stood around, threatening those of us who were bystanders.

I was playing basketball as a junior in high school when an opposing player suddenly threw the ball down and came after me, swinging his fists. I took a blow to the mouth. The ring on his finger cut my lip and cut my trumpet playing days short at the same time. I wasn't a stranger to violence.

Yet seeing the inside of Mom's house destroyed was a slam to the head. Seeing the dark blood of my mother, who poured out her life raising me, pooled on the carpet snapped my eyes wide open. The police officer said that only a few dollars in loose change seemed to be missing. That was another slap. The tragedy and the waste associated with violence hit home.

Later that week, I went back into our old house to meet the claims adjusters. While we talked amid the carnage, two men arrived. "We're here to replace the damaged carpet," said one. They sliced through the carpet about one yard from each side of the center of the two bloodstains. They tugged the carpet away from the floor. Underneath, there was a pool of sticky gore that was at least one yard in diameter.

I could feel my legs get shaky. The fragile illusion that I had held all week—that my mother had not suffered after being bludgeoned—was ripped away with the carpet.

She must have lain there a long time as her heart pumped her life's blood into those pools that ran underneath the carpet, I thought. The ugliness beneath was far wider than what showed on the surface of the carpet.

I thought that unforgiveness might rear up in me again. Instead I felt only a huge sense of sorrow for my mom's suffering. Strangely, I felt a new wave of compassion for the youth who committed the murder. It was clear that he needed forgiveness even more than I had originally thought. In my soul, I could only cry out to God. I hoped that he might have mercifully spared my mother consciousness. I prayed for mercy on her murderer. The guilt of what he had done must be torturing him.

DETOXIFYING THE SOUL

Seeing the blood beneath the carpet was one of the strongest, most persistent mental images that I've ever had. Since that day, I have thought even more about forgiveness than ever before. Standing eye to eye with the horror, ugliness and waste of murder changed me. I knew experientially how low we humans can descend. I also knew experientially how much we need forgiveness.

I have often spoken publicly about my mother's death. People have asked many times, "How can you possibly forgive?" Some people have suggested that somehow I must have some special courage or character trait that helped me forgive.

I don't think so. I know my own heart. I know the struggles that I have gone through trying to forgive. I don't always succeed. In fact, I fail too often. I hold unforgiveness too long.

Students once hurt me by giving me low teacher ratings. I struggled for months to forgive them. In my reflection I had to admit that whether I received super teacher ratings from every class was not very important in life's priorities. Faculty members have criticized some of my actions as chair of the department of psychology. I struggled for months to forgive them. A professional colleague criticized my character. I struggled for over a year to forgive him. I have experienced rejections, betrayals and slights, just as we all have. I have held onto some grudges for years.

Yet here is the miracle. When I had to forgive the horrible, hard-to-forgive murder of my mother, I did it within a day.

I am sad to say, from the point of view of my self-esteem, it was not positive character that let me forgive quickly. In many ways, being able to forgive is a gift and a mercy from our precious Lord, which we do not deserve or work to earn. Sometimes we forgive because we initiate forgiveness. Sometimes we forgive because it seems to happen to us. Sadly, sometimes we struggle and cannot forgive emotionally, even if we can grant decisional forgiveness.

I knew my character flaws and was all too aware of some of the petty unforgiveness that was beneath the surface. I saw the yuck in my own heart that others cannot always see. My acts were similar to the blood *on* the carpet. My soul was like the blood *beneath* the carpet.

The toxic waste in our own soul can be far greater than what others can see. Yet—and this is the hard news—it is that unseen toxicity that needs to be cleaned out before we can detoxify our relationships. Before I can begin to detoxify the unforgiveness within, I must be willing to admit that I am unforgiving. I have to look at my heart squarely and admit that I have a heart disease. I need to forgive myself from my heart.

Getting forgiveness from God. But forgiving myself, if I am still unforgiven before God, is not a solution to my problems. I make things worse by convincing myself that I don't need to confess and seek God's merciful forgiveness.

So before I try to forgive myself, I must confess my sin to the Lord. I know that "if we confess our sins, he is faithful and just and will forgive us our sins and purify us from all unrighteousness" (1 Jn 1:9). The unrighteousness that God forgives can be of two types. In one, a person's relationship with God has not been redeemed by Jesus' saving work on the cross. By accepting Jesus' salvation, the person is forgiven of all sins by God (Jer 31:31, 33-34; Ezek 16:60-63; Lk 24:46-47; Acts 2:38; Col 2:13; 3:13). That makes the person a Christian believer. However, even Christians commit sins (1 Jn 1:8, 10). Those are dealt with through bringing them directly to Jesus, whose blood covers the individual sins we commit (1 Jn 1:7). That divine forgiveness is the second type of purification from unrighteousness.

Forgiving myself decisionally. After receiving forgiveness from God, though, we often still don't forgive ourselves. We can realize that divine forgiveness has been granted, which is the equivalent of receiving divine decisional forgiveness. God grants us forgiveness. However, we may emotionally still *feel* unforgiven because we condemn ourselves. Telling ourselves that we should not feel unforgiven might help some people, but not others. Telling ourselves that we need simply to appropriate the forgiveness God has granted might work for some, but not others. Reminding ourselves of Scriptures that tell us we have been forgiven if we have confessed to God (1 Jn 1:9) might help some of us, but not others. We need to forgive ourselves. (That adds nothing to our divine forgiveness, but it deals with our self-condemning thoughts and feelings about ourselves.)

Some people simply cannot let go of their self-condemnation. Let's say that I do something I think is horrible. Suppose I lose my temper and yell at my administrative assistant. I then feel guilty and ashamed. I pray and confess the sinful act, read Scripture that assures me that God forgives me, and have friends tell me that I am forgiven, but I still feel terrible. I need to forgive myself, which is the equivalent to emotional forgiveness.

We do not have to forgive ourselves *before* we can forgive a transgressor. Yet for the sake of our mental well-being, we should forgive ourselves *as well as* forgiving our transgressor if it is going to make much difference in our lives, relationships or communities. Self-condemnation not only can make us miserable but also can make it more difficult to restore our relationships.

We underestimate how hard it is to forgive ourselves. Three reasons make self-forgiveness especially hard. First, it's hard to admit that we've done wrong. I prefer to think of myself as someone who "makes mistakes" or "means well" or "isn't perfect." Second, I do not like to think that I could plan to do wrong intentionally. I don't like to admit to negative motives.

Third, to forgive myself, I am in two roles at the same time. I am the victim; I realize that my sinful act damaged me at the core of my being. But I am also the transgressor; I did the sinful act. That dual role makes self-forgiveness complicated.

I can simply grant forgiveness to myself (as transgressor), which is decisional forgiveness. I can thus say that I won't try to make myself feel bad or won't continue to punish myself for my transgression. That decisional self-forgiveness doesn't change my negative unforgiving emotions arising from my self-condemnation.

Forgiving myself emotionally. Forgiving my own transgressions is little different than forgiving someone else's. I can employ the REACH steps. For example, in the case of yelling at my administrative assistant, I should first recall (R) the incident vividly. Importantly, I should spend substantial time empathizing (E) with myself. Why did I lose my temper? I was under a lot of stress. My boss was pressing for a project immediately. I had been criticized by two colleagues earlier that morning. I got a speeding ticket the day before. My administrative assistant was particularly annoying. He refused to do a job I had assigned to him, and when I returned from a meeting, he was on the computer playing solitaire. If I look deep within myself, I can see that I was not only reacting to his insolence but I was envious of his relaxing while I was working. Deep down, I probably wanted to punish him for being relaxed. That is an ugly motive that I do not like to admit, but if I can see how my envy developed, I can perhaps forgive those darker motives.

By empathizing with myself, I treat myself with the same respect I treat others. That might help me move through the A, C and H steps of REACH and forgive myself for losing my temper.

When I get there, I usually think, *Ah, I've forgiven myself. I'm glad that's done.*

But usually it isn't done. I still feel self-condemnation.

What's left? As it turns out, forgiving our acts, and even our motives, is only part of forgiving ourselves. The harder part—the part we usually fail to consider—is that we cannot forgive ourselves for being the type of person who could do the evil. We can forgive our *acts*. We often cannot forgive our own *character*.

So I admit to myself: I did yell at my assistant. I did act out of envy. I have forgiven that behavior and that motive. But I don't forgive myself for being the type of person who would do those things. My acts and motives were not consistent with my self-image. Forgiving myself for tarnishing my self-image is difficult. How can I do that?

Self-acceptance. To forgive ourselves, we need to be forgiven. We need to find out that we are forgivable—that we are acceptable even with a crooked halo. Someone from outside of us needs to be able to forgive us. The kind of self-forgiveness that we can generate in ourselves by thinking that we must be forgivable is usually not enough to cleanse us. It can remove some spots but does not do deep cleaning.

For some people, we're all that we have. Others have a loved one who can help us believe we're forgivable and thus help us forgive ourselves. That loved one can help us admit the weaknesses of our character. He or she can encourage us to grant merciful forgiveness for what we did, and even more, for who we are. We know that we can always turn to God for forgiveness. Divine forgiveness can help us forgive and accept ourselves.

If you need divine forgiveness, seek it. If you are struggling with self-condemnation, can you find someone you trust enough to talk with? Even if you can find no listening ear, you can pray, and you can write to yourself in a journal. By talking about your painful character flaws with a trusted friend, God or your journal, you are taking a big step, equivalent to the R and E steps, toward REACHing forgiveness of yourself for your own character weaknesses.

As you see, forgiving yourself is not easy. Accepting your own imperfections might be even harder. Sometimes people struggle for years in psychotherapy to forgive and accept themselves. It can be a lifetime work. We all are imperfect and knock our halos askew regularly. Sometimes we seem to throw them in the mud and grind them beneath our heels. The hard truth is that we must pick up the dirty halo and squarely look at the mud. The halo won't spontaneously clean itself. We must courageously face our character under the gentle yet truthful guidance of the Holy Spirit.

When we're over the hump and have begun to forgive ourselves, or perhaps while we are still struggling to forgive and accept ourselves, we cannot remain still. We must act if we are to rescue a relationship that is plunging downhill. We must reverse the negative slide.

RELATIONSHIP RUPTURE

Unforgiveness is being trapped in a sudden squall—buffeted, battered and beaten. It is fearing that you will never escape or that you will escape only to find yourself headed for the rocks, angry and resentful at the storm, bitter at your luck.

Suddenly, as abruptly as the squall began, it passes. You sail into sunshine. You forgive. Of course, there is damage still to repair—flapping sails to secure, water to pump from the bilge, loose sheets, wet charts, a malfunctioning guidance system and a wrecked radio. It isn't going to be easy to get home to safety and security. But the stark difference between squall and sunshine gives hope. And hope makes all the difference.

John Gottman, a psychologist at the University of Washington in Seattle, has studied marriages for over thirty years.[1] He has shown that when marriages deteriorate, they usually do so in four predictable steps. I have found those steps to be just as true for friendships, work relationships and parent-child relationships as for marriage.

The first step involves criticism. At first, people criticize each other in their mind. Then the criticism becomes verbal. Second, defensiveness appears as the person hears the criticisms. The defensiveness is initially mental, but over time it becomes verbal. Criticism plus defensiveness equal arguments. The third step in relationship rupture is contempt. With contempt, the person changes the view of the relationship. Whereas criticism and defensiveness both tend to be specific to acts and qualities of the other person, contempt is directed to the person himself or herself. In the fourth stage of relationship rupture, couples can either stonewall or enter into war. A person who has been hurt many times does not wish to be hurt again. To avoid being hurt, some people turn their hearts into stone walls. As Simon and Garfunkel said, "A rock feels no pain." Each person's attitude is, "You can't get to me. Whatever you say will bounce off just as if it had struck a stone wall." For others, pain is made tolerable by hurting the other person; war erupts.

Straws and camels' backs. A direct connection seems to exist between being positive and feeling happy with the relationship. Gottman found, however, that as he observed married couples precisely, dramatic differences in their relationship were likely, depending on a couple's ratio of positive to negative interactions. If one couple had ten, seven or even five times as many positive interactions as negative, they were usually happy. But when couples had a ratio of positive to negative interactions below five, it usually was not four-to-one. Instead it was one-to-one or one-to-two.

At five-to-one, an abrupt transformation occurred, as if a rope had snapped. People above the five-to-one break generally saw the relationship positively. People below the break saw mostly the negative.

When good families or friendships turn sour, they usually erode slowly (like marriages). In a relationship on the edge, one negative event can push the people over the threshold to a negative, pain-filled relationship. The straw breaks the camel's back. It's as if the two people whip off their rose-colored glasses and slam on dark glasses. Through those, they can see only the negative in each other and the relationship. They develop contempt for the other *person*, not just the other person's behavior. The relationship is in serious trouble and can quickly degenerate to where each person divorces himself or herself from feelings or turns himself or herself into a stone wall. Only a dramatic turnaround can prevent a rupture.

In a positive relationship, people might be unforgiving toward each other, although usually small hurts are either forgiven, quickly forgotten or forborne. But if the relationship slides into troubled waters, partners find that it becomes harder to overlook the negative. They ruminate about the negative. Rumination is, of course, at the core of unforgiveness. The relationship fills with resentment, bitterness and perhaps even hatred.

Reconciliation requires detoxification. When a relationship has gone bad, usually increasing doses of poison have been injected through toxic interactions. Finally, toxins make the relationship sick.

To reconcile, we must reverse the buildup of relationship poison as we climb from stonewalling (or war) to contempt to defensiveness to criticism. We must move further so that infrequent criticism again is the norm. At some point, as we forgive and claw our way, inch by inch, out of our relationship sickness, a sudden transformation usually occurs. One day the relationship looks rocky; the next, the way is paved. We find our rose-colored glasses. They may have some smudges on the lenses, but they let in a lot more light than the dark glasses.

When we are reconciling, we must assess our relationship to determine whether it has deteriorated through those four stages that Gottman identified. If so, we need to detoxify our communication to move it to a higher stage. While we would all prefer instant, total relationship detoxification, usually we must settle for moving back up the cascade step by step.

Move from stonewalling or war back to contempt. For example, if we have gotten to the stage of stonewalling, in which we have deadened our feelings toward the other person, then we must try to recover our feelings. We must decide whether to risk having a serious discussion with each other or someone else about the relationship. If so, we commit ourselves not to hurt the other person during the discussion. We can adopt a cease-fire, even if we are at war, and try to have a discussion. If we're successful, we can at least get back into contact with each other.

Obviously we must protect ourselves from harm during a discussion. We know that if we do not do anything differently, the relationship poison will move past stonewalling or war to death of the relationship.

To detoxify, it's helpful to consider what will be lost if the relationship crumbles. Will parents lose contact with children? Will long-married couples lose years of positive shared memories? Will business partners lose financial stability? Will friends lose pleasant relations with each other? The goal for each person should be to re-engage.

By feeling again, we take a risk. We risk being hurt. But by risking, we may find our relationship restored.

We might get angry with each other, feel pain, feel frustration. Of course, no one likes to feel those negative feelings. Despite this, if we're attempting to scale stonewalling hearts, then feeling anger and pain is actually a positive step. Pain indicates that we still have some feeling for each other.

Rudy and Dorrie sat in my counseling office. Their closed postures reflected their closed hearts toward each other. Beginning the eight weeks of counseling they had agreed to, they weren't interested in repairing their marriage. They were looking for a validation of their incompatibility that could be traded for a low-guilt divorce.

Then Rudy went away to a business conference and attended a seminar on business communication. On the flight home, he reached a decision, which he dropped like a bomb into the counseling.

"I realized that my life was like a refrigerator. Our marriage was cooling in one compartment. My passion for my job was freezing in another. I don't even like to watch television anymore. I don't want to live this way."

Dorrie faced Rudy for the first time all hour. "I think that's the most vulnerable statement I've ever heard you make." Her compliment was mixed with criticism, but fortunately Rudy responded to the compliment, not the criticism.

"I want us to get our marriage out of the cooler. I'm worried that if we do, we'll fight. But anything is better than being on a slab in a morguelike refrigerator."

Dorrie began to cry.

Rudy and Dorrie were far from being happily married, but they had at least moved back into the land of the living. Rudy's measured vulnerability started their conversation. Dorrie's vulnerability kept them talking. For a while, they were able to express themselves instead of living walled-off refrigerator lives.

At this point, a quick granting of forgiveness that doesn't touch the heart would be merely a cold forgiveness. Surface forgiveness can be one more stone in the stone wall. Surface forgiveness often comes from a snow-covered heart. Warm-hearted forgiveness is different.

Move from contempt back to defensiveness. If the relationship hasn't deteriorated all the way to stonewalling, or if it has moved up from there and is in the stage of contempt, then we generally feel that the other person's character flaws are causing the problem. We must move away from this belief if reconciliation is to occur.

We should recall the good things that the person has done. We tell ourselves that those acts are just as much a part of the other person's character as are the flaws. When we are upset, we see more flaws than strengths in the other person or in the relationship. It's helpful (but hard) for us to remind ourselves that we're not perfect either.

Hector and Jennifer seemed to loathe each other. Their contempt dripped from every evaluation of the other. They were headed for divorce.

Strangely, it was country line dancing that got them back together. Jennifer had been going to a community center to dance with her friends. Hector despised dancing. Then Hector's best friend Julio and his wife started going dancing. They invited Hector and, in a "moment of weakness," as he later described it, he agreed to go.

In spite of his prejudice against dancing, he got hooked. Then he and Jennifer began to drive to the dances together. The big change happened in Hector. He realized that if he could be so wrong in his contempt for line dancing, then maybe he was wrong about some of Jennifer's other habits and personal qualities as well. That mundane opening moved them into serious conversation. Talk and shared fun helped them repair some of the damage to their marriage.

It might be helpful to recall the words of Aleksandr Solzhenitsyn, who said, "If only there were evil people somewhere insidiously committing evil deeds, and it were necessary only to separate them from the rest of us and destroy them. But the line dividing good and evil cuts through the heart of every human being. And who is willing to destroy a piece of his own heart?" A related quote is by Thomas à Kempis: "Be not angry that you cannot make others as you wish them to be, since you cannot make yourself as you wish you to be."

Move from defensiveness back to criticism. If we find ourselves in the stage of relationship rupture in which we are extremely defensive, we will often snap back into a negative mindset when we even think that the person is criticizing us. To reconcile, we first need to recognize how our defensiveness gets in our way.

How defensive are you? Take the Defensiveness Self-Test in table 11.1. If you scored 15 to 20, you are very defensive. Once you recognize how defensive you are, you need to defuse yourself. Instead of snapping back into negativity or snapping back verbally at the other person, you can soothe your anger by taking a few deep breaths. Deep breathing calms the body by activating the parasympathetic nervous system, which calms us. Once you're calm, you're ready to examine the criticism to which you're having this knee-jerk reaction. If you think there's any truth to it, admit the truth to yourself and try not to provoke the other person.

There is no one right way to react to every criticism, but I have found, through my own mistakes, that certain ways are always unhelpful. If I go blind with rage and blast the person who criticizes me, I almost always will pay a price later that is out of proportion to the relief I got from exploding. If I criticize the other person in return, it usually leads to escalating hostility. If I bear a grudge and punish the person later, it not only hurts my relationship with the person but damages my own integrity.

When I am criticized—and, as anyone in a leadership position knows, criticism is frequent and often viciously personal—I try to ask myself what my goals are for the relationship. Do I really want to mend damages? Or do I just want the relief of emotional catharsis regardless of the consequences?

Most of the time I decide to stifle my defensiveness and stay calm. Most of the time, my desire for reconciliation takes precedence over my wounded ego.

Table 11.1. How Defensive Do You Feel? Test Yourself

As you ponder a particular relationship, answer these questions.

Circle the One That Applies

1. Do you feel misunderstood by the other person?	Often Sometimes Never
2. Do you have silent arguments in your head with the other person?	Often Sometimes Never
3. Do you wake up in the middle of the night and not get back to sleep because of the silent arguments with the other person?	Often Sometimes Never
4. Do you feel criticized by the other person?	Often Sometimes Never
5. Do you feel that the other person is violating your basic rights?	Often Sometimes Never
6. Do you feel angry at the other person?	Often Sometimes Never
7. Do you argue with the other person?	Often Sometimes Never
8. Do you think you never get the last word when you talk to the other person?	Often Sometimes Never
9. Do you feel attacked by the other person?	Often Sometimes Never
10. Do you feel sorry because you have acted negatively toward the other person?	Often Sometimes Never

How to Score Your Defensiveness Self-Test

Total the number of times you circled "Often"
and multiply by 2. Put your answer
here.   _____

Total the number of times you circled
"Sometimes" and put that total here.   _____

Add the two and put the sum here. This is
your defensiveness score.   _____

If your defensiveness score is:

15-20	you are highly defensive
6-14	you are somewhat defensive
0-5	you are not defensive

For instance, I offended a faculty member in my department by not recognizing the contributions she had made to arrange a large public lecture. She confronted me. My mind swirled with justifications, but deep down I knew she was right. I swallowed my ego and didn't lash back by bringing up times when she had dishonored me. I publicly apologized to her.

Of course, sometimes we are accused of wrongdoing when we know we did no wrong. My daughter Becca wanted me to attend a school play she was in. I told her I would come. A freak spring snowstorm hit the Shenandoah Mountains, and the highway patrol closed the interstate over the mountain, which prevented me from getting to her play. Naturally, Becca was disappointed and hurt that I couldn't come. When I talked with her, I was able to acknowledge that I had hurt her and apologize, even though I realized that I hadn't done anything wrong.

Move from criticism back to normalcy. Criticizing others is a tough habit to break. It's easier if we focus on the other person's good qualities instead of his or her negative, aggravating traits. Or we can consider what pressures the person might be under. We can try to discern what is pushing the other person to act in ways that we find aggravating. Then we can try to ease some of those pressures to help the person be less stressed. In the best case, it's helpful to think about what we might have done to incite the person to act negatively. If you discover some provocation, apologize for what you did.

If you're like me, you probably read the last two paragraphs and nodded. You may have even thought, *Sure, that sounds like a great idea. Think of the positive. Try to figure out what is going on behind the scenes.* But you won't succeed unless you actually make this intention concrete. I tell people in my workshops to make a list of the other person's good qualities and another list of the pressures on him or her. It's hard not to feel at least some empathy when you're looking at a list in black and white.

Yesterday I had a small confrontation at work. It wasn't the first with this person. Sadly, I would have flunked the defensiveness test if I had taken it. I had been critical. So I took my own advice. I made a list of the person's positive qualities. I considered the pressures the person was under. I even examined my own behavior and (gulp) realized that I needed to apologize, which I did via e-mail. Tonight the person acknowledged receiving the e-mail, and our relationship took a giant step toward reconciliation.

So instead of reading quickly through these steps, apply them. Is a relationship at work going sour? Make a list of the person's positive qualities. Is a parent-child relationship more negative than you want? Examine your own behavior.

Revisiting the War of the Watch. In the War of the Watch, we saw Johann and Hans's relationship deteriorate. They accumulated negative events and violations of trust until the relationship slid over the precipice. They criticized each other and reacted defensively toward each other. Each felt nothing but contempt for the other. Johann was contemptuous of Hans for stealing the watch from his mantel. Hans was contemptuous of Johann for stealing the watch from their father's house before the father was even buried. They each turned into stone walls.

Through their children's relationship, Johann began to move toward reconciliation. His stone wall was chipped away when Annamarie told him about her growing acquaintance with Fred, Hans's son. Johann reacted in anger, but at least he was *feeling* something. Johann and Hans met with each other and talked. Even though anger flared up at the end, at least they moved beyond their earlier contempt for each other. When Annamarie questioned whether the criticisms levied by Hans against Johann were true, instead of reacting defensively, Johann actually considered whether they were true. He began seriously to consider acting differently toward Hans. Both Johann and Hans moved beyond criticism by meeting on neutral ground. By the time Johann invited Hans to his home for dinner, they had begun to walk across the Bridge to Reconciliation. They had begun to detoxify their relationship. Next they needed to detoxify their expectations.

DETOXIFYING NEGATIVE EXPECTATIONS

Reconciliation involves restoring damaged trust. But what if a person does something that violates our trust again? Perhaps he or she does a little thing. Still, it is a violation of trust. What should we do? Should we give up and write off the effort to reconcile as doomed to failure because the other person is flawed beyond redemption? Or can we plan a more positive way to manage failures in trustworthiness?

When people have developed a history of hurts and offenses, those wounds often are beneath the skin, apparently healed over but tender to the touch. They can be reopened at the slightest provocation. Expectations are still poisoned.

William Faulkner said in *Requiem for a Nun,* "The past is not dead; it's not even past." This truth is nowhere more evident than in responses to the Holocaust. Jews and non-Jews alike are committed to remembering the evil that humans are capable of and have perpetrated against other humans.

In fact, such human rights violations occur on a large scale throughout the world, even today. We know of the horrors in places like Cambodia, Sierra Leone, Rwanda, Laos, Sudan, Guatemala, Chile, Bosnia and Kosovo. In each conflict, each side tells its own history. In Rwanda, the Hutus and Tutsis teach their separate histories to their children. Is it a mystery what will happen when this generation of children, with their separate histories, become adults? Armed with separate blame-splattered histories, each side will be primed for new bloodletting.

Despite the almost worldwide sense of guilt over the Holocaust, there is always danger that such events will become "simply history." If we forget or minimize the Holocaust, the moral and emotional power that might prevent such atrocities from recurring will be lost. Yet by remembering we sometimes expect the worst.

This necessary tension was dramatized on the world stage in 1985. In the beginning scene of the first act, the chancellor of West Germany, Helmut Kohl, invited President Ronald Reagan to come to Germany to participate in the fortieth anniversary of the end of the war in Europe. The ceremony was intended to be a sign of reconciliation between the United States and Germany. The impact on Jews was drastically underestimated. In the ensuing four months, President Reagan responded to the invitation. He announced that he would participate in the reconciliation ceremony but would not visit a concentration camp because it might reawaken old memories and stir up leftover and always-simmering pain from the Holocaust.

Reagan's announcement was criticized by Jews and non-Jews alike. People demanded to know why the president did not want to visit a concentration camp. Behind this denunciation seemed to be a fear that the Holocaust would be officially (and later privately) forgotten. Critics were upset that the soldiers of Germany would be honored but the (Jewish) victims of Germany would not.

On April 16, 1985, President Reagan announced that he would visit a graveyard in Bitburg to honor the German dead there. He portrayed the dead in that cemetery, though they were Germans, as victims of Nazism, just as the Jews had been victims of Nazism. He did not realize that there were forty-nine SS soldiers—members of Hitler's special security force— buried in that cemetery. Critics accused Reagan not just of trying to sweep the Holocaust under the rug but also of honoring some of the worst perpetrators.

Three days later, on April 19, 1985, Nobel Peace Prize laureate Elie Wiesel, who was a survivor of a prison camp, was slated to receive the Congressional Gold Medal, the highest honor that Congress bestows on civilians. Wiesel gave an impassioned speech aimed directly at Reagan. Wiesel argued that Reagan's moral commitment should be to the victims of the SS and not to SS perpetrators of crime against humanity. Wiesel described scenes that he had seen as a prisoner at Auschwitz. He argued that the issue was not politics but good versus evil. Wiesel acknowledged that President Reagan was seeking to restore relations between the United States and the German people. He said that he did not believe in collective guilt or collective responsibility. Rather, he held the killers (the SS) responsible for their acts. Wiesel criticized Reagan's lack of sensitivity to the victims of the Holocaust. Reagan admitted that he was moved by Wiesel's passion. Yet he did not cancel his plans to visit Bitburg.

In both Germany and the United States, public opinion crystallized around this issue. In the Senate, a scant majority of Senators condemned Reagan's decision. Public polls on the issue in the United States were divided. By the end of this episode, when Reagan finally had laid the wreath at Bitburg, a number of leaders, both in the United States and Germany, had made public statements about reconciliation and about the necessity of remembering the evil that had been done in the Holocaust. At Bitburg, Reagan said, "Many of you are worried that reconciliation means forgetting. I promise you, we will never forget." He went on, "We celebrate today the reconciliation between our two nations that has liberated us from that cycle of destruction."

The experience at Bitburg conveys graphically on a national scale that hurts do not magically go away simply because they are past. Certainly, the Holocaust is worthy of our memory. *How* we remember makes all the difference. Memories can be brought up with a venom of bitter unforgiveness, in a spirit of righteous and haughty indignation, or in a spirit of firm but well-meaning confrontation, as with Wiesel's confrontation of Reagan. Traumatic and emotion-laden memories pop unbidden into our minds. They can push us quickly back into ruminating and unforgiveness, and they can result in our telling stories in which we are victims of harm or prejudice. We cannot stop the traumatic and emotional memories from arising. We can derail the negativity before it gets up a head of steam if we detoxify our thoughts, expectations and speech.

Evidence of the need to detoxify. Memories of past transgressions arise when we experience a new (similar) hurt, when we are under stress or when we are reminded of the old transgression. Merely remembering an old wound is not a sign that we need to detoxify our relationship. How do we know if we need to do this? There are some telltale signs. We (1) reproach the transgressor by bringing up past hurts instead of merely dealing with the current hurt, (2) make an overly harsh reproach, (3) attack the other person rather than sticking to the issue, (4) hear bitterness in our voice or (5) cannot let go of a past hurt.

When we see the need to detoxify our mutual bitterness and resentment, the issue is usually not merely one of forgiveness but of reconciliation as well. That is, we need to restore trust.

The most common sign of the need to detoxify that I see in my workshops is the urge to unload emotional memories of hurt and betrayal. If you unload a litany of past betrayals, it's called "kitchen sinking" because we hit the transgressor with everything but the kitchen sink. The transgressor is flooded with too many issues to deal with. If you catch yourself kitchen sinking, stop and deal with a single current violation of trust. The two of you can more likely work out an understanding and rebuild trust if you deal with one issue until it's resolved.

Developing helpful expectancies. If we want to reconcile with someone, we need some plan for dealing with failures in trustworthiness. Such failures are almost inevitable. Once our trust has been broken, we're often sensitized to look for violations in trustworthiness. We may perceive betrayal where objectively none exists. The other person is usually just as sensitized and often, at the slightest opportunity, thinks we have broken trust.

When we think that the other person has not been trustworthy, we're usually quick to conclude that reconciliation has failed. The other person's lack of perfection is taken as proof positive that he or she never intended to change, is unable to change, is unwilling to change and cannot be trusted ever to change.

If reconciliation is to succeed, we must see failures in trustworthiness as not only unsurprising but expected. This attitude is hard to maintain. We might admit that we are not trustworthy 100 percent of the time, but if we mess up, we cut ourselves huge amounts of slack. When we notice our own betrayals of trust, we are clearly aware of the pressures and good rea-

sons that forced us to behave as we did. But we have a hard time understanding the pressures on the other person. We take the other person's
failures as proof of an ustable, negative personality.

Instead of being thrown by failures in trustworthiness—either our
own or the other person's—we should think of these failures as opportunities to practice forgiveness. Theologian Henri Nouwen said, "Forgiveness is love practiced among people who love poorly." See the other
person's failures in trustworthiness as opportunities to build your own
forgiving disposition. See your own failures as opportunities to practice
humility. When transgressions rip apart relationships, forgiveness is the
seamstress who reweaves the jagged tear in trust, thread by thread. Forgiveness restores the unraveled seam of love and irons out the wrinkles
of residual anger.

Latitude and gratitude. The process of reconciliation is one step backward and two steps forward. In our fantasies, progress is continuous and
rapid, but in real life, progress is herky-jerky. When reconciliation takes
one step backward, we should try to practice an "attitude of latitude." We
try to tolerate the other person's imperfections and failures because we are
aware of our own propensity to fail at times. We try to extend toleration to
the other. Sir Arthur Wing Pinero said, "It is only one step from toleration
to forgiveness."

When reconciliation takes two steps forward, we try to practice an "attitude of gratitude." We notice progress by the other person. We say aloud
what we notice. We thank the person for being willing to work toward
reconciliation.

Failures of trustworthiness are alarm bells. If the other person hurts
us, we don't sit on our hands awaiting an apology, but we approach with
open arms (not closed fists). We look for ways to help the other person
save face. If we transgress, we offer explanations that do not deny, justify
or excuse untrustworthy behavior. We apologize and make restitution. It
is not fair to place the burden of reconciliation on the back of the person
who's been hurt. Instead, let us remember the wise saying of psychologist
Jack Corazzini, "It's not so much what you did. It's what you do about
what you did."

When people have had marital troubles, the renewed love between
them can be as fragile as a spider's web. Davis and Ramona came to our
marriage-enrichment workshop from the community. They had almost di-

vorced over Ramona's overinvolvement in work. The children had flown from the nest five years earlier. Ramona threw herself headlong into a career she felt had been on hold during the years the kids were growing up. Even then, Davis had considered her driven. He longed for the empty nest so the couple could recapture the halcyon days of their early marriage. Ramona's increased time at work made him bitter.

They had attended counseling successfully and had begun to reconnect with each other. But their bonds were few and far between. When they saw the advertisement about an enrichment group on forgiveness, they jumped at it.

When the two-weekend workshop was half over, Ramona canceled a date with Davis because she needed to work late. She was behind on paperwork. Davis was alarmed and felt betrayed. At the group, he brought up his sense of betrayal. Ramona told her side. She reminded him that they'd gone to the movies the night before. The group helped Davis see how he could practice his attitude of gratitude for the dates they were having and his attitude of latitude for the small "betrayal."

We see another example in the movie *Sabrina,* a story of reconciliation after a grievous wrong. Sabrina is a chauffeur's daughter who goes to Paris and becomes a sophisticated young woman, though still without money.

The family for which the chauffeur works has two sons, an older one named Linus and a younger one named David. Sabrina is infatuated with David, an incorrigible playboy. Linus, a sensible and ruthless businessman, is concerned that Sabrina may be a financial liability for the family if David falls for her. Linus is interested in promoting a union between David and a woman whose father owns a large business that would be advantageous to the family. So Linus lures Sabrina into falling in love with him. Then, even though he has also fallen in love with Sabrina, he attempts to take Sabrina to Paris so David's marriage and merger can take place in her absence.

At the last moment, Linus has an attack of conscience and confesses to Sabrina. Sabrina is deeply wounded. As they talk about the rejection, she asks how Linus could do such a terrible thing—a gentle reproach. Linus's explanation is sensitive and contrite, yet Sabrina cannot forgive his gross violation of trust. She heads to Paris alone.

David's playboy heart has finally been awakened by seeing Sabrina's pain, so he steps in as leader of the company. Linus, now free of his duty to the company, is liberated to love. He races Sabrina to Paris. Will she accept him? Will they reconcile?

In the climax of the movie, Sabrina forgives the immediate hurt, gets over her contempt for him, puts defensiveness and criticism on hold, and starts to rebuild the love that was damaged by the violation of trust.

The unanswered questions, of course (because the movie ends too quickly for resolution), concern reconciliation. Will they be able to develop an attitude of latitude and an attitude of gratitude toward each other? Can they fully detoxify their relationship? Can they deal with future violations of trust? In *Sabrina,* a deep hurt is forgiven. But will total reconciliation occur? They have walked almost all the way across the Bridge to Reconciliation. Will they complete the trek? We are left to wonder.

On the border. In the 1980s, Watts, a section of south central Los Angeles, was the scene of extreme violence between two youth gangs, the Bloods and the Crips. These gangs lived in two nearby neighborhoods, and the warfare between the two was often fatal to gang members and bystanders.

Between the two neighborhoods, Aqeela Sherrills lived in a smaller community. The members of the Bloods and Crips moved back and forth across Aqeela's neighborhood. Aqeela couldn't be blamed for wanting to escape that neighborhood. Escape he did. He went east to college. At college he became convinced that he was created to make a difference in the neighborhood battles between the Bloods and Crips. So he returned to Los Angeles. In 1989, he began to organize members of his neighborhood to march into both Bloods and Crips home ground with a message of reconciliation—"Peace for Peace's Sake."

"Both groups tolerated us," Aqeela said. "They allowed us to march. They even listened to our rhetoric. But nothing seemed to change.

"Eventually we met the football great Jim Brown." (Many remember Jim Brown for his role in the film *The Dirty Dozen.*) "Jim Brown allowed us to come to his house. We had the run of the place. He listened to our message and encouraged us to talk. He was a big brother for our group. For six months, he simply listened and accepted us.

"Over that period, Jim Brown developed his own vision of how changes might occur. One night, six months later, he shared it with a group. An organization called Amer-I-Can was born. Amer-I-Can aimed to steer young men toward positive goals." In Amer-I-Can, older, wiser men mentor younger men.

Aqeela and his group were swept up into Jim Brown's vision. They began to believe that they could make a difference. They could help broker peace. Aqeela and his brother Daude held a meeting to motivate the group to go directly to the Bloods and Crips and try to start talks that would lead to a truce between the gangs.

"Yes, we were worried. We literally were afraid for our lives," Aqeela said. "But I said to the group, 'We are on the border between the neighborhoods. We should be the ones who stand in the middle between the Bloods and Crips and bring the neighborhoods together.' By the end of the night, we decided to march into both territories and bring a message of reconciliation." The message eventually led to a "peace treaty" between the Bloods and Crips. After much sacrifice on each side, it led to reconciliation.

Aqeela's is a story of two steps forward and one step back. He stepped back when he left Los Angeles for school in the East, but he stepped forward when he moved back to L.A. He stepped forward again when he organized the group to try to make a difference in the neighborhood. He retreated when the group did not seem to make an impact. He and his fellow group members retreated once again into the safety of meeting with Jim Brown. But through Jim Brown's vision and the courage of the members of Aqeela's group, they stepped forward into the gap between the Bloods and Crips and contributed a vital part to the forging of that truce and later to the reconciliation of the neighborhoods.

Reconciliation almost never seems to move in a straight line. It zigzags down the field like Jim Brown zigzagging down the pavement in *Dirty Dozen*. Sometimes we trip and fall; sometimes we become discouraged and want to retreat completely from the prospect of reconciling. Yet if we can persevere, sometimes we can forge a reconciliation that is accepting and respectful of both sides—and that brings both sides together into a relationship that was not possible before. Into that relationship we must try to build devotion, the last plank across the Bridge to Reconciliation.

DISCUSSION QUESTIONS

1. Explain why the author thinks that forgiving oneself is very difficult and why people usually underestimate how hard it is. He does not believe that one must forgive oneself or change one's self-concept to accept the newly flawed portion of the self

in order to forgive others. Do you agree, or does self-forgiveness come before reconciliation?

2. List Gottman's four steps experienced when marriages (and other relationships) deteriorate. Are you in any relationship that is moving down the cascade toward relationship breakup? What can you do to repair the damage?

3. What was your score on the Defensiveness Self-Test?

4. Summarize in thirty-five words or less the Bitburg incident. What lessons did you learn from the incident that you can apply in your family, work or church life?

5. What is the point of Aqeela Sherrills's story? Can you learn other lessons from that story?

6. What are the Scripture passages that support our need to confess our sins to one another? Do they mean that you must confess to the one whom you harmed? Hypothetically, imagine a man who has had multiple affairs. One of those affairs was with his wife's sister. The affairs have been secret for years. When his wife finally announces that she wants a divorce, he decides he needs to confess all of the affairs to her, including the one with her sister. Is he following Scripture, or is he simply hurting her in the most hateful way by stealing her friendship with her sister? Scripture says he should confess, but to whom?

12

Devotion

We are what we repeatedly do.
Excellence, then, is not an act but a habit.

ARISTOTLE

To reconcile is to do more than decide to reconcile, discuss transgressions, and detoxify the relationship from previous damage and harmful expectations. Those three planks get us within an arm's distance of the center of the Bridge to Reconciliation. We might even be able to leap across the divide into reconciliation, but our foothold might be precarious. To meet in the center, we must build a final plank: devotion.

Plank four, devotion, is built from four boards that fit tongue in groove. We must (1) resolve our grief over what we have lost, (2) build love through empathy, (3) decrease the negative and (4) increase the positive. Look at figure 12.1.

Reconciliation is restoring trust where trust was lost. We grieve what we've lost. Whether you lose a person or something less tangible (such as trust), you can grieve your loss in ways that hamper or help your future adjustment. If you ignore the loss of trust, you'll continue to have doubts about the future of the relationship. To cover over the loss with a veneer of smiles would leave the wounds beneath the surface untended. Most people want to resolve the loss of trust with a new commitment. That requires an effective resolution to the grief.

RESOLVING GRIEF

Whether we are forgiving or unforgiving strongly affects both how we'll grieve and our character after we have grieved. I saw the connection between forgiveness and grief as I grieved my mother's death. You have seen the story of my forgiveness for her murderer unfold throughout the book, but the story would not be complete without describing how I grieved her death.[1]

The stages of grief. For two weeks after I found out about the murder, my emotions were in turmoil. I went through the funeral and murder investigation on auto-pilot. Emotions popped up unexpectedly. Sadness—I missed her. Guilt—I should have phoned more often. Fear—I'm a forty-nine-year-old orphan; what does that mean for me?

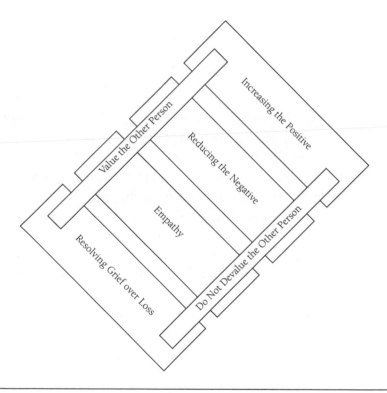

Figure 12.1. A close-up of the underside of devotion

Returning home to Richmond, I withdrew into a protective emotional shell. I poked my head out only to talk with Kirby. I deflected discussions about my feelings.

My first two weeks were consistent with research on grieving. The beginning of grief is usually a period of emotional turmoil and vulnerability.

Typically, for the next year, when we grieve, we repeatedly tell a story over and over in our minds about ourselves and the person. We might think, *If only I had made my loved one wear a seat belt, he would not have been killed in the accident.* In reality, we probably had never been able to make him wear a seat belt. We had no control over whether he wore a seat belt. But "if only . . ." thinking is the core of the obsessive mental review we undertake as we grieve. We think about our story at night. Events unexpectedly trigger memories. As we retell the story, it evolves. A detail changes here, another detail the next time.

At the same time, we seem compelled to tell others the story of the loss. If you have been on the receiving end of these stories, you know how frustrating they can be. A friend describes her childhood relations with her recently departed father. You sympathize. The next day she tells the same story. You sympathize again. The day after that, it's still the same story. By the fifth time, only your essential humanity prevents you from shouting, "Get over it! Get a life!" You want to scream and pull out your hair. By the tenth time, you don't want to see the person. She'll just tell the story again. This is called compulsive social review. It's a normal part of grief, but it's tough on friendships.

I was a textbook case. I knew about compulsive social review, and I did not want to drive my friends and family crazy. So I did not talk much about my grief to them. I'm sure they were relieved. However, repeatedly in my public talks I told the story of my mother's murder and of my experience with forgiving.

After I had told the story five times or so, though, I started to chastise myself. *I don't need to tell about Mama's murder at this conference,* I would think. But when the conference was in full swing, in the midst of my talk, I would tell the story anyway. That compulsion lasted for almost a year after my mother's death. At the time, I did not understand why I kept telling the story. I thought that perhaps I had developed a morbid fascination with her death. I hadn't. It was simple grief. I was doing exactly what I needed to do to get over her death.

Why do we obsessively think about and compulsively tell others the story of our loss? Because we are working hard to make sense out of our life without the loved one. We are seeking a story that makes sense. At first, this story doesn't quite fit. As we tell it over and over, it evolves. One day, *voilà!* The story makes sense—not in a logical way but in an emotional way. Perhaps after six months, perhaps a year, maybe two, our obsession with figuring out the meaning of a loss ceases. We become at peace with our story.

Whether we forgive or don't is crucial to our final story, and it helps shape our character. Suppose we're grieving the loss of love in a romantic relationship, headed toward divorce, have been jilted or simply feel trapped in a cold and passionless relationship. During grieving, we constantly review our story. If we are unforgiving, the story is filled with rumination about unfairness, bitterness, hatred, rage, hostility and resentment. We are obsessed with unforgiveness. We compulsively share our bitter story with our family and friends.

We are programming into our brain a story of bitterness and unforgiveness that will take years to undo. It transforms our personality, making us bitter, unforgiving people. We are also straining our friendships. When we keep talking about unforgiveness, friends and family support us for a while. They know that we've suffered. Yet their tolerance for hearing bitter, hateful, resentful stories is limited. We drive away the very people whom we need to support us when we compulsively tell unforgiving stories.

On the other hand, if we forgive from the heart quickly, we grieve differently. Our obsessive thoughts are filled with empathy, compassion, sympathy and love. We picture ourselves as being forgiving. We feel compassion. We visualize ourselves, within the midst of one of the most difficult personal experiences that people can have, as showing positive character traits and as exhibiting love.

If we forgive deeply but quickly, we tell others a balanced story, not a false story that says, "I never thought anything bad of this youth who killed my mother. I condone this crime." False forgiveness is syrupy and unbelievable. It extracts its price from a social network. It makes friends want to spit out the saccharine sweetness. It doesn't attract the social support we need. Real forgiveness says, "A genuine wrong was done. I could hate him for what he did. Instead, I choose to understand. I see him as a human, not merely an object of my hatred, not merely a betrayer of trust." That story is more nourishing for our character (and goes down better with our friends).

Grieving ends when we come to a resolution with the story about the loss. We finally arrive at a life-narrative that lets us understand at a deep level a plot in which we are the central character. Forgiveness is the twist in the plot that allows us to tell a story that helps us move forward. Unforgiveness is either an unfinished story or one we never want to reread. Forgiveness wraps up the loose ends. I have summarized the roles of unforgiveness and forgiveness in grieving in table 12.1.

Table 12.1. The Roles of Unforgiveness and Forgiveness in Grieving

Stage	Numbed Shock	Obsessive Thought, Compulsive Talk		Resolution
		Obsessive Mental Review	Compulsive Social Review	
Story	Ripples of shock cause our story of life to disintegrate. What will life be like without this person or relationship?	We retell the story repeatedly in our minds, trying to formulate a new understanding. Small changes happen with retelling.	We retell the story repeatedly to others trying to formulate a new understanding. Small changes happen with retelling.	We settle on a new story of how life will be. This includes changes in our self-concept and in our network of supporters.
Role of Unforgiveness	Initial emotions lay the groundwork for the development of unforgiveness.	If we mentally rehearse unforgiving thoughts and emotions, we feed a self-concept as bitter, resentful, and angry.	If we socially rehearse unforgiving stories, we strain friendships and turn the tone of the relationship negative.	We can harden our self-concept as unforgiving and drive away friends.
Role of Forgiveness	Forgiveness can replace initial emotions and prevent unforgiveness from ever developing.	If we mentally rehearse forgiving thoughts, we feed a self-concept as empathic, forgiving and compassionate.	If we socially rehearse forgiving stories, we do not add negativity to the demands already on friends to listen and support.	We can create a firm self-concept as forgiving and maintain a positive support network.

Grieving my loss of reputation. I'm sometimes ashamed of the petty hurts that happen in academic life. Yet that world is where I live much of the time.

It was early in my career. One of the students whose work I had supervised was defending his master's degree thesis. In those meetings, students present their written thesis to a committee of professors and observers. They describe their research and answer questions posed by the professors. In this case, the defense was not going well. One professor was being particularly hard on the student, who was struggling.

At the end of the painful meeting, the student is always asked to step outside while the committee decides whether the student passed or failed. Students who pass are assigned a grade of A or B. Almost all students receive a grade of A.

As the doorway swung shut, the "difficult" professor erupted. "This is inferior work," he blasted.

Another professor chimed in, "I thought the student wrote well and gave a good talk." He said to the "difficult" professor, "What did you find to be disturbing?"

"The student missed a whole line of research on the topic. It was not even mentioned. In my lab, I have studied this topic for five years in at least ten studies."

I felt my stomach sink. I had not thought to direct my student toward that professor's research. The "difficult" professor looked directly at me. "I'll pass the thesis with a B because I don't expect a student to know better. But the person who really deserves the B is you, Ev."

I could feel my face flush. Of course, he was right. I had blundered. I was shamed by the public critique.

Over the next weeks, I grieved my loss of reputation. Psychology departments are small communities. Word got around fast. I was sad and mad. I began to ruminate. I didn't want to look the "difficult" professor in the eye. I fussed and fumed as Kirby and I went on nightly walks.

About six months later, I realized that unforgiveness and unresolved grief were poisoning me. The "difficult" professor seemed to have forgotten the event. It was just another thesis defense in his long academic career. I could see how offended he must have been that I hadn't remembered his research even though we worked together daily.

Finally, I forgave him for his shaming critique. I accepted the event as a painful learning experience. I grieved the loss of my reputation. In the end, I saw myself as an inexperienced professor. I wasn't perfect. I could learn. I could forgive even when I was shamed for my mistakes. That story helped me move on and let me later approach the professor and reconcile with him.

To reconcile requires that we grieve whatever we feel we have lost. Forgiveness helps resolve the grief in a way that allows us to move toward building love.

BUILDING LOVE

We usually think of love as romantic love or love of family. I recommend a broader definition. Love is being willing to value and unwilling to devalue people. Love can be built in any relationship. To complete the Bridge to Reconciliation, we set our goal as valuing the person who hurt or offended us. First, we must understand how the person would perceive love. We try to understand how he or she would feel valued. To avoid devaluing the person, we try to understand what acts he or she would perceive as devaluing. Then we try, as much as it depends on us, to increase the positive and decrease the negative interactions between us. As John Gottman's research reveals, good relationships usually have a ratio of positives to negatives of at least five to one.[2]

Determine what the other person would perceive to be love. When Kirby and I were first married, we sometimes misunderstood each other's acts of love. Typically, I would come into the kitchen, where she was cooking dinner. I would put my arms around her, hug her close and perhaps give her an affectionate squeeze and caress. She would squirm away, say, "I love you," and go back to cooking. I would grunt and move away. Both of us were unsatisfied.

In thinking back to our histories, it's easy now for me to see what was happening. I was reared in a home where we didn't talk about love. Dad wasn't as nonverbal as the husband who said, "I told her I loved her when we got married, and I'll let her know if things change." But he came close. My mother and father were physically affectionate with each other, and I have vivid pictures of my dad squeezing my mom, surprising her with a kiss on the neck or giving her an affectionate pat on the bottom as she leaned over. I learned that a husband shows love through loving touch and affection.

When I visited Kirby's family for the first time, however, I saw strange behavior I had a hard time understanding. Before we got into the house, one member or another of Kirby's family said, "I love you." I left after a brief visit feeling like I had never heard the phrase "I love you" used so many times in such a short period. Kirby had learned to show love by saying it.

Early in our marriage, we each tried to put the Golden Rule into practice: "Do to others what you would have them do to you" (Mt 7:12). I showed Kirby love through physical affection, and Kirby told me often how much she loved me. But I wasn't getting enough physical affection, and Kirby wasn't hearing "I love you" as often as she longed to. *All she wants to do is talk about it,* I thought. *Ev just wants to paw me 24-7,* she thought. I really wanted Kirby to understand that I perceived love through physical affection, and I wanted her to show me love in that way. She really wanted me to tell her, "I love you." We changed our ways. Now, thirty years later, she's all over me. And I love it. (So does she.) I tell her "I love you" a lot. We both smile more often.

In *The Five Love Languages,* Gary Chapman identifies five ways in which people like to have love shown to them.[3] We have already mentioned words of love and encouragement (Kirby's primary love language) and physical touch and affection (mine). For others, spending quality time is a love language. Quality time includes talking about things that both partners consider important or doing things together that both enjoy. Acts of loving service—such as when we do something nice, get meals ready or help with a burdensome chore—are ways some people show and perceive love. For some, gifts convey love. Knowing that a loved one has spent time and money selecting the perfect gift is evidence of thoughtfulness, love and valuing. In sum, to build love we first identify how a person perceives love and then show our love in that way.

While Chapman's five languages of love are not the only ways that people can show love, they are among the most common. To understand how to show love, rank the five languages of love as you think your spouse, children or friends would rank them. Then ask each person if you understood correctly. The person might have a different perception, and this conversation can help you understand him or her more accurately.

Even in relationships outside the home, you can use the languages of love. At work, for example, some colleagues like to be encouraged verbally, while others feel that such encouragement is patronizing. Some colleagues enjoy a pat on the back. Others don't want to be touched. Some colleagues enjoy spending quality time with coworkers. Others limit their non-work socializing to family friends and relations outside of work. Some colleagues enjoy your doing acts of service for them. Others feel that your service to them communicates that you do not trust or respect them. *(What, she doesn't think I can do it myself?)* Some colleagues enjoy receiving gifts of appreciation. Others look on this with suspicion and distrust. Analyzing your workplace can help determine which language of love to use when relationships need repair.

Decreasing negative interactions. As we've discussed, when a relationship is troubled, the ratio of positive to negative interactions between the people is usually well below five to one. Let's assume the ratio is one to one. People have ten positive and ten negative interactions on an average day. The fastest way to change the ratio, moving it closer to the ideal of five to one (or higher), is to decrease the number of negative interactions. For example, if partners who had the ten-to-ten ratio were to decrease negative interactions by a mere eight, the ratio would be ten to two, which is five to one. In order to change the ratio to five to one by increasing positive interactions, however, they would have to have forty *additional* positive interactions each day. To make rapid changes in a negative relationship, first try to decrease the negative.

Increasing positive interactions. On the other hand, there are many problems associated with decreasing negative interactions. For one, it's difficult to get the other person to notice what you're *not* doing.

Suppose you and I are in a negative relationship. I feel the urge to criticize you, but I refrain from doing that. You won't notice anything different. You won't know that I am trying to make the relationship better. We'll end the day feeling more positive toward each other because we have had fewer negative interactions, but you won't perceive that I'm trying to change. Therefore, you might attribute the change to the weather or to your own attempts to make the relationship more positive.

On the other hand, if I do positive acts that I know you'll like, you'll notice. Those acts are so positive and perhaps unexpected, they'll stand out. You'll see that I am making a good effort. The problem is, I must do forty of those to make a difference.

Obviously, if we are to change the ratio fast and powerfully, we need to do both: decrease the negative *and* increase the positive. Think of love as being like money. If I do a loving act, that places one love dollar in our love bank. If I do a negative act, however, it removes five love dollars. (This is an adaptation of a metaphor used by Willard Harley Jr.)[4] Based on your understanding of the other person's love language, try to increase your deposits to the person's love account while decreasing those five-dollar withdrawals.

RECONCILIATION DURING A FAMILY SQUABBLE

I overheard a conversation between my wife and our then-seventeen-year-old daughter Katy Anna. The conversation began innocently. Katy Anna announced that she intended to go with her cousin Carol to downtown Richmond to advise Carol on purchasing a dress for their senior home-coming dance. Kirby was surprised. She didn't think that the trip was a good idea because Katy Anna hadn't done her chores—cleaned her room, packaged some books to send away or written thank-you letters for some gifts.

"I'll do those this afternoon or tomorrow," said Katy Anna.

"You said that earlier in the week," ventured Kirby. "The chores are still not done."

You can probably imagine the flow of this conversation. It progressed along what one might expect would be normal parent-adolescent lines. Kirby kept insisting that the work needed to be done because it was the responsible thing to do. She encouraged Katy Anna to put off her pleasure until she had done her work. Katy Anna, on the other hand, kept pointing to times when she *had* been responsible. She enumerated several times when she had done her work and also socialized with her friends.

Such talks are filled with high emotion. Both sides are tense. In our home (thank you, Lord), these occur infrequently. My stomach was tight just overhearing the conversation.

I was keeping a low profile. (You can call this wisdom or—probably more accurately—being chicken.) As I listened, I was so proud of my family. Kirby kept asking Katy Anna what she was feeling and thinking. Kirby has always been an encouraging listener, and even though the interaction was difficult, she encouraged Katy Anna multiple times to share her feelings.

Katy Anna also was behaving with great maturity. Instead of getting an-gry and sullen and clamming up, as many teenagers do, she hung in there and explained her feelings. "I feel like I have to obey many more rules than most of my friends," she said. "I see my older sisters and brother having much more freedom than I do. I realize that they're older than I am, but it's hard being the youngest child."

Kirby would reflect back Katy Anna's frustration and continue to affirm that she understood Katy Anna's struggle. Kirby also explained that her heart's desire was to help Katy Anna develop maturity. Katy Anna ac-knowledged Kirby's care and concern.

After talking for thirty minutes, they worked out an agreement. I was amazed at the love and mutual respect they showed for each other. Reconciliation is all about deciding to talk, talking gently in love, empathizing, repairing any hurt feelings (sooner rather than later) and building a sense of loving devotion that both people feel.

RECONCILIATION FIFTEEN YEARS LATER

Remember Susan from chapter eight? She worked through the Pyramid Model to REACH Forgiveness and fully forgave her father, who was diagnosed with prostate cancer. She was able to turn loose fifteen years of unforgiveness by vividly imagining forgiveness for one symbolic act—the Friendly's episode in which her father embarrassed her in front of her friends.

Still, the prospect of facing the old man made her stomach knot. She wasn't sure the relationship would work out. As it turned out, things didn't go as she had planned. Let's walk over the Bridge to Reconciliation with Susan as a review.

Susan weighed the questions about reconciliation. Should she visit him? What would he be like? Would he be as gruff and preoccupied as he'd always been? Susan didn't even know how to empathize accurately. After fifteen years of no contact, she was out of the habit of worrying about him and what he thought.

"What if he dies and we've never even talked?" she asked her best friend, Marta.

Marta stirred her coffee thoughtfully. "You've lived without him for fifteen years. You'll probably feel bad for a while." She took a sip. "But you'll survive."

"Marta, you're always so philosophical. But I don't want merely to survive."

"Yeah, I know. You think that because you've forgiven him, you can suddenly make everything right just by showing up. Well, you're my good friend, and I don't want to see you hurt."

"I don't think I'll get hurt," said Susan.

"You always say that, but this guy hasn't changed. He's the same insensitive jerk who pulled you out of Friendly's that time back in high school. You're setting yourself up to get wiped out."

"I want to try," said Susan. "I'm not going to bring up the past if he doesn't. I'll just visit and see how things develop."

"Yeah, right. They'll develop."

Susan was nervous as she phoned. "He's not here," a grave male voice said. "He'll be back about six. Why don't you come then? Or maybe after supper?"

"Do you think he'll mind if I just show up?"

"No problem. I know he'll be here. We eat about 6:30. Come before or after." Susan nervously scribbled the address and directions. It was not a high-rent district.

Susan thought about the benefits of a time-limited visit. "I'll come by around six."

The place is a dump, thought Susan as she parked her blue Ford Taurus out front at 6:00. The sign by the doorbell said Out of Harm's Way. She punched the bell.

The door opened to a man in his late thirties, brown beard, jeans and a T-shirt advertising Diet Pepsi.

"I phoned earlier, uh . . ."

"About Ted, right?" The voice was grave—older than the face appeared to be. "He's on the third floor in 3D."

"Uh, what is this place? An apartment building, or what?"

"It's a recovery house for alcoholics. We help each other."

Great, Susan thought as she made her way up the two flights of stairs. She took a deep breath at the top. She saw 3D on a door on the right side of the hall.

Her father's eyes, in a withered face, came into view as the door opened to her knock. "Susie," he said stepping backward and letting the door swing inward.

"Susan," she corrected. "Everyone calls me Susan now."

"Well, you'll still be Susie to me," he said sharply. "Anyway, come in."

The one-room apartment was dominated by a rumpled, unmade bed. Susan's father gestured at a dirt-colored, once-plaid recliner. "Chair?"

They settled in—Susan's father at the chair by a wooden table, Susan in the recliner.

"How are you?" she ventured.

"Been better," he said.

You're not making this easy for me, she thought.

"I don't need sympathy," he said.

Susan started to shoot back a retort. She paused. "I know," she said.

"I expect you got the message that I have prostate cancer."

"I did. Hazel Hendrick phoned me."

"Ran into her at the hospital. She was visiting. I was getting checked to see if I was fit for surgery. I told her to tell you if she ever saw you."

"How bad is the cancer?" asked Susan.

"They don't think it's worthwhile to operate. It's already in my system. Just a matter of time. Stage three, they say."

"Dad, I'm sorry."

"No you aren't, Susie. I gave you a hard time growing up; you gave me a hard time. I think that not speaking for fifteen years is clear evidence that you aren't sorry."

Susan looked down. "I wasn't very mature. I'm older and, I hope, wiser now."

"We're both older," he said. "I wanted to at least say goodbye. I guess I didn't want to leave you with all bad memories."

"I have tried to forgive you, and . . . I understand that I was a handful too. I'm sorry. I hope you can forgive me."

"So you *tried* to forgive me. Does that mean you couldn't?"

"I did, and do, forgive you."

"I wasn't much of a dad to you. Then after your mom died, the social drinking got out of hand. After a couple of years, I got into treatment. Then I came here."

"Dad, I hate to see you living here. Can I do something? Give you some money so you can move? Can I help?"

"Susie, I told you I don't need sympathy. In fact, I *choose* to live here. I actually support this house financially."

"You do?"

"Yeah. I always worked hard. I saved over a million in stocks. When I became an alcoholic, this house and these people helped me. So when I got back on my feet, I started to help the house. I set up an endowment of a half million. It provides enough in interest to keep the house going. It will after I'm gone as well."

"I'm touched," said Susan.

"I wanted to tell you face to face that I'm leaving you the money I have left, except for that endowment. I know that money won't buy back the years we missed, but maybe it's a start at making up. Can you accept a late gift from a dying old man?"

Susan felt a tear run down her cheek. She nodded.

"Thanks. You've made me happier—" he paused until Susan looked up—"Susan."

OVERCOMING OBSTACLES TO RECONCILIATION

At this point in the young history of the scientific study of forgiveness and reconciliation, we do not know how to get around or climb over all the obstacles to reconciliation. We are finding more about how to help people forgive faster and deeper and reconcile more permanently.

I recall a classic cartoon in which two scientists are standing in front of a blackboard filled from top left to bottom right with equations. In the middle is one blank line with a dotted line connecting the top and bottom halves of the equations. Beside the line is printed, "About here a miracle occurs." One scientist says, "Do you think we need to be a little more explicit about that?"

I have tried to be more explicit about this miracle of forgiveness and reconciliation throughout this book. I've drawn from Scripture to create a theology of forgiveness, and I've drawn from our scientific studies to integrate a psychology of forgiveness (and to a lesser extent, reconciliation) within the theology. Forgiveness and reconciliation are not panaceas. We frail and fallible humans cannot forgive and reconcile as we ought. We depend on the mercy, grace and love of the triune God. We work within God's providence. Along with forbearance, social justice, a system of laws, a method of resolving differences, an intentional effort to reconcile, as well as engagement in a community of Christians, forgiveness and reconciliation are woven together into one strand of Blake's Golden String:

> I give to you the end of a Golden String
> Only wind it into a ball
> And it will lead you in to Heaven's Gate
> Set in Jerusalem's Wall.

I have tried to help you grasp that String when you struggle to find it, so you can wind it close to your heart.

THE LIMITS OF A SCIENCE OF FORGIVENESS

I have described some of the findings from our scientific studies of unforgiveness, injustice, justice and forgiveness. We have discovered ways that help people move through the Pyramid Model to REACH Forgiveness. We have found how to pause on the Bridge to Reconciliation to decide whether, when and how to reconcile, to discuss transgressions softly, to detoxify the poison in the relationship, and to build devotion. We have learned a method of explicit reconciliation that guides us plank by plank into a meeting in the center of the bridge.

Our scientific findings help support much wisdom drawn from writers in the humanities and theology. I have illustrated some of this wisdom in quotes scattered throughout the text and at the beginning of each chapter.

We now better understand that forgiveness is rooted in other-oriented love. A stalk of empathy sprouts branches of compassion, brings forth leaves of altruism and humility, and eventually yields the succulent fruits of forgiveness and (perhaps) reconciliation (depending on whether two types cross-pollinate). The Lord created the seeds, sends water, sunlight and nutrients in the soil to nourish the plants, and provides the life force for its growth. We learned (in chapter two) that many fruit trees grow in the garden to quench the hunger created by injustice and unforgiveness. Some fruits—like social justice, fair laws, just decisions and policies, and unselfish forbearance—are also sweet. They go down well alone. They also make a tasty fruit salad when combined with forgiveness. Other fruits—revenge, harsh punitive justice, projection of our own unforgiveness onto the one who hurt us—are bitter. Their sour taste withers our guts and hearts.

In the end, though, a science of forgiveness—even when coupled with knowledge of forgiveness from theology and the humanities—can take us only so far. It's a long plunge from a hurt and unforgiving heart into the refreshing water of a heart at rest in forgiveness. Knowledge won't make us jump. We can stand at the brink knowing how to forgive but not willing to jump.

In the classic movie *Butch Cassidy and the Sundance Kid*, Butch (Paul Newman) and Sundance (Robert Redford) were pinned down by bounty hunters who chased them with the tenacity of the Energizer bunny. Escape required them to jump into a river below.

"Let's jump," says Butch.

"Nope," says Sundance, drawing his pistol. "We'll fight."

"We'll be killed."

"Yep, but we'll fight."

Often we take that stance rather than risk forgiving. Pressed for a reason, Sundance explains he won't jump because he can't swim. "The fall will probably kill you," says Butch encouragingly.

There was nothing else to do. The force of Butch's courage encouraged Sundance to take the plunge. It was risky. It was hard to do. But they plunged in, floating the river together, and were free. Together.

Forgiveness and reconciliation are all about getting together. We get together with God, and our loving Lord helps us get together with others, even when our relationships are in ruins. As Rumi, a mystic Persian poet, observed, "Where there is ruin, there is hope of treasure." God can uncover the relational treasures when we are joined to him. As I have noted throughout, Jesus said, "I am the vine; you are the branches. If a man remains in me and I in him, he will bear much fruit; apart from me you can do nothing" (Jn 15:5). Yet, the apostle Paul writes, "I can do everything through him who gives me strength" (Phil 4:13).

We are never told that forgiveness or reconciliation will be easy. Thomas Paine, one of the founders of freedom for the USA, said, "That which we obtain too easily, we esteem too lightly." Opening ourselves to granting other-oriented forgiveness is not easy. No friend, family member, author or television personality can do it for us. Marilyn Ferguson said, "No one can persuade another to change. Each of us guards a gate of change that can only be opened from the inside." When we allow that gate to be opened through the power of the Holy Spirit, we step through it and leap outward to plunge into the cool, refreshing freedom of forgiving. Perhaps just as important, we also encourage and bless the other person with the gift of forgiving that is for giving.

DISCUSSION QUESTIONS

1. What are the three stages of grieving? (One stage has two sub-stages.) Have you experienced a serious loss (of a person or relationship) that involved those stages?

2. Why is the ratio of positive to negative interactions important, and how high should the ratio be for a good relationship to exist?

3. What roles does empathy play in building devotion in a relationship?

4. What is love? How is it defined? How should you show love to people who are important to you? Can you come up with an example in which your way of demonstrating love was not the way a person could receive love?

5. Looking back over the book, did the author present a picture of forgiveness that was

thoroughly consistent with Scripture yet enriched by drawing on a scientific approach? That was his goal, but everyone may not agree that the goal was achieved or that the goal was even one that should have been pursued. What do you think?

6. What are the three most important facts or lessons you learned from the book? Write them, and then share one with the group.

Notes

Chapter 1: Why Forgive?

[1] Michael E. McCullough, Steve J. Sandage and Everett L. Worthington Jr., *To Forgive Is Human: How to Put Your Past in the Past* (Downers Grove, Ill.: InterVarsity Press, 1997).

[2] Christopher Carrier, "From Darkness to Light," *Reader's Digest* (May 2000): 101-6.

[3] Cynthia Ozick, "Cynthia Ozick," in *The Sunflower: On the Possibilities and Limits of Forgiveness* (New York: Schocken, 1998).

[4] Throughout the book I disguise personal cases unless their case information has been presented in some public forum. The disguise might involve changes in age, gender, ethnicity and other identifying information, and it usually involves using a pseudonym.

Chapter 2: Unforgiveness, Justice and Forgiveness

[1] Everett L. Worthington Jr., "Is There a Place for Forgiveness in the Justice System?" *Fordham Urban Law Journal* 27 (2000): 1721-34.

[2] Antonio R. Damasio, *Descartes' Error: Emotion, Reason, and the Human Brain* (New York: Avon Books, 1994).

[3] Ibid.

[4] Everett L. Worthington Jr., "Unforgiveness, Forgiveness, and Reconciliation in Societies," in *Forgiveness and Reconciliation: Religion, Public Policy, and Conflict Transformation,* ed. Raymond G. Helmick and Rodney L. Petersen (Philadelphia: Templeton Foundation Press, 2001), pp. 161-82.

[5] Roy F. Baumeister and Julie Juola Exline, "Self-control, Morality, and Human Strength," *Journal of Social and Clinical Psychology* 19 (2000): 29-42.

[6] Julie Juola Exline, Everett L. Worthington Jr., Peter C. Hill and Michael E. McCullough, "Forgiveness and Justice: A New Frontier for Social Psychological Research," *Personality and Social Psychology Review* (2003): in press.

[7] Frederick A. DiBlasio, "The Use of Decision-based Forgiveness Intervention Within Intergenerational Family Therapy," *Journal of Family Therapy* 20 (1998): 77-94.

Chapter 3: The Christian Foundation of Forgiving

[1] David Stoop, *Real Solutions for Forgiving the Unforgivable* (Ann Arbor, Mich.: Servant, 2001).

[2] Frederick A. DiBlasio, "Scripture and Forgiveness: Interventions with Christian Couples and Families," *Marriage and Family: A Christian Journal* 2 (1999): 247-58.

[3] Elliott Dorff, "The Elements of Forgiveness: A Jewish Approach," *Dimensions of Forgiveness: Psychological Research and Theological Perspectives,* ed. Everett L. Worthington Jr. (Philadelphia: Templeton Foundation Press, 1998), pp. 29-55.

[4] DiBlasio, "Scripture and Forgiveness."

[5] Everett L. Worthington Jr., Jack W. Berry and Les Parrott III, "Unforgiveness, Forgiveness, Religion, and Health," in *Faith and Health: Psychological Perspectives*, ed. Thomas G. Plante and Allen Sherman (New York: Guilford, 2001), pp. 107-38.

[6]Julie Juola Exline, Everett L. Worthington Jr., Peter C. Hill and Michael E. McCullough, "Forgiveness and Justice: A New Frontier for Social Psychological Research," *Personality and Social Psychology Review* (2003): in press.

[7]Julie Juola Exline, A. M. Yali and M. Lobel, "When God Disappoints: Difficulty Forgiving God and Its Role in Negative Emotion," *Journal of Health Psychology* 4 (2002): 365-79.

[8]Neil Krause and Berit Ingersoll-Dayton, "Religion and the Process of Forgiveness in Late Life," *Review of Religious Research* 42 (2001): 252-76.

[9]Jennifer Ripley, Everett L. Worthington Jr., Jack W. Berry, Nathaniel G. Wade, Sandra Gramling, David E. Canter, Robert Nicholson, Charlotte vanOyen Witvliet, Lynn O'Connor, Gary Oliver, Les Parrott III and Mark A. Yarhouse, "Religious Commitment and Beliefs and the Big Five Personality Factors as Predictors of Trait and State Forgiving," Unpublished manuscript, Regent University.

[10]Jo-Ann Tsang, Michael E. McCullough and William T. Hoyt, "Psychometric and Rationalization Accounts for the Religion-Forgiveness Discrepancy," *Journal of Social Issues,* in press.

[11]Michael E. McCullough and Everett L. Worthington Jr. "Religion and the Forgiving Personality," *Journal of Personality* 67 (1999): 1141-64.

[12]Ripley et al., "Religious Commitment and Beliefs."

[13]Robert Wuthnow, "How Religious Groups Promote Forgiving: A National Study," *Journal for the Scientific Study of Religion* 39 (2000): 125-39; L. L. Toussaint, D. R. Williams, M. A. Musick and S. A. Everson, "Forgiveness and Health: Age Differences in a U.S. Probability Sample," *Journal of Adult Development* 8 (2001): 249-57; Donald F. Walker and Robert L. Gorsuch, "Forgiveness Within the Big Five Personality Model," *Personality & Individual Differences* 32 (2002): 1127-38; Krause and Ingersoll-Dayton, "Religion and the Process of Forgiveness."

[14]Everett L. Worthington Jr. and Jack W. Berry, "Character Development, Virtues, and Vices," in *Human Nature, Motivation, and Change: Judeo-Christian Perspectives on Human Nature,* ed. William R. Miller and Harold D. Delaney (Washington, D.C.: APA Books), in press.

[15]Jack W. Berry, Everett L. Worthington Jr. and Lynn O'Connor, "Altruism and the Structure of Virtue Preferences," unpublished manuscript, Virginia Commonwealth University.

[16]Wuthnow, "How Religious Groups Promote Forgiving."

[17]Larry Christensen, *Paradoxes* (Undated audiotape, Berkeley, Calif.: 120 Fellowship, 1970).

[18]Gregory Jones, *Embodying Forgiveness: A Theological Analysis* (Grand Rapids, Mich.: Eerdmans, 1995).

[19]David Augsburger, *The Freedom of Forgiveness* (Chicago: Moody Press, 1988).

[20]Roy F. Baumeister, Julie Juola Exline and A. Stillwell, "The Victim Role, Grudge Theory, and Two Dimensions of Forgiveness," *Dimensions of Forgiveness: Psychological Research & Theological Perspectives,* ed. Everett L. Worthington Jr. (Philadelphia: Templeton Foundation Press, 1998), pp. 79-104.

[21]Wuthnow, "How Religious Groups Promote Forgiving."

Part 2: How to REACH Forgiveness

[1]Evan J. Brownstein, Everett L. Worthington Jr. and Jack W. Berry, "Workplace Transgressions," Unpublished manuscript, Virginia Commonwealth University.

[2]Everett L. Worthington Jr. and Jack W. Berry, "Can Society Afford Not to Promote Forgiveness and Reconciliation?" in *Promoting Social, Ethnic, and Religious Understanding and Reconciliation in the 21st Century,* ed. Robert L. Hampton and Thomas P. Gullotta (Washington, D.C.: Child Welfare League of America; 2003), in press.

[3]Everett L. Worthington Jr., "Is There a Place for Forgiveness in the Justice System?" *Fordham Urban Law Journal* 27 (2000): 1721-34.

Chapter 4: R: Recall the Hurt

[1]Deborah Cox, Sally Stabb and Karen Bruchner, *Women's Anger: Clinical and Developmental Perspectives* (New York: Brunner/Mazel, 1999), pp. 102-3.

[2]J. W. Pennebaker and M. E. Francis, "Cognitive, Emotional, and Language Processes in Disclosure," *Cognition and Emotion* 10 (1996): 601-26.

[3]Nathaniel G. Wade and Everett L. Worthington Jr., "Content and Meta-analysis of Interventions to Promote Forgiveness," unpublished manuscript, Virginia Commonwealth University.

Chapter 5: E: Empathize
[1]R. W. Levenson and A. M. Ruef, "Empathy: A Physiological Substrate," *Journal of Personality and Social Psychology* 63 (1992): 234-46.

[2]Wanda M. Malcolm and Leslie S. Greenberg, "Forgiveness as a Process of Change in Psychotherapy," in *Forgiveness: Theory, Research, and Practice,* ed. Michael E. McCullough, Kenneth I. Pargament and Carl E. Thoresen (New York: Guilford, 2000), pp. 179-202.

[3]Stanley Milgram, *Obedience to Authority* (New York: Harper & Row, 1947).

Chapter 6: A: Altruistic Gift of Forgiveness
[1]Andrew Murray, *Humility: The Beauty of Holiness* (Old Tappan, N.J.: Revell, 1997).

[2]Elias Chacour and David Hazard, *Blood Brothers: A Palestinian Struggles for Reconciliation in the Middle East* (New York: Chosen, 1984).

Chapter 7: C: Commit Publicly to Forgive
[1]Richard D. Marks, "Firststone: A Biblical Forgiveness Intervention for Pastors and Christian Counselors," *Marriage and Family: A Christian Journal* 2 (1999): 307-12.

[2]J. W. Pennebaker, ed., *Emotion, Disclosure, and Health* (Washington, D.C.: American Psychological Association Press, 1995).

Chapter 8: H: Hold On to Forgiveness
[1]Daniel Wegner, *White Bears and Other Unwanted Thoughts: Suppression, Obsession, and the Psychology of Mental Control* (New York: Guilford, 1994).

[2]Walter Mischel and H. N. Mischel, "A Cognitive Social Learning Approach to Morality and Self-Regulation," *Moral Development and Behavior: Theory, Research, and Social Issues,* ed. T. Lickona (New York: Holt, Rinehart & Winston, 1976).

[3]Roy F. Baumeister and Julie Juola Exline, "Self-Control, Morality, and Human Strength, *Journal of Social and Clinical Psychology* 19 (2000): 29-42.

Chapter 9: Decisions
[1]Jennifer S. Ripley and Everett L. Worthington Jr., "Comparison of Hope-Focused Communication and Empathy-Based Forgiveness Group Interventions to Promote Marital Enrichment," *Journal of Counseling and Development* 80 (2002): 452-63.

[2]Diana Baumrind, "The Discipline Controversy Revisited," *Family Relations: Journal of Applied Family & Child Studies* 45 (1996): 405-14.

[3]Miroslav Volf, *Exclusion and Embrace: A Theological Exploration of Identity, Otherness, and Reconciliation* (Nashville: Abingdon, 1996).

[4]F. LeRon Shults, Steven J. Sandage and Lisa J. Kiser, *The Faces of Forgiveness: Searching for Wholeness and Salvation* (Grand Rapids, Mich.: Baker, 2003).

[5]Frans de Waal, *Peacemaking Among Primates* (Cambridge, Mass.: Harvard University Press, 1990); Frans de Waal, *Chimpanzee Politics: Power and Sex Among Apes* (Baltimore, Md.: John Hopkins University Press, 1989).

[6]M. Portegal and R. J. Davidson, "Young Children's Post Tantrum Affiliation with Their Parents," *Aggressive Behavior* 23 (1997): 329-41; J. Dunn and C. Herrera, "Conflict Resolution with Friends, Siblings, and Mothers," *Aggressive Behavior* 23 (1997): 343-57.

[7]Howard Zehr, *Changing Lenses: A New Focus for Crime and Justice* (Scottsdale, Penn.: Herald, 1990).

[8]Raymond G. Helmick and Rodney L. Petersen, eds., *Forgiveness and Reconciliation: Religion, Public Policy and Conflict Transformation* (Philadelphia: Templeton Foundation Press, 2002).

[9]Everett L. Worthington Jr. and Dewitt T. Drinkard, "Promoting Reconciliation Through Psychoeducational and Therapeutic Interventions," *Journal of Marital and Family Therapy* 26 (2000): 93-101.

[10]Everett L. Worthington Jr. and Nathaniel G. Wade, "The Social Psychology of Unforgiveness and Forgiveness and Implications for Clinical Practice," *Journal of Social and Clinical Psychology* 18 (1999): 385-418.

Chapter 10: Discussion

[1]L. Gregory Jones, *Embodying Forgiveness: A Theological Analysis* (Grand Rapids, Mich.: Eerdmans, 1995).

[2]A. M. Stillwell and Roy F. Baumeister, "The Construction of Victim and Perpetrator Memories: Accuracy and Distortion in Role-Based Accounts," *Personality and Social Psychology Bulletin* 23 (1997): 1157-72.

[3]Steven J. Sandage, Everett L. Worthington Jr., Terry L. Hight and Jack W. Berry, "Seeking Forgiveness: Theoretical Context and an Initial Empirical Study," *Journal of Psychology and Theology* 28 (2000): 21-35.

[4]June Price Tangney, "Humility: Theoretical Perspectives, Empirical Findings and Directions for Future Research," *Journal of Social and Clinical Psychology* 19 (2000): 70-82.

[5]Pietro Pietrini, Mario Guazzelli, Gianpaolo Basso, Karen Jaffe and Jordan Grafman, "Neural Correlates of Imaginal Aggressive Behavior Assessed by Positron Emission Tomography in Healthy Subjects," *American Journal of Psychiatry* 157 (2000): 1772-81.

[6]Everett L. Worthington Jr., Charlotte vanOyen Witvliet, Jack W. Berry and Nathaniel G. Wade, "Unforgiveness, Forgiveness, Justice, and Health," paper presented at the meeting of the Society for Behavioral Medicine, Washington, D.C., May 2001.

Chapter 11: Detoxification

[1]John Mordechai Gottman, *Why Marriages Succeed or Fail . . . and How You Can Make Yours Last* (New York: Simon & Schuster, 1994).

[2]*New York Times*, May 6, 1985.

Chapter 12: Devotion

[1]Everett L. Worthington Jr., "Unforgiveness, Forgiveness and Grief," *Wings* 7 (2000): 13-16.

[2]John Mordechai Gottman, *Why Marriages Succeed or Fail . . . and How You Can Make Yours Last* (New York: Simon & Schuster, 1994).

[3]Gary Chapman, *The Five Love Languages* (Chicago: Northfield, 1995).

[4]Willard F. Harley Jr., *Love Busters* (Old Tappan, N.J.: Revell, 1993); Willard F. Harley Jr., *His Needs, Her Needs: Building an Affair-Proof Marriage* (Grand Rapids, Mich.: Revell, 1994).

Subject Index

Scripture Index